7/2012

D0016529

Globalized Arts

Globalized Arts

The Entertainment Economy and Cultural Identity

J. P. SINGH

Columbia University Press   *New York*

Columbia University Press
Publishers Since 1893
New York   Chichester, West Sussex
Copyright © 2011 Columbia University Press
All rights reserved

Library of Congress Cataloging-in-Publication Data
Singh, J. P., 1961–
Globalized arts : the entertainment economy and cultural identity / J. P. Singh.
p.   cm.
Includes bibliographical references and index.
ISBN 978–0–231–14718–7 (cloth : alk. paper) — ISBN 978–0–231–51919–9 (e-book)
1. Arts and globalization. 2. Culture and globalization. 3. Arts—Political aspects.
4. Arts—Economic aspects. I. Title II. Title: Entertainment economy
and cultural identity.

NX180.G56S56 2010
306.4'7—dc22

2010014598

References to Internet Web sites (URLs) were accurate at the time of writing.
Neither the author nor Columbia University Press is responsible for URLs that may
have expired or changed since the manuscript was prepared.

For
Chuck

Contents

Contents

Figures

Tables

Preface

For as long as I can remember I have suffered from a deep feeling of
anxiety which I have tried to express in my art. Without anxiety and
illness I should have been like a ship without a rudder.

—Edvard Munch

What is the difference between creative and cultural life? Both art and
culture provide meaning to our lives, of course. Both may be located in
the maelstrom of a deeply interactive world—its technologies involving
people in intense communications and rapidly revolving representations.
Human anxiety regarding these interactions informs both art and culture;
an artist's angst about the self or a culture's anxieties about its identity are
prenatal twins. But, as this book shows, to call something cultural involves
social and political deliberations. Creativity begets art, but politics connect
art to culture. The creative voice must therefore be distinguished from the
cultural voice and identity. We find ourselves in the midst of several global
debates that tug at our notions of cultural identity, and the symbolic nature
of creative expressions is deeply contested in these debates.

The following pages examine global cultural politics as it arbitrates the
implications of symbolic creative expressions. The latter are mostly limited
to fine and performing arts, entertainment industries, and cultural tourism. However, these expressions parallel and make salient global anxieties
regarding cultural identity in a host of other areas. Global deliberations
on the flows of creative expressions thus embody more than one kind
of fear amid all kinds of other flows—movements of people, products,
and ideas—and creative products are especially important in this regard.

They are the symbols that represent these anxieties and thus salient in our global politics.

This book links creative expressions to the vociferous debates on the politics of cultural identity that are currently raging the world over. These moves parallel the salience of issues of cultural identity in politics, which can range from earnest efforts to address cultural discomforts to outright hypocrisy in presenting or, as the book shows, in deliberately not presenting some entertainment-economy phenomena as "cultural." The book deals with the clashes among national identities favored by states, other types of group-identity politics in society, and the need for creative industries such as film, television, performing arts, and cultural tourism to locate themselves in global markets.

The book closes as it begins. It warns us against elevating cultural policies to some innocent and unquestionable purpose of enriching our lives with arts and entertainment. At the level of politics, we should be concerned with cultural policies that promote some singular and exclusionary identity through the arts. An exemplar is the national museum that celebrates a national culture at the risk of excluding or marginalizing minority cultures. In the United States, we ought to be careful in thinking that a department of culture will only enhance the case of arts funding. A look at cultural ministries worldwide would show the kinds of political manipulations in these agencies that valorize particular kinds of cultural identities. In France, the only identity for which statistics can be kept is national identity. Its Muslim and other minorities remain uncounted and, by any account, marginalized. How can France's ministry of culture speak of cultural diversity, as it does vociferously in various international deliberations or negotiations, when it won't even count its minorities?

The book had a curious start. I was trying to *pitch* a manuscript on international negotiations to the editor at Columbia University Press and for illustration spoke at length about its chapter on creative industries. It was about Hollywood and described some colorful politics and personalities. We had a rather lengthy discussion on the ways in which artists and their arts are manipulated in global negotiations regarding cultural identity. We went tangentially into a conversation about other articles I had written on global cultural politics and policies. At that point I told the editor that the book on the manipulation of creative expressions in global deliberations had not been written but I did have on hand a book on international negotiations in general. Write it then, said this editor at Columbia, write the book on the global politics of creative expressions. As you can see, I have done so. Thanks first and foremost to my editor, Anne Routon, for encouraging and inspiring me to write this book. She has helped every step of the way with incisive and straightforward feedback.

Inspiration, despite its dramatic aura, has quotidian elements. At a practical everyday level, for the purposes of this book, it involved the slow delineation of ideas, mulling over thoughts, erasing sentences, and executing minor decisions. I was trying to transcend the facile notions that flows of creative expressions, especially through commerce, destroy cultures and cultural identity. This would pit me against the ready acceptance of the idea in many intellectual circles that "true" creativity and culture must be located away from commerce. Deliberative cultural politics in these accounts involves only citizen activists and artists. Instead, this book finds that both commercial networks and citizen deliberations are necessary for creative expressions to flourish and for cultural politics to be democratic. Helping me argue this stance with conviction and carefulness are fellow intellectuals, in academia and otherwise, who listened and read or otherwise provided useful feedback. I would especially like to thank Françoise Benhamou, Tyler Cowan, Mima Dedaic, Patricia Dewey, Joni Cherbo, Jo Dickison, Harvey Feigenbaum, Jeff Hart, Vijayendra Rao, Jeff Peck, and Margraret Jane Wyzsomirski. Feedback received from anonymous reviewers of the manuscript both at an early stage of the manuscript development and at the end was immensely helpful. They all helped me go beyond the quotidian to find my creative voice.

Article versions of the book chapters were presented at several iterations of the following conferences: International Studies Association, American Political Science Association, Association of Cultural Economics International, International Conference on Cultural Policy Research, and Social Theory Politics and the Arts. Many of these conferences were held in great creative cities—Istanbul, Vienna, and Chicago, to name a few—and I was happy to be there. I am grateful to the International Studies Association's International Communication Section for awarding me with their best article prize for the paper that forms the basis of chapter 4 in this book. It was a needed boost at that time to know that I was headed in a meaningful direction with my research. The three cultural policy conferences named above involve small interdisciplinary communities of scholars who can speak across academic turfs and engage in thoughtful conversations about the arts and cultural policies. I would like to thank the audiences at these conferences for their feedback but especially Peter Cowhey and Ken Rogerson. The Film in Trade Evenings sponsored by the Curb Center of Vanderbilt University that Carol Balassa convenes in Washington, D.C., have been enormously useful in getting a sense of policy trends in creative industries. I am grateful to my colleague Mima Dedaic, who called chapter 1 "a harmonized interdisciplinary accord."

I have also been fortunate these last few years to serve on the UNESCO Expert Group on the Measurement of the Diversity of Cultural Expressions and the UNESCO Taskforce on Cultural Statistics. Participation in these forums introduced me to many of the best minds on culture policy from across the world. Our discussions further emboldened me to think that measuring culture is incredibly hard, if not impossible, and involves sidestepping or tripping over all kinds of politics. Therefore, the argument in this book veers more toward the creative rather than the cultural. I would like to thank the following people in UNESCO: Guiomar Alonso Cano, Lydia Deloumeaux, Simon Ellis, and Jose Pessoa. A trip to UNESCO, Paris, at the end of 2009 just as I headed toward the final set of revisions was enormously useful in clarifying concepts and adding missing details to the many negotiations discussed in the book. The U.S. ambassador to UNESCO, David Killion, went out of his way to render all kinds of help for which I am enormously grateful. I have also had occasion to meet with a number of officials in the World Trade Organization and the World Intellectual Property Organizations and thank them for their help. Chapter 3 is adapted from my book *Negotiation and the Global Information Economy*. This was the chapter that prompted me to start thinking about cultural politics. The chapter reflects conversations with numerous European Union and U.S. government officials who participated in the creative-industry negotiations in the WTO and UNESCO. A few other sections in this book are adapted from other publications. Chapter 5 borrows from "Culture or Commerce? A Comparative Assessment of International Interactions and Developing Countries at UNESCO, WTO, and Beyond," *International Studies Perspectives* 8 (2007): 36–53. The section on the sex industry in Thailand is adapted from "Sex Workers and Cultural Policy: Mapping the Issues and Actors in Thailand" (with Shilpa A. Hart), *Review of Policy Research* (March 2007). Many people who helped with the preparation of these articles are acknowledged in the original articles, but many of them also provided ideas for subsequent revisions. These include Don Abelson, Donna Ghelfi, Todd Nissen, Martin Roy, Pierre Sauvé, Lee Tuthill, and Jayashree Watal. I also thank numerous cultural policy officials in Belize, China, Costa Rica, India, Senegal, South Africa, and Uruguay who provided all manner of assistance for this book. Many thanks to Michael Haskell for attending to the book's production with great care at Columbia University Press.

I would like to thank the participants in three graduate seminars at Georgetown that allowed us to engage in disparate literatures. These seminars were politics of cultural representation, international cultural policies, and cultural economics. Several graduate assistants also helped me collect materials and provided feedback on the chapters. These include Jehan Agha, Marcus Holmes, Becky Jakobs, Andrea Salvatore, Teresa Schlafley, Kim Singletary, and Sarah Thompson. Two competitive grants-in-aid for this book from the Georgetown graduate school enabled me to travel to UNESCO offices in Paris and funded a trip to West and South Africa that allowed me to witness firsthand the tremendous creativity of artists and the struggles among many officials to keep art alive. The scintillating mbalax sound at Youssou N'Dour's club Thiossane in Dakar was the highlight of this trip. A WTO assignment to Colombia and Uruguay showed the ingenuity of creative producers in these countries. A jaunt over to the small production company Metro Films in Montevideo will cure anyone of the notion that small countries lack production capacities or access to global networks.

I have thought about this book these past few years as I enjoyed several opera performances, found myself at fascinating arts festivals, watched the pictures at many an exhibition, immersed myself in cultural tourism, listened to music, and recited poetry. I have shared these magical moments with my life partner, Chuck Johnson, whose support for my intellectual work is beyond words.

Most of all, art is its own muse. Thank goodness!

Abbreviations

CARICOM	Caribbean community
CNC	Centre National du cinéma et de l'image animée
DBS	Digital broadcast satellites
DCMS	Department of Culture Media and Sport (UK)
EACEA	Education, Audiovisual, and Culture Executive Agency (EU)
EBU	European Broadcasting Union
EC	European Commission
EEC	European Economic Community
EU	European Union
FEPACI	Pan-African Federation of Filmmakers
FERA	European Federation of Audiovisual Workers
FESPACO	Panafrican Film and Television Festival (Ouagadougou, Burkina Faso)
FT	*Financial Times*
GATS	General Agreement on Trade in Services
GATT	General Agreement on Tariffs and Trade
GNS	Group on Negotiation for Services
INCD	International Network for Cultural Diversity
INCP	International Network on Cultural Policy
IPC	Intellectual Property Committee

MAI	Multilateral agreement on investment
MFN	Most Favored Nation
MNC	Multinational corporation
MPAA	Motion Picture Association of America
NAFTA	North American Free Trade Agreement
OECD	Organization for Economic Cooperation and Development
RIAA	Recording Industry Association of America
TRIMS	Trade-Related Investment Measures
TRIPS	Trade-Related Aspects of Intellectual Property Rights
TWF	Television Without Frontiers
UNCTAD	United Nations Conference on Trade and Development
UNDP	United Nations Development Programme
UNESCO	United Nations Educational, Scientific, and Cultural Organization
UNWTO	United Nations World Tourism Organization
USTR	United States Trade Representative
WIPO	World Intellectual Property Organization
WTO	World Trade Organization
WTTC	World Travel and Tourism Council

Introduction

The Creative Voice and Cultural Identity

> Perhaps the immobility of things that surround us is forced upon
> them by our conviction that they are themselves and not anything else,
> by the immobility of our conception of them.
>
> —Marcel Proust

The anxieties of globalization are ubiquitous, from simmering favelas to favored salons. These anxieties are usually about losses to "local" ways of life as a result of deepening connections with the "outside" world. The following pages attend to the politics of collective identity that seeks to address these global anxieties. They detail how creative expressions from the arts and entertainment industries—now estimated to be over $1.7 trillion in world output—become the vessels of collective cultural identities. As creative expressions circulate globally, they unleash or enhance concerns regarding the dissolution of identity, in turn emboldening political actors to enact specific cultural policies. *Simplemente Maria*, a telenovela from Colombia, can bind together Spanish-speaking people around the world but also appeal, as it does, to a host of other audiences. Similarly, Hollywood's *Matrix* garners large audiences but can also inspire protests regarding cultural domination.

Globalization, the growing yet intangible connectedness among people and ideas, is driven in large part by the tangible palpability of material or economic existence. But such connections scarcely give individuals pause to make sense of the technologies and expressions that make possible a new world. In such a maelstrom, the anxiety and longing for a meaningful life, often manufactured with nostalgia or frustration or both, are understandable. It has happened before. At the dawn of the industrial revolution, the fascination with the machine was coupled with fears about its serendipitous monstrosity. Mary Shelley's Frankenstein embodied such anxieties.[1] So did the Paleolithic cave dweller who set out to scratch her representations on the cave walls. "Man's first expression, like his first dream, was an aesthetic one. Speech was a poetic outcry rather than a demand for communication. Original man, shouting his consonants, did so in yells of awe and anger at his tragic state, at his own self-awareness and at his own helplessness before the void" (Newman 1947). What took place in caves next to real fires now glows from theatrical stages and LED screens. In the words of Postman: "Our media are our metaphors. Our metaphors create the content of our culture" (1985, 15).[2]

This book explains the origins of cultural policies that result from the politics around creative expressions, such as those produced through fine and performing arts, entertainment industries, and cultural tourism. These politics are increasingly global and reveal the ways in which an artist's expression or a creative industry's output becomes a purveyor of cultural identity or a way of life for a group. It is important to examine these politics carefully: the marriage of art and politics reveals powerful agendas regarding identity. All too often it is assumed that cultural policies attached to arts and entertainment speak to our highest aspirations as human beings. They may, in fact, speak to our basest instincts if the creative expressions upheld by these policies actually exclude and marginalize "other" people and lead to a politics of hatred.

The conversion from the creative output to policies about collective identities entails a deliberative politics that involves various stakeholders—some with entrenched interests, others with emerging agendas and burgeoning passions. This book examines these deliberations or discussions at the global level of cultural-policy elite and politicians, domestic and transnational civil society, international organizations, and the creative producers. States involved in shaping global rules are *primus inter pares*: their actions at the global level and refracted in national discussions are especially important. Cultural politics are almost always dramatic, festooned with colorful statements and personalities. These politics then result in particular cultural policies that states and other international actors enact to protect or enhance particular notions of cultural identity. While these cultural policies are made explicit through subsidies, quotas, tax incentives, and the like, at a deeper level the context for these measures lies in

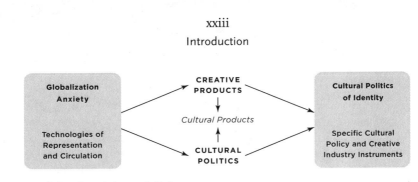

Figure 0.1   Creativity and Culture

cultural politics of identity through which these measures are deliberated. The identity debate is old; only the global context is new. Mary Shelley's Frankenstein and Barnett Newman's cavemen lived through the old debates. Nevertheless, the debate is revisited here to draw out insights on the politics of cultural identities through a rapidly evolving globalization. Figure 0.1 illustrates the argument, and table 0.1 defines the major terms used throughout this book.

There is a plethora of literature on the grand politics of cultural identity; this book intentionally makes a less-than-grand contribution. The existing literature describes global identity politics as a clash of civilizations, as a battle between market forces and recessive ethnic identity (*Jihad vs. Mc-World*), or as commodified and packaged through commercial means in a global consumer culture.[3] I set aside these grand narratives to focus instead on creative expressions, examining the micropolitics of identity from the national to the international levels. The book's empirical chapters detail the politics surrounding creative expressions and the ways in which the creative becomes the cultural. Such a focus is missing in the grand narratives of identity mentioned above or in cultural-studies literatures obsessed with finding a commercial hue in every shade of identity—describing any kind of identity merely as another layer of commodification and evidence of the growing power of commerce invading every aspect of human life. Creative expressions, while speaking to micropolitics, have an important stature in an age concerned with identity and culture. A Hollywood film, a Bollywood song, or a Latin American telenovela is not just a creative product: in the realm of politics, it becomes an embodiment of a cultural identity.

Creative expressions, which the following chapters deal with in detail, parallel most textbook definitions of creative industries as comprising a *core* group of creative arts (performing and fine arts, museums) and then overlapped by successive layers of *affiliated* creative activities with a high

TABLE 0.1

Definitions

- *Creative expressions or products*: Fine and performing arts; entertainment such as films, TV, music, radio; design such as architecture and advertising; specific types of tourism. Also referred to as creative goods and services. The shorthand term "arts," as in the title of the book, is also used throughout the text.
- *Creative industries*: the economic organization of inputs and outputs for producing creative products. The 'value chain' encompasses creativity/imagination, production, distribution, exhibition, preservation/archiving. The term 'audiovisual' industry is used in the World Trade Organization.
- *Cultural politics*: Political deliberations among a variety of political actors that endow collective meanings to creative expressions. This book specifies an ideal type for deliberations that involves political actors in problem solving through a high degree of trust, transparency, and inclusion.
- *Cultural representations or products*: Creative expressions endowed with meanings borne from cultural politics.
- *Cultural identity*: Any sense of group or collective identity, including local, national, and international cultural identities. Might include notions of race, gender, sexuality, class, nationality.
- *Cultural policy*: In a *general* or *macro* sense it refers in this book to any institutional support for assigning cultural identity boundaries. Creative arts policies, not the subject of this book, provide institutional support without reference to cultural identity. In an *instrumental* or *micro* sense cultural policy refers to specific institutional support mechanisms such as grants, subsidies, quotas, tax and philanthropy incentives, and capacity building.

---

commercial element (entertainment industries such as film and televisions, games and toys, cultural tourism) and, finally, some elements of artistic design in several *ancillary* industries such as furniture, textiles, architecture, or advertising.[4] This book focuses primarily upon entertainment industries and cultural tourism, as they unleash the greatest controversies across the globe, but it also attends in certain places to fine and performing arts. Most texts employ the term "cultural industries" instead of "creative industries," which in these texts stand for aesthetic and design industries.[5] However, cultural products and industries, by definition, must be endowed with meanings regarding collective identities. I consider the term "creative industries" to be more politically neutral.

Allow me to be even more clear about what this book does *not* attempt: this is not a book on the effects of market production on cultural identity.

There are several texts (detailed later) on the efficacies or, conversely, the pathologies, of market capitalism for cultural products.[6] While this book is broadly sympathetic to market processes, my intent is not to venerate markets but to make salient the politics that mediate between the production of creative expressions (through markets or technological or other means) and the types of cultural identity that arise as a result.[7] As detailed later, such politics may not be terribly deliberative if they simply allow cultural-policy elites to legitimize their prefabricated positions rather than allowing problem solving to take place among a variety of stakeholders, bolstered by transparency and trust (Singh 2008b, chapter 7). Chapters 1 and 2 will detail the relevant market-driven and technologically driven production systems for creative expressions and the way they privilege particular cultural politics.

Chapter 1 examines, first, the deliberative cultural politics that lead us from the creative to the cultural and, second, the significance of creative expressions amid global anxieties. Chapter 2 details the political economy and technological changes underlying these representational practices, while the four chapters following it provide the empirical substantiation for my claims.

Globalized Arts

Cultural Politics and Global Anxieties

Despite the guilty, fearful silence at the front of the auditorium, few could hear what Funda Eser was saying: that when the angry girl tore the scarf off her head, she was not just making a statement about people or about national dress, she was talking about our souls, because the scarf, the fez, the turban, and the headdress were symbols of the reactionary darkness in our souls, from which we should liberate ourselves and run to join the modern nations of the West. This provoked a taunt from the back rows that the entire auditorium heard very clearly.

"So why not take everything off and run to Europe stark naked?"

—Orhan Pamuk, *Snow*

The road from the production of creative expressions to their realization as policies enacted to protect cultural identity is paved with politics. The ultimate aim of this book is to warn against the kinds of politics that revolve around some singular elite notion of culture. Art and politics are not innocent allies: the politics of identity they yield need to be questioned. Winslow Homer's American landscapes speak to a ruggedly innocent national identity venerated in many American discourses; however, we need to investigate the notion of a national cultural identity, especially when creative expressions no longer obey national mantras. This does not mean giving up on culture: it only means that the quest for identity and a cultural voice need not be moored to the ship of the nation-state.[1] The institutions and processes through which cultural politics and deliberations take place are described in the next section. The rest of the chapter examines the salience of identity politics and cultural anxieties in globalization.

Creative Expressions and Globalization

Creative expressions are the most visible symbols in understanding human identities. They mark and embody the passage of time and the way of life for individuals. A statue, a stanza, or a city's architecture may well reveal to us many things about its creators or the groups that have successively inhabited or experienced such forms. Representations—linguistic, visual, musical, or otherwise—are, therefore, practices created and interpreted by individuals. Being representations, they can be shared, inherited, and left behind as legacies. On Christmas Day, 1989, Leonard Bernstein conducted Beethoven's Ninth Symphony (*Ode to Joy*) in Berlin to celebrate the fall of the regretfully eponymous wall. Earlier, in 1972, the Council of Europe and, in 1985, the European Union, had adopted the symphony as the European anthem.[2] In this regard, Beethoven's Ninth provides a punctuated equilibrium to Europe's restless quest for a common identity. In Potsdamer Platz, the fall of the Berlin Wall was also greeted with other music, including Pink Floyd's *The Wall*.[3]

Creative expressions reflect but also constitute our reality; the mirror tells us who we are. Who are we, then, when surrounded by several mirrors, each showing a different and changing portrait? Institutions of power often take individual or group identities to be fixed; their task is to affix it further through evocations of historical memory, as in Beethoven's Ninth. But identities are always in a state of flux, and the fall of Berlin Wall serves as a physical reminder. The ability to demarcate the contours of identity is a form of metapower: itself borne out of interactions with people and their creative representations. Such is the power of representation or art; expressions beget power by providing an identity to the issues they enact. Once the contours have been set, what we do with our identities is business as usual. No wonder, then, that art calls forth such passions and reasons everywhere.

Globalization has given metapower to actors hitherto not present in our living rooms. Who decides which representations are creative? How do these creative representations become cultural- or group-identity artifacts? Whose culture? What can we make of global cultures and global societies in these debates? These are questions to which I attend in the following pages. Like a postmodern narrator, let me provide the denouement right here. As always, the right to call something cultural is being contested, as it should be, in globalization debates. Globalization has stirred up the demarcations of identities anchored to the ship of the Westphalian nation-state that emerged in the modern world as the preeminent actor. The flux of identities was largely settled in 1648 by the peace of Westphalia. Commerce, technology, and social imaginaries converged to produce in the nation-state the legitimate political organization for governance (Anderson

1983).[4] In Europe, the initial boundaries of the nation-state were primarily linguistic, demarcating people as English, French, German, or Italian. For this very reason, when this Europe adopted *Ode to Joy* as its anthem, it asked the conductor Herbert Von Karajan to come up with an instrumental version devoid of Schiller's poem by this name, sung in German in Beethoven's symphony.

While the nation-state fights for dominance and legitimacy in a plurality of actors in the twenty-first century, the representational metaphors are in flux again. A dozen yellow stars now encircle the middle of the European Union's blue flag. Likewise, identities are afloat: sometimes affixed to the nation-state, otherwise paddling toward other identity markers—civilizational, linguistic, religious, diasporic, indigenous, ethnic, sexual, global. Representational practices with local flavors find, or are created for, global audiences. The plight of poverty and its effect on children are shown in films such as *City of God* from a favela in Brazil, *Tsotsi* from a South African township, or *Salaam Bombay* and *Slum Dog Millionaire* from a chawl in Mumbai. They now compete in representational politics with the *La Boheme* of La Scala or a *Pearl Fisher* from the Palais Garnier. The capital C of high culture and the small c of popular culture can be seen in contest or collaboration or both.

In their struggles to dominate or, at times, to profit their constituencies, the various international actors—nation-states, international organizations, commercial enterprises, societal groups and movements—deploy or destroy, as the case may be, a variety of representational practices. The salience of public diplomacy in the United States after September 11, 2001, promotes the "soft power" or persuasive and positive appeal of being "American" through the seductive charms of its films, music, and other creative expressions. Meanwhile, in other parts of the world, these "charming" exports, as they appear to the nation-state that promotes them, may be typecast as cultural imperialism by other nation-states or actors. Such debates can lead to protests against Hollywood's presence in various parts of the world. In other parts, even local representations may become part of destructive rituals, as in the Taliban regime's destruction of the historic Bemiyan Buddhas in Afghanistan or protests against Hollywood films in South Korea. At a less destructive level, these quarrels feature lively moments in the so-called "cultural flows" at local, societal, national, and international levels. At stake are not just the commercial and technological practices that sustain these flows but also the meaning of cultural identity itself when the local and the global—that is, the Janus-faced twins of representational practices—turn around and stand face to face.

The Politics of Cultural Policy

The path creative expressions tread toward becoming symbolic bearers of cultural identities wends through political institutions and deliberations. The end point is policies that favor one form of cultural identity over another. In the age of globalization, these deliberations are informed by anxieties about creative expressions flowing across borders, both territorial and extraterritorial—anxieties that come from fears of the unknown. These fears or cultural anxieties reflect the challenges to collective identities from accelerated flows of various creative expressions and representations. The territorial origins and destinations provide a physical dimension to the flows of creative expressions. However, creative expressions also possess an extraterritorial dimension and challenge, as they always have, the boundaries of what it means to have a self, a family, a community, a society, or a network. It would be a truism to note that identity politics are in a flux today as people challenge the cultural boundaries of their identities.

Who invokes culture? In which political or social space is it being invoked? How is the invocation contested or deliberated? By whom? For what purposes? The anthropologist Virginia Dominguez (2000, 22) writes that an analysis of cultural politics needs to move beyond a repertoire of objects and their distribution in society "toward asking *what is being accomplished* socially, politically, discursively when the concept of culture is invoked to describe, analyze, argue, justify, and theorize." In an essay that immediately follows Dominguez's, in the same volume, the sociologist Paul DiMaggio (2000, 38) notes that "people's choices of expressive goods are profoundly cultural and social." In other words, individual acts of consumption are not independent of social and cultural preferences. The Dominguez-DiMaggio challenge is to think of creative artifacts and cultural policy as socially constructed and instituted processes related to social and cultural preferences rooted in the kind of identity politics that I outlined earlier. These ideas link cultural-identity policies with specific cultural-policy measures that are enacted to promote these identities. Nevertheless, this is not an assault on individual rationality or freedom. By focusing on deliberative and discursive acts, one merely moves toward a model of cultural policy while not necessarily negating individual choices. I take it as given that creative expressions and their consumption can be individualistic but nevertheless socially informed.

The chapters that follow evaluate cultural-policy contests or deliberations from an ideal type, namely that of problem-posing deliberations, which may include individuals, groups, or institutions. Ideal types are necessary not only to provide a method of evaluation but also to underscore my normative argument around nonoppressed creative voices. This argument leans upon inclusive and impartial policymaking where groups solve problems rather than prioritizing precrafted solutions that are always partial to one group or another. Cultural policy explicitly favors particular (cultural-identity-based) creative expressions. When the meaning of cultural identity is rapidly changing, it becomes unclear whom cultural policy should favor. An ideal type that allows all groups to participate and engage in problem solving offers a process for crafting an appropriate cultural policy.

Cultural deliberations will invariably run into a contest between segmentations of a historical identity and permutations available in the future. While cultural practices may run deep in history and be objectified or even reified through institutional objectifications, they are, being group phenomena, the result of social construction. What one believes to be high culture, such as opera, for example, has received centuries of political support from elite cultural institutions. Seyla Benhabib (2002, 5) notes that participants in any culture "experience their traditions, stories, rituals and symbols, tools, and material living conditions through shared, albeit contested and contestable, narrative accounts." We now find ourselves in a contest where the meanings and influences of elite and popular cultures are being redefined. Any narrative of cultural policymaking must then account for the power of those in contest.

Cultural Deliberations

Ideally, deliberations involve assaying alternatives in political spaces that allow for trust, transparency, and inclusion among the stakeholders or participants. Nevertheless, power often shapes outcomes. If power is diffuse, contests among individuals and groups can yield indeterminate results or a slow search for solutions; if power is concentrated and outcomes are dictated by the powerful alone, results can be overdetermined and rigidly derived.[5] However, power also has a transformative dimension, especially in an interactive deliberative context in which the deliberations themselves effect changes in the identity of the participants and the meaning of the issue they are discussing. This notion of *metapower* attends problem-posing deliberations in which successive interactions among participants changes the issue dimension and the identities of the participants. As the term implies, in "problem-posing deliberations" outcomes reflect discursive deliberations accomplished through persuasion.[6] They are not predetermined solutions revealing the prerogative of those with instrumental or structural power to effect their favored outcomes.[7] Furthermore, in problem-posing deliberations, the absence of instrumental coercions does not always result in a win-lose format. Instrumental persuasion may be present in problem-posing deliberations as well, but it is transformative in making participants cognizant of alternatives.

The notion of problem-posing deliberations presented here rests upon Freire's notions of dialogic action and Habermas's notions of communicative action.[8] Freire notes that problem posing can only take place in an atmosphere of trust and empathy, in which the participants "name their world" and find a cultural voice through successive communications. For Habermas, communicative action is deliberative, transparent, and inclusive. Instrumentality, on the other hand, is purposive and therefore cannot effect problem-posing deliberations. Clearly, Habermas is positing communicative action as an ideal type. In practice, deliberations can start with instrumental rationalities and lead to problem posing and persuasion once sufficient trust has been established among participants.

Three criteria define the ideal type for deliberation: trust, transparency, and inclusion. Trust is the belief in the legitimacy of the process and the space in which deliberations are taking place. Legitimacy, in terms of a socially constructed due obedience, may or may not encompass normative conduct, but due obedience does specify at least a minimal habitual acceptance of results (Hurd 1999).[9] Transparency similarly varies in deliberations and poses a particular problem. Collective action is easier among small groups that can meet without the spotlight of the media. There may still be space for a small group meeting to effect consensus, but transparency creates due process. Finally, inclusion is especially important for any deliberation and must speak to all the parties affected. In practice, inclusive participation often means chains of delegation—people participate indirectly through delegations or representatives. In a communicative context, Iris Marion Young (1996) avers that inclusion can result from acknowledging existing forms of greetings, rhetoric, narratives, and storytelling from the marginalized "other" voices. Appiah (1994, 161) calls these forms "positive life-scripts," organizing narratives about people's lives that offer dignity and inclusiveness. Trust, transparency, and inclusion together create conditions for problem-posing deliberations or the weighing of alternatives through persuasion. As will be seen later, the three conditions are notably present at the international level, where diffused power is the norm, or in domestic contexts, where democratic institutions are present. The absence of trust, transparency, and inclusion, especially in situations of concentrated power among a few actors, invariably leads to coercion or manipulation. Nevertheless, even in democratic contexts, deliberations around cultural identities are particularly tricky (Benhabib 2002, Benhabib, Shapiro, and Petranovic 2007). Two or more cultures in negotiation may not know each other and may meet within a climate of mistrust and fear. As I alluded to before, the anxieties of globalization make this particularly difficult.

Two narratives drawn from the U.S. context may help to illustrate the claims I have just made. In *Slim's Table* (1992), Mitchell Duneier presents an ethnography of a group of black mechanics that regularly meet at the cafeteria Valois in Chicago's Hyde Park neighborhood. In the opening chapter, Slim, one of the mechanics, reaches out to Bart, who grew up in the segregated South. But Duneier notes that Slim's "attitude of caring exists within a framework of barriers to closeness set up by Bart" (15). Bart's upbringing cautions him against interacting with Slim and his friends, therefore causing him anxiety. Despite Bart's barriers, "Slim's caring behavior had pushed Bart to the limits of his potential for tolerance, friendship and respect" (21). *Slim's Table* is a powerful testimony to the successive degrees of trust, transparency, and inclusion within interactive environments. It shows how individuals may move toward Taylor's multicultural politics of mutual recognition of one another's dignity and esteem (1994). Thomas Frank's *What's the Matter with Kansas?* (2004) presents the opposite: the manipulation of anxiety by the political elite to breed mistrust and exclusivity. Frank documents how voters in Midwestern states such as rural Kansas have overlooked their own history of radical politics to vote for a particular type of conservative cultural politics coming out of evangelical churches: "railing against abortion and homosexuality and gun control and evolution" (75). These are the political economies of our anxieties that Glassner describes in converting our "moral insecurities" into "symbolic substitutes" (1999, xxviii). He notes that social psychology validates the thesis that people want their vague and ambiguous notions to be replaced by something definite and symbolic. Here, anxieties born out of material and economic issues are buried under fiery cultural politics. During the 2008 presidential campaign, Barack Obama's comment that rural voters cling to guns and religion touched off a storm of protest regarding his elite credentials and his looking down on rural voters.[10] Meanwhile, the morally conservative wing of the Republican Party, as personified in the vice presidential nominee, Sarah Palin, sought to exploit these anxieties further by focusing on divisive cultural issues.

In the context of globalization anxieties and cultural-identity politics, problem-posing deliberations are hard to effect. First, the pervasive anxieties reveal the limits of the human capacity to make sense, at least in terms of identity, of the creative expressions that surround us and our inability to present the self in a coherent narrative. For existential philosophers, the quest for identity—through alienation, a sense of nothingness, and anguish—informs the freedom of being. In Sartre's famous words, we are "condemned to be free." Despite the anxiety of existence and identity, Giddens notes that the individual minimizes risk by relying upon existing social relationships—becoming a " 'reflexive self', a narrative project that is sustained through the constant reintegration of local involvements, system necessities and global concerns" (Abbinett 2003, 30). The possibility of a coherent identity under these circumstances is bleak indeed. A recent commentator (Saatchi 2008) summoned Freud's law of ambivalence in the context of (English) national identity and globalization: "The law states that it is possible for human beings to love and hate the same object at the same time; and that these contradictory feelings lead to frustration, which leads to anger."[11] Anxiety, frustration, and anger make the self emotionally vulnerable and perhaps even open to manipulation. If the self turns to familiar networks of trust, how is trust to be evaluated normatively? What if the familiarity results in racism? Problem-posing deliberations through trustworthy communicative action must, then, involve a dialogue among interlocutors where one party is not assigned an inferior status.

Culture and Hybridity

Cultural hybridity is the problem to be posed or deliberated through cultural policy. Hybridity refers to the intermixing of various influences in art. In the midst of global cultural influences, reactions to hybridity vary across societies. In some cases, it is embraced, and its existence celebrated through notions of diversity or multiculturalism in cultural policies. In terms of this book, an example would be a society's ability to exchange and absorb diverse creative expressions both from within and outside its borders. Relevant cultural-policy measures would encourage open exchanges and encourage creative freedoms. However, quickly evolving hybridity provides the impetus for negotiations and deliberations in political systems to resolve social tensions. They can get resolved in an atmosphere of progressive degrees of trust (*Slim's Table*), or they can devolve into outright manipulation (*What's the Matter with Kansas?*).

At a general level, cultural policy is a direct reflection of the politics of cultural identity. The all too visible battle for economic resources (grants, subsidies, quotas, tax cuts) is often a battle for institutionalizing one or the other notion of a cultural identity (see figure 0.1). For example, it takes an act of U.S. Congress to erect any public monument in Washington, D.C. The city's monuments thus reflect the nation's image. It is in the interest of cultural-policy stakeholders to make creative arts, commercial or otherwise, serve the cause of cultural policy. There are various means of doing so: advocacy, legislation, creating arts institutions, financing, and grants, to name a few. Of course, not all art serves the cause of a cultural identity, and thus there exists a perennial tension between creative expressions and cultural identity. Nevertheless, just as the central bank in any country exercises considerable moral authority, known as suasion in economics, to provide indicative policy to constituent banks, governments lead through suasion in cultural policy as well; direct support for culture is merely one aspect of this leadership. Others include the public spaces—executive, regulatory, legislative, judicial, media—in which these deliberations take place. For example, President Obama and First Lady Michelle Obama have increased the profile of arts in general by surrounding themselves with arts advisors and making careful selections for the art to be displayed in the White House, which includes a number of avant-garde pieces and works by African American artists. According to the *Washington Post*: "They seem to redress past imbalances in the nation's sense of its own art" (Gopnik 2009). Another observer remarked: "What pieces Barack and Michelle decide on has wide-ranging implications about what art and artists should be on the public's radar, and could affect what those artists' work is worth" (Ackerman 2009).

The politics of culture identity is now increasingly complicated for governments. Globalization poses a particular challenge to a government's suasion and its ability to exercise control through resource distribution. A nation-state must now coexist with competing actors from within and outside its ranks. Local or subnational groups and organizations may challenge a nation-state's mandate or sense of purpose. At the international level, cultural flows and institutions sit parallel to nation-states. The United Nations Educational, Scientific, and Cultural Organization, for example, is often characterized—derisively at times, depending on the speaker—as an international ministry of culture that likes to frame the agenda for national cultural policies. But, there are other institutions that are also often examined with suspicion. The World Trade Organization seeks to liberalize flows of commodities, including creative arts, among its member states. In the last two decades, nation-states have fought faux battles, supporting either the UNESCO or WTO agendas, which are often taken to be in conflict with each other: governments often view UNESCO as supporting national efforts to preserve particular cultural identities while WTO is regarded as diluting these identities by enforcing free flows of creative expressions. That the same government often supports cultural flows through WTO while signing on to UNESCO instruments speaks to the competing influences and schizophrenia among governments.

Culture and Markets

Two implications follow from the profound ideological challenge to cultural policy posed by the WTO: the triumph of commercial flows and the weakening of the nation-state. Creative expressions may be produced through government patronage, commercial means, or both.[12] The WTO represents not just freer trade but also, in terms of cultural policy, the increasing commodification of creative output. Commodification here means the conversion of creative human experiences into commercial commodities and the increasing expansion of such consumption in everyday life. Herein lies the ideological divide to which I will return in the conclusion. The production of creative expressions through commercial means provides alternatives to artists and creative producers who were once at the mercy of limited markets or patronage systems. The starving artist is, after all, a cultural metaphor for the languishing state of the arts in any society. This same commercialization, for others, is the end of creativity, as commerce is viewed as a set of routinized and ritualized practices that binds both the producers and consumers in monotonous tasks and unending bouts of greed.[13]

The second challenge posed by commercial flows is that while such flows may or may not strengthen particular cultural expressions, they might weaken the hold of the nation-state over such expressions, even where commerce seems to be taking its cues from the nation-state or the state is directly or indirectly involved in their production. In cultural-policy deliberations, government measures have ranged from patronage to particular creative expressions because they cannot be sustained through market means (grants for fine and performing arts, usually), direct ownership and production (national museums or broadcast networks), patronage provided to thwart market incursions from other places (protecting national cinemas through quotas), and patronage provided to complement market means (subsidy schemes). Government cultural policies can also be market friendly through fiscal measures such as tax incentives and reduction of regulations (O'Hare, Feld, and Shuster 1983). Market systems may also encourage a state's ideological power; the so-called triumph of global liberalism can be characterized as an ideology favored by powerful governments, such as that of the United States. The historian Victoria de Grazia (2005) notes that America's consumer and commercial revolutions increased its cultural exports and extended the soft power of the government to convert others to this market-based ideology.

As globalization challenges systems of patronage and market-based networks proliferate, the denouement may not favor any particular outcome. First, the triumph of market systems may not be a triumph of the United States. De Grazia (2005) closes by noting that the United States, which gained from spreading its capitalist ideology, must now compete with other states that have caught up. "Though the United States may still be the single most dynamic force behind today's global consumer culture, it no longer exercises a sufficient technological edge to monopolize innovations in either production or consumption" (476). Second, globalization demonstrates that these deliberations take place between creative output and the formation of policies that affect cultural identity. Neither creative expressions nor cultural identities necessarily obey the logic of identity favoring the nation-state or other patronage systems. Artists receiving funding from a local arts organization may question local power, while those receiving funding from international organizations or funding sources may also question their benefactors' aims and intents. Third, if nation-states cannot dictate identity politics through their cultural policies, how will cultural identities be imagined? I stay close to the empirical ground in this book in noting that national identities remain strong but are overlapped by all kinds of other identities.

One Last Critique

Cultural policy, the institutional interventions that make creative expressions relevant to group identities, may be understood in narrow as well as expansive ways. In an expansive way, cultural policy involves the cultivation of particular tastes in people in an effort to fulfill specific societal purposes. As such, cultural policy transcends creative expression to include the education system as whole. In fact, here culture is understood as a way of life, and thus cultural policy seeks to preserve or, at times, create a particular way of life for people. Several cultural-studies theorists take cultural policy as propagation of ideology through education and art to make docile subjects out of those who are governed (Miller and Yúdice 2002). The concept recalls the Marxian concept of the state as the committee for the management of the interests of the bourgeoisie, the Gramscian notion of hegemonic ideologies that make subjects out of those governed, and the Barthes-Foucault notion of governmentality wherein the state cares for individuals in such a way that those governed fail to doubt the state's sense of purpose by, at times, internalizing oppression. Markets, more or less, are also posited as oppressive structures that gain from governmentality and, as in the Marxian viewpoint, the state appears to be in cahoots with the capitalist in the purposeful production of a particular culture. Commodified cultural expressions here profit the capitalist and help the state govern by homogenizing or taming the subjects.

At such a grand level, cultural-policy studies, even if traced through painstaking ethnographies and genealogies, as Foucauldian analyses tend to do, is unaware of any potential of falsifiability or the examination of conditions under which it could possibly be mistaken. Under this schema, culture is "performative" and "expedient" and encompasses "strategies implied in any invocation of culture, any invention of tradition, in relation of some purpose or goal" (Yúdice 2003, 38). The sine qua non resource is globalization itself, which allows the state to maintain a national identity and for capital to profit from an international cultural division of labor (Yúdice 2003). This is a compelling analysis that not only underscores the misuses of cultural policy but also constructs an ethical perspective based on cultural activism that challenges the state-corporate nexus at a global level. Nevertheless, it flounders in its grandiosity in pronouncing any act of creativity not informed by critical activism as merely capitalist cultural policy by any other name.[14] That said, I share a sense of purpose with cultural studies in being skeptical when the term "culture" or "cultural policy" is invoked. However, I part company with certain analyses, to which I will return in the conclusion, that pronounce an ideological denunciation of market systems.

Anxiety and the Salience of Identity Politics

The anxieties of globalization are my starting point for a description of the salience and constitution of cultural identities. Globalization anxiety, as I noted before, refers to fears regarding the loss of collective identities as a result of increasing flows of people, things, ideas, or creative expressions. Cultural politics, as described in the last section, mediate the gap between anxiety and identity. This section describes the two ends, anxiety and identity, surrounding cultural politics (see fig. 0.1). We can also imagine a feedback loop between types of cultural policies and identities and the further exacerbation or mitigation of globalization anxieties.

Cultural identity, a sense of groupness, invariably reflects a political purpose in trying to effect goals for the group in question. Cultural identity needs cultural politics to realize itself. Quite obviously, for identity to be defined in the singular, as in nationality, for example, one institution's political prerogatives, the nation-state's in this instance, must override those of others. Historically, state patronage of the arts had this goal in mind. If identity politics are in flux again, the nation-state must defend its sense of purpose and legitimacy. In terms of art, creative expressions must be aligned or realigned with the prerogatives of the nation-state. That the state will succeed in, or with, its arts is not a fait accompli. The ability of the state to affix cultural boundaries to creative expressions amid pronouncements of anxiety remains dubious or mixed at best. The publicly funded National Air and Space Museum of the Smithsonian failed, amid a much-publicized controversy, in its attempt in 1995 to revisit and analyze the dropping of the bomb in Hiroshima with its exhibit of the plane *Enola Gay*. After this controversy, the museum "heard rumors that conservative superpatriots in Congress sent anonymous staff members to inspect Smithsonian exhibitions, looking for 'un-American' displays or wall texts" (Kammen 2006, 286).

The rise of the politics of cultural identity in a rapidly globalizing era is not puzzling. To note that identities are changing is simply a statement of the obvious. The puzzles lie in the forms identity takes and the processes underlying the transformation.[15] This is the metapower of affixing identity around particular parameters from which other cultural policies follow. Metapower looks underneath the quotidian to uncover how the actors and their issues came to embody meanings through successive interactions and their reflection on representational practices. In our case, metapower politics would reveal how, for example, the last movement Beethoven's Ninth Symphony, *Ode to Joy*, became the embodiment of Europe's hopes. Somewhat analogous insights can be found in sociology. For example, that nations are involved in a struggle for power is a routine insight. It lies at the level of what Giddens calls the practical consciousness: the symbolic but routinized ritual through which nations interact with each other (Giddens 1984). The ritual itself does not tell us how nations came into being as embodiments of specific meaning, which is the stuff of discursive consciousness for Giddens.[16] Rituals, representations, and the languages through which we interact embody reality but only through successive "objectifications," the stages of socialization and their institutionalization (Berger and Luckmann 1966).

The Cultural Politics of Symbolic Representation

The events examined in this book deal with symbolic representations and the struggles by groups to define them as cultural or to wipe out their existence in the name of cultural identity. Sociologists and anthropologists generally take symbolic representations, from those of the cave dweller to the ones emanating from a television set, as the most complex and deeply meaningful forms of objectivation. "The symbolic universe is conceived of as the matrix of *all* socially objectivated and subjectively real meanings; the entire historic society and the entire biography of the individual are seen as events taking place *within* this universe . . . so that the individual may 'locate' himself within its most solitary experiences" (Berger and Luckman 1966, 96).

When an artist introduces symbolic representations that challenge us to rethink our *location* or "place" in the world, he can produce a variety of reactions from introspection to outright social hostility. As the meaning of things that we took for granted begins to change, anxiety might take the place of sureness. The controversies generated around Robert Mapplethorpe's photographs in the United States in the late 1980s, especially the 1990 legal challenges leveled at Cincinnati's Contemporary Arts Center for allegedly "pandering obscenity," are among the many episodes that questioned some fundamental assumptions about the display of symbolic representations. The Mapplethorpe controversy was itself part of debates centered on the budget of the National Endowment for the Arts in the United States and its role in funding "American" art.

Mapplethorpe's challengers inhabited the right wing of the American political establishment. Interestingly, the American left was at the same time leading its own challenges against particular types of symbolic representations. Self-professed multiculturalists, especially in the English literature departments of U.S. universities, questioned literary and artistic representations that canonized the work of Caucasian male creators while marginalizing those of women and of minorities. To be sure, they were questioning the canon, not the politics of the authors included in the canon. Shakespeare had stood at the dawn of merchant-led capitalism questioning and transforming all kinds of social roles in Elizabethan and Tudor England, just as Mapplethorpe did four centuries later. The more general point is that the Shakespeare being questioned in the late twentieth century is the symbolically objectified Shakespeare, a particular strain of "Western" cultural traditions. The multiculturalists ranged from those who wanted to expand the canonical repertoires to include non-Western, marginalized, or non-Caucasian voices, to those who argued that the idea of a canon itself was a hegemonic or reactionary practice or those who located in Shakespeare noncanonical but more progressive and subversive practices.[17] There is also a more general point: symbolic representations are important and, therefore, contested in all political hues. The historian Michael Kammen begins an engrossing book on art controversies in the United States by noting that they "matter because they are so symptomatic of social change as a highly visible but contested process" (2006, xi).

Debates around creative expressions within nation-states have not gone away but are increasingly overlapped by controversies surrounding flows of creative expressions across borders or those affected by international trends and influences. Globalization presents an opportunity for examining not just new symbolic representations and the way cultural identities are constructed around them but also the conceptual processes by which we understand identity. The politics of creative expressions examined here foreshadow the anxieties of globalization underlying them. It is in this sense that Appadurai begins a text on globalization (2000) by locating the anxiety in the U.S. academic world. Underlying these anxieties are the globalized flows "of objects, persons, images and discourses" leading to what he calls "relations of disjuncture" or disruptions in the ways of life or the ideas with which we make sense of it (2000, 5).

Geertz (1973) analyzes the Balinese cockfight not in routinized functional terms to provide a commentary on social hierarchies in Bali but as "a metasocial commentary upon the whole matter of assorting human beings into fixed hierarchical ranks and then organizing the major part of the collective existence around that assortment" (448). Now imagine walking into a cockfight as the village struggles to maintain its meaning not just against the "modernizing" Indonesian state that, Geertz notes, regarded the cockfight as "traditional" but also against a whole host of other symbolic representations unleashed by the global "relations of disjuncture" noted above. It is the interactions that arise from such disjunctures and the anxieties thereof that provide clues to the metapower inherent in interactions around symbolic representations. Generally, it is easy to enact particular representational dramas in isolation. Interacting cultures, however, produce tremendous anxieties and disruptions in narratives (Goffmann 1959).

Globalization and Identity

Globalization's disjunctures or disruptions in people's narratives provide fascinating stories of various kinds of identity politics. Memorable opening salvos came from post–Cold War theorists who bemoaned the "order" produced though a balance of power and located its fallout in identity terms: Samuel Huntington's famous essay (1993) predicted that the new sources of conflict will be cultural and civilizational. Specifically, in the words of the Singaporean diplomat Kishore Mahbubani, whom he quoted, Huntington posited this conflict as between the West and the Rest, the Confucian-Islamic Alliance, which does not share such Western cultural values such as constitutionalism, democracy, and free markets. Meanwhile, a liberal interpretation of civilizational dynamics came from Barber's *Jihad Versus Mc-World* (1995), which represented the *Gemeinschaft* versus *Gesellschaft* conflict as between tribal and religious identities versus those defined through commodity-led global capitalism. Unlike Tönnies, however, who predicted that *Gesellschaft* would triumph over *Gemeinschaft*, Barber outlined a conflict between the two camps, solitary consumers without a social identity to bind them confronting armies of jihadists who "gather, in isolation from one another but in common struggle against commerce and cosmopolitanism, around a variety of dimly remembered but sharply imagined ethnic, religious, and racial identities meant to root the wandering postmodern soul and prepare it to do battle with its counterparts in McWorld" (164). The anxieties unleashed through the televised images of the falling Twin Towers in Manhattan on September 11, 2001, seemed to confirm the tragic and pathological apotheosis of these struggles.

Against the backdrop of the civilizational constructs, with their emphatically grand and linear insights, theorists of myriad scholarly persuasions examine with a questioning ambiguity the rise of cultural politics as the breakdown of ways of life or structures of meaning that might be called culture (Lapid and Kratochwil 1996). The sociologist Hannerz speaks of "information overload" and "information anxiety" as processes of disjuncture that make it hard for people to manage their "cultural inventory" (1992, 32). In seeking to avoid the term "messy," he notes the multifaceted aspects of "cultural complexity." Niezen (2004) notes that globalization could be understood as "a permanent state of uncertainty" between universal and particular values. Niezen's view is more nuanced than that of Barber, locating resistance to the McWorld free-trade-based cultural values also among other universalists such as those who gathered in late 1999 in Seattle to protest against the meetings of the World Trade Organization. Castells's important contribution to thinking about cultural identity in terms of globalization also locates the identity politics of various social movements as reactions against globalization: "When the world becomes too large to be controlled, social actors aim at shrinking it back to their size and reach" (1997, 66). The international legal scholar Tania Voon notes: "The fear that cultural identities, traditions, and rituals are under threat is part of a broader anxiety about growing interconnectedness and faster rates of change in life" (2007, 248). These narratives are counterparts of the old debate over whether interdependence leads to animosity or harmony. The former view is epitomized in Hobbes or Sun Tzu, the latter in the Vedas and Rousseau.

Most views are unable to distinguish the bellicose and irenic elements, epitomized in Fernand Braudel's words as "the stimulating impact of strangers" (1963/1993, 10). Both views are also variously cited in interpreting Rudyard Kipling's famous verse from "The Ballad of East and West":

> OH, East is East, and West is West, and never the twain shall meet,
> Till Earth and Sky stand presently at God's great Judgment Seat;
> But there is neither East nor West, Border, nor Breed, nor Birth,
> When two strong men stand face to face, tho' they come from the ends
>   of the earth!

Globalization's complex identity politics can be examined through representational places or spaces, flows, interstices, or a combination of these. Spaces may be physical, conceptual, or virtual spaces wherein identity politics are played out. Anthropologists call these cultural spaces. Representational flows may be particularly apt at examining the coming together of various spaces, while interstices may be apt for featuring borderline conflicts historically or geographically. Regardless of the choice made, identity accounts feature considerable ambiguity and a resistance to any single narrative. Qualitative narratives of identity tend to show considerable negotiation of boundary conditions, resistances, and awakenings and an emphasis on the conceptual shifts made. This is perhaps best revealed in books with the phrase "The Idea of" or "The Invention of" in the title.[18] While territorial claims remain important in affixing identity, emotional and imaginary ties expand extraterritorial tensions (Berezin and Schain 2003). Thus, the idea of France must now coexist with the idea of Europe; the idea of a local community, with that of diasporas and networks. Singular notions of identity, in other words, must coexist with multiple markers of identity and hybridity. Along with the "idea of" books, there is a plethora of books analyzing hybrid, syncretic, and creolized identities in analytical narratives, fictional and nonfictional, ranging from Anderson's *Imagined Communities* (1983) to Zachary's *The Global Me* (2000).

The quantitative dimensions of these identity politics reveal similar overlaps and ambiguities. Most international polls tend to find support for globalization around the world. One poll in 2007, which asked if "globalization, especially increasing connections in our country with others around the world, is mostly good or mostly bad," found the highest levels of support among export-led economies such as China (87 percent) and

Israel (82 percent) and below 50 percent support only in three countries (Mexico, Russia, and Philippines).[19] Nevertheless, another survey in 2006 covering sixty-four countries found that, on average, only 38 percent of the respondents considered globalization to be good for their countries, with numbers ranging from 71 percent in Africa to 35 percent in Latin America. At the same time, most respondents in Europe and North America held that globalization is neither good nor bad.[20] Interestingly, most polls conducted solely in the United States on the effects of international trade on the U.S. economy tend to provide negative support for its effects on U.S. investments, jobs, and competitiveness.[21] The findings in Hermann, Tetlock, and Diascro (2001) confirm that U.S. politicians are unable to shield themselves from "populist anxieties" regarding international trade but, nevertheless, Americans in general support trade as long as they think it does not make them worse off (192). Surprisingly, contrary to many Americans' views of the Muslim world, a poll in seven predominantly Muslim countries found that majorities supported globalization in six of them.[22] While these economic indicators are not about identity per se, they may reveal the anxieties regarding the effects of globalization in the United States. National-level data on noneconomic indicators reveal similar ambiguities. One poll asked Europeans in five countries if they thought of their identity as European, international (non-European), regional, or national. In France, a 52 percent majority of respondents thought of their identity primarily in national terms, whereas in Germany only 22 percent did so.[23]

In an interconnected world, the fault lines of identity politics do not lie between some form of identity that is primeval or primordial and one that we might consider modern but rather in the contestations around hybridity and the possibility of global identities.[24] For every "true" American there is a mongrel, a hybrid, tracing his or her "roots" to a mix of cultural influences. The results, in terms of cultural politics, at least, are often arbitrated by institutional power holders seeking or with access to resources and spaces of deliberation.

Exposition

The pages that follow explore how the politics of cultural deliberations lead to the ascendance of one or another notion of cultural identity in politics. The elephant in the room is, of course, national cultural identity, which, depending on the context, is being resurrected, obliterated, surpassed, or complemented by other identities. Earlier in this chapter I spelled out the three conditions for problem-posing deliberations: trust, transparency, and inclusion. Their presence is directly proportional to levels of conflict resolution and transformative understanding. Their absence leads to manipulation and coercion. The deliberations themselves are about resource allocation, whether through patronage systems or market means.

The chapters that follow spell out the logic of cultural-policy deliberations that span the themes of this book. Chapter 2 examines the economic and technological roots of cultural politics. It also examines cultural policy and creative industry instruments, specifically patronage versus market-network systems, to argue that the latter are slowly but surely supplanting the former, though in some instances there is still room for patronage. More important, nation-states, through their control of several types of national and international institutions, control the spaces wherein these deliberations take place. Chapters 3 and 4 attend to the principal cultural conflict of our time, namely, the formation of global rules governing the flows of creative products. They foreshadow the influence of national cultural-policy elites and entertainment industries in these deliberations, which often blame unfettered markets for a loss of (national) identity. Chapter 3 analyzes the deliberations at the World Trade Organization, and chapter 4, at UNESCO and the European Union. Chapter 5 deals with the production of creative expressions in developing countries, where entertainment industries often turn to global commercial networks for production support as well as for a realization of a cultural voice. Chapter 6 shows the contradictions in cultural policies, which often suspect global flows and yet welcome cultural tourists. It also tries to show that what is called "cultural" is also a human construct by pointing out that sex work in Bangkok, for example, is a direct result of Thailand's cultural tourism policies. The conclusion returns to the broad themes of this volume, originating in global anxieties and politics of cultural identity, to speak of cultural voices as overlapping articulations of various types of identity inherent in any individual and evoked in creative expressions. The normative model seeks to distinguish creative expressions from cultural politics: creative expressions can be produced through a variety of means. Cultural voices often reflect these expressions, but they can also be the opposite—the manipulation of the creative voice to fit elite purposes.

2

Value, Markets, Patronage

A bird doesn't sing because it has an answer, it sings because it has a song.

—Maya Angelou

How are creative expressions valued, and what means encourage their production? How do evolving technologies affect creative output and cultural valuation? How, for example, should we value a dance performance? Limiting ourselves to its costs and revenues would be narrow, if not outright vulgar or trivial in some contexts, and would miss the aesthetic or symbolic importance of dance. Questions of value and production both link and delink creative expressions from cultural representations and the institutional contexts within which these representations are constructed, sustained, and debated. As I explained in the previous chapter, while creativity is an exercise in imagination, skills, and resource mobilization, cultural identity is linked with these expressions only through the pulling and hauling of deliberative cultural politics. Figure 2.1, a detail of figure 0.1, shows how questions of value link creative products with cultural products

Given the multiple and wide-reaching influences inherent in globalization, the ability of cultural politics to affix any creative expression with a salient cultural identity is always questionable. The economic, technological, and institutional networks that sustain creative activities further complicate the creativity-culture nexus. They may not always sustain particular notions of cultural identity, despite social or political impetus to do so. However, the obverse scenario also holds: political and social pressures

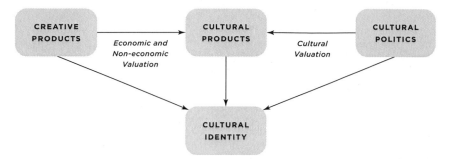

Figure 2.1   Valuation and Identity

to maintain particular notions of cultural identity may also direct creative output. For example, at the behest of the postcolonial Indian state, classical Indian music and dance moved from religious significance and patronage to the secularized proscenium of "national heritage."[1]

The question of value allows creative products to be redefined as cultural products. What lends value to a creative product? Even if the artist denies it, the institutional context is important for the production of value. The institutional context informs, constrains, or expands the choices available to the artist. In this sense, the artist is merely the supplier of value. Art must also be demanded: here, the social-institutional context becomes important. We admire, hear, see, touch, or collect art—all of which are consumption practices, in the parlance of the economist—not just because of some innate aesthetic sense but also through tastes cultivated from sociopolitical influences.

There is also increasing flexibility in terms of the networks that make possible particular types of creative products, especially as market networks increasingly supplant state-led patronage networks. Both the patronage and market networks are now also global in nature, leading to ever greater degrees of hybridity and cross-fertilization. Once, patronage led to worries over the freedom of the lonely artist, but the new worries concern cultural commodification in which artistic content may be diluted or dumbed down for mass consumption and production.

Economic reasoning is the point of entry for this chapter. Value, price, and production *can* be understood from an economic perspective in which individual preferences determine both the price as well as the levels—quantitative *and* qualitative—at which art gets produced. Economists, therefore, are "value-neutral": they make no judgment regarding the quality of art that is demanded and supplied in a marketplace. In a world in which only the market mattered, normative claims regarding other ways of valuing of art would be unnecessary—in such a world, there would also be no society or politics. Especially in the case of representational practices, social and political institutions step in to regulate and rank artistic practices. These institutional practices are not synonymous with market ones, but the connection between the two is undeniable. State patronage of the arts may be undertaken in the name of the market's inability to sustain particular arts or to realize their value, but more often than not, such calculations are informed by political imperatives that may have nothing to do with economics. For example, support for national monuments and heritage may have little to do with the underlying economics.

This chapter first disentangles the economic, technological, and sociological claims regarding artistic value and output. In doing so, it provides the material basis for the cultural politics discussed in the last chapter. Together all these factors outline a political economy of art in which sociopolitical institutions often appropriate economic arguments to favor particular representational practices or cultural identities (the end points of both figure 0.1 and 2.1).

The chapter also seeks to show that even though cultural politics change individual preferences into sociological or cultural preferences, economists need not be afraid of social preferences, even though individual preferences form the bedrock of their thinking. Consumption preferences are not merely "constrained" by institutions; as sociologists show, they are themselves social institutions. The *effects* of preferences can be taken as given, but the *origins* of preferences, which is especially important to understanding the genesis of artistic representations, lies in the realm of sociology. Rather than presenting value and price merely from an individualist perspective, I seek to connect it to social and political practices.

A further complication in the sociopolitical practices within which art is valued and produced is that these practices must be placed in a global perspective. Thus, what is to be valued and how it is to be produced often now takes on global dimensions. It is in this context that the previous chapter referred to the global anxieties about representational practices. The questions of artistic value and output that an eminent economist once termed "frivolous activities" (Caves 2000, vii) may not be as frivolous when tied up with powerful narratives of cultural identity.[2] Thus, this chapter is not so concerned about the most efficient means of producing art or whether states or markets produce diversity; rather, it is concerned about the political and economic processes that sustain art and the way they are linked or delinked from particular notions of cultural identity and diversity.[3]

Value: Creative or Cultural?

Cultural value is not synonymous with creative value, although the two are often conflated. Cultural value arises from political processes that seek to rank the symbolic importance of creative expressions in terms of a national or other form of group identity. Creative value speaks to the ranking of the creative output in material or nonmaterial terms to the artist and her audience. Furthermore, as noted before, with creative work price is often only a crude if not erroneous measure of value. For example, the market value of a piece of art is a material ranking while the importance of that artwork to a particular art critic may be a nonmaterial ranking. Given that these rankings may be a mixture of both, markets are but one way of resolving the divergent expectations in value between the producers and the consumers. Quite often, even what the economic actor—the famous homo economicus of neoclassical political economy—does is initially settled in social and political institutions. In real life, resource allocation to the arts is a product of both market and political motivations.

Through the process of market valuation, economics links the relative desire to produce or sell an art object with the preference ordering of the consumer who will buy it. Even a unique art object's scarcity and related price are ultimately contingent upon consumers' valuation. If the demand is high, the art object will fetch a high price. Markets are nothing more than auction houses, really; in fact, art markets represent one of the few places where physical auctions still take place as bidders enter their successive evaluations of art through their price offers. Sotheby's and Christie's are the glamorous icons of these art markets. EBay is a sophisticated digital version of this auction; hawkers on a street corner in New York or New Delhi are another example. These auctions are unique in various ways. For one, they are contingent upon individual valuations; in this case, their normative valuation is expressed in terms of price. Prices, in turn, express the relative satisfaction or utility to a consumer of owning an art object or of selling it for the producer. Bruno Frey (2000, 23) aptly sums up the economic valuation of art:

> The concept of art, as understood by economists, starts with the preferences of the *individual*. This distinguishes the economic concept of art fundamentally from other definitions of art which derive from quite different principles, e.g. from a notion of aesthetic beauty based on deeper philosophical grounds. It also strongly differs from the concept of art defined by art experts (art historians, museum curators, conservationists, art critics and journalists, gallery owners and artists themselves), who have superior professional knowledge of the various aspects of artistic activities and therefore derive the authority to pass judgment about what art is. According to the economic approach, the individual preferences for art are recorded, but no normative judgment about it is given: art in this sense is what people think art is.

As an elaboration on what determines the market value of art, the economic evaluation is indispensable. Nevertheless, it is fraught with problems. Art markets are often distorted, even economically, through public support measures ranging from subsidies to taxation incentives to outright protectionism. A market valuation is hardly ever a qualitative measure of what people think art is. More important, artistic value is not synonymous with market value. Creative processes are much more: they may reveal what economists term as value intrinsic to art. "What do we mean when we say that Monteverdi's operas or Giotto's frescoes are valuable in the history of art? In neither case does an appeal to individual utility or to price seem appropriate" (Throsby 2001, 26). The economist David Throsby resolves this paradox in terms of cultural value, which I will discuss later. For now, it is important to note that creative output—imagination realized in various ways—may follow market incentives, but it may also be produced just for art's sake—or, in the words of Maya Angelou, "because it has a song." Artistic freedom and institutional incentives are important for creative output. But even when lacking these incentives, art can still ooze out of our anxieties and blossom from our hopes. Maya Angelou's creativity speaks of racism, patriarchy, class, and sexual pathologies. Great works of art have come out of prison cells, Holocaust camps, or prehistoric cave walls.

More often than not, the valuation of creative output is made in terms that are cultural, not economic. The concept of intrinsic value is itself illustrative if we ask, 'intrinsic to what'? Throsby (2001, 28–29) more or less equates creative value with cultural value. This disaggregation of cultural value into components speaks to culture as ways and habits of life for groups of people:[4]

- Aesthetic value, or properties of beauty or art shared in a culture
- Spiritual value, or value to a religious group
- Social value, expressed in terms of identity and location
- Historical value, reflecting things as they were within a culture through time
- Symbolic value, as a purveyor of representational meaning
- Authenticity value, accruing to the original work

When cultural artifacts are not imbued with a sense of power, the criteria of cultural value can seem innocent and pious. St. Peter's basilica is not just culturally significant for Catholics or for humanity as a whole but is also vested with the power of the Vatican. The indelible contribution of sociology, anthropology, and cultural studies to thinking about cultural value lies in presenting culture in power terms. Many of the techniques that Throsby recommends in understanding value—especially mapping, thick description, and expert appraisal—all start with an acute sensibility for social and political power hierarchies. *What markets are to prices, power hierarchies and deliberation are to cultural value.*

Value, Power, and Culture

Power, as outlined in chapter 1, can be understood instrumentally as either constraining or expanding particular possibilities for action. In a metapower sense, power constitutes the identity of the actor or issue. Metapower helps us uncover how the actors and their issues came to embody specific meanings through successive interactions. Metapower, therefore, precedes instrumental power. It is especially important for understanding the origins or construction and meaning of preferences before these preferences are constrained through further action. Economists generally take preferences as given and then study their resolution or effects. At the level of understanding cultural value, such notions of preferences are unhelpful; we need to know how group preferences came into being and whose power is most privileged in these preferences. For cultural-studies theorists, value, power, and culture go together. An example is the cultivation of taste through educational and other institutions, especially when such taste normatively ranks high culture above pop culture.[5] Therefore, to understand preference formation and its effects, instrumental and metapower notions are needed.

The notion of symbolic power in Bourdieu (1993) details not only the distribution of cultural artifacts in society but also a diffusion of the ways in which they are received and understood in society. His concept of *habitus* relates to the way in which cultural representations and practices are self-generating while that of *field* relates to the hierarchical organization of social and political institutions that rank cultural production. An understanding of cultural value from the perspective of a way of life must include both the diffusion and ranking of cultural production. Thus, while Throsby notes symbolic *value*, Bourdieu notes symbolic *power*. Value in the latter case includes power diffused through the institutions that regulate and rank cultural production. However, while Bourdieu is useful for thinking about cultural value, this is not synonymous with the valuation of all creative work. Several studies, including detailed ethnographies, show that the meaning of art varies for individuals from deeply personal to socially significant.[6] Halle (1993) provides an ethnography of art collections in the homes of 160 upper-, middle-, and working-class families. The meaning of art in these homes is deeply personal and challenges conceptions such as Bourdieu's, where all art seems to be ranked and regulated through diffused power.

While economic theory has traditionally been concerned with the preferences of the individual, it is not entirely innocent of the concept of institutionally determined preferences. New institutional economics starts with collective preferences and interactions as sources of long-term economic growth and change. These preferences may be influenced through informal institutions like customs and traditions, or formal ones like markets and regulatory authorities (North 1990). Furthermore, these institutionally defined preferences emerge from complex environments and may not be the most efficient, in the economists' sense of producing the greatest good for the greatest number. The analysis of long-term collective action in Olson (1982) points to the power of small organized groups over that of society to effect institutional change in their favor, given that a society as a whole faces many problems of collective action. As the power of few overrides the power of many, countries in the long run make inefficient choices by locking in a few personal rather than a vast number of impersonal choices. North (1994, 366) notes that "most societies throughout history got 'stuck' in an environment that did not evolve into the impersonal exchange essential to capturing the productivity gains that came from the specialization and division of labor that have produced the Wealth of Nations." Sociologists critique such market analyses to show that the impersonal and arms-length relationships of the markets are in fact culturally specific and intersubjectively understood by those who participate in them (Granovetter 1985).[7] This does not take away, however, from the central insight from institutional economics that preferences are not always efficient, in either a cultural or an institutional sense, and may reveal the power of the few over the power of the many. For my analysis, it is important to remember that in forming cultural policy, elite and creative producers may have organized to effect cultural policies in their favor. In mapping these preferences, it is important to show how the preferences of these particular individuals may or may not intersect with other social groups. It may very well be that the protections afforded to French or Canadian film industries do in fact correspond to national preferences, but it is also possible that this may not be the case. Furthermore, collective preferences evolve and, as pointed out by new institutional economics, learning is the key to understanding long-term change.

To understand the origins of cultural preferences and their role in shaping the value of art, markets provide some grounding, but so do informal and formal institutions. Later, we will see how a focus on institutions is especially helpful in understanding the links between preferences and cultural identity.

Production: Property Rights and Democracy

Whether for the sequestered poet in a prison cell or the networked Hollywood producer, the path from creativity to output takes resource mobilization and, importantly, an environment conducive to creativity. The prisoner must have an instrument to scratch her poems on the prison walls and must conjure the emotional and physical strength to do so. The tasks of the Hollywood producer may be onerous in other ways. In both cases, appeals to culture and identity may be embedded in the creativity, or they may be made to attract resources. While human beings turn to creativity in all situations, it is also conceptually and empirically known, as I explain later, that well-specified, market-oriented property rights and political incentives that allow for freedom will enhance creative industry.

Resource mobilization results in transaction costs, and these tend to be high for creative goods and services. The concept of transaction costs goes beyond the materials that go into producing a good. They are the administrative, legal, distribution, and marketing costs usually associated with any good arising, as it were, from the transaction itself. A few examples include the 1 percent or more of charges that credit card companies charge sellers or buyers for an electronic transaction, or that only 15 percent of the total cost of a home-delivered pizza goes toward what we eat; the rest is transaction costs. It is now fairly well known that societies and polities that keep transaction costs low actually produce higher growth rates. However, just as the transaction cost of a home-delivered pizza is going to be higher than perhaps selling lemonade at a street corner, so also creative goods and services have characteristics that make transaction costs high. Even an incarcerated poet faces high transaction costs in obtaining writing materials, avoiding a long incarceration, or distributing the work outside the prison.

Creative goods and services contain unique characteristics. For example, "cost disease" refers to the increasing costs of arts production: a Schubert quartet in 2010 will sound similar and take the same input of four musicians as it did nearly two centuries ago, but musicians are now a professional class and will accordingly command higher wages (Baumol and Bowen 1966). This is different from other products where less costly inputs are found through successive innovations leading to a long-run decline in costs. Second, high transaction costs cause dilemmas for production. Caves (2000) specifies these dilemmas well: artistic productions contain high degrees of uncertainty and risk, are likely to be produced by nonconformist individuals, bring together multiple skills, are highly differentiated, ask for a high degree of coordination to produce, and are durable products that can accrue revenues for years to come, if successful. Goods with high risk and uncertainty carry higher transaction costs; thus, incentives to produce them not only need to be well specified but can also be complicated. These incentives and guarantees, at the level of rules governing production, are known as property rights.

The key to keeping transaction costs low is well-specified property rights that make it easy to mobilize and deploy resources. An artist who can receive patronage from the state reduces market-based uncertainties and risk—although it also makes her beholden to the dicta of the state. As an institutional form, markets possess several advantages in encouraging innovation and production, even while there may be dispositions favoring state intervention in the case of artists. Douglass North, whose analysis of property rights in the rise of Western Europe is considered seminal, notes that successful countries like England and Netherlands worked out property rights that reward efficiency and innovation while relatively unsuccessful countries like France and Spain were not able to do so (North and Thomas 1973; North 1981). In particular, while the rising commercial classes checked the power of the state in England and Netherlands, in France and Spain the state increased its powers. In France especially, an elaborate bureaucracy developed whose regulatory capacities were unmatched. Adam Smith in his *Wealth of Nations* (1776/2003) referred to late-seventeenth-century France under Louis XIV and his finance minister, Colbert, as a venal society that would turn France into a nation full of shopkeepers as opposed to the innovation and industry of those across the English Channel.[8] The state-business relationship is one factor in reducing transaction costs; freedom to innovate is another. Colbert's France regulated everything from people's diets to the number of hours artists should paint to the number of warps and woofs in textiles. In an anecdote often repeated, one businessman supposedly pounded his fists on the table and demanded, "*Laissez-nous faire*," a remark now attributed to the origins of this phrase of free trade. In a similar vein, Cummings and Katz (1987, chapter 1) notes that while the rise of the bourgeoisie in England led to the proliferation of painting as these new classes began to collect and patronize art, in absolutist states such as those ruled by the Habsburgs and the Bourbons, royal patronage played a major role in producing art on "a grand scale," such as the opera houses and related institutions in Vienna and Paris.[9] Meanwhile, the Florentine Renaissance is taken as an example of the freedoms given to industry and artists by the Medici family and a rising class of wealthy merchants.[10] A final factor often taken into consideration in reducing transaction costs is competitiveness. The Florentine Renaissance may have come about as a result of the competitiveness among Italian city-states. Competitiveness is understood here as an informal institution constraining the ability of business to exploit consumers.

In general, property rights supply the institutional matrix, the formal and informal practices and rules, within which productive activity takes place: "The cost of transacting reflects the overall complex of institutions—formal and informal—that make up an economy or, on an even greater scale, a society. This overall structure ultimately shapes the cost of transacting at the individual contract level, and when economists talk about efficient markets, they have taken for granted an elaborate framework of constraints" (North 1990, 66).

This framework of constraints obviously calls attention to the political and sociological factors that make a market possible. Cultural understandings, therefore, both give rise to and facilitate the operations within a market: "Mental models are the internal representations that individual cognitive systems create to interpret the environment; institutions are external (to the mind) mechanisms individuals create to structure and order the environment" (North 1990, 3). Nevertheless, economists do not really provide much depth to these cultural understandings, which are the subject of scrutiny among sociologists and anthropologists. To these scholars, the seeming autonomy of economic agents in markets is, in fact, embedded in cultural practices that are well understood: "Culture is not a once-for-all influence but an ongoing process, continuously constructed and reconstructed during interaction" (Granovetter 1985, 486).[11] Such analyses point not only to the limits of strategic action or rationality as understood by economists but also to the origins of preferences in cultural practices. Guyer (2004), for example, shows that what appear as non-market-based or nonrational practices in historical equatorial Africa were an elaborate framework of symbolic representational practices, easily understood by the participants and analogous to any market system in Europe or otherwise, that allowed economic transactions to take place. Guyer understands rationality as reason but then embeds it in cultural understandings.

A sociological or anthropological understanding of markets and the origins of preferences enhances understanding of creative practices and their links to culture. Locking creativity in a system of state patronage may produce a certain aversion to markets, but we cannot automatically assume that art would be of an inferior quality under patronage systems. Great works of art have been produced in the service of a state, for which the only reasonable explanation is the elaborate system of cultural understandings that produced this art. Culture-specific preferences can reduce uncertainty and provide impetus to a particular type of artistic practice much the same way that a genre of films based on a particular formula (such as sex, violence, or melodrama) guide a film studio in garnering profits.[12]

Nevertheless, awful art can also be produced by dependence on the state. Patronage can produce moral hazard if it always leads to one type of work being favored over others. The film *Amadeus* makes much of the way the composer Salieri used his royal connections to rise above Mozart in the artistic circles of Vienna, even though Mozart was the superior composer. However, Cowen (1998) notes that although Mozart was buried in an unmarked pauper's grave, he was a reasonably successful artist of his time, which may have led to his ability to take risks with his artistic practices. In this sense, Salieri could not afford to take risks.

French grand opera, which flourished roughly between 1830 and 1870, is a precursor of formulaic production: five acts with an obligatory ballet and a great deal of spectacle on stage. From Rossini's *William Tell* in 1829 to Verdi's *Aida* in 1871, grand opera defined the cultural life of the growing middle classes in Paris.[13] What's more, grand opera was both a commercial success and heavily subsidized and sanctioned through state patronage. The early histories of grand opera present it as a perfect union of art and business in the post-Napoleonic era, when financing opera became difficult (Crosten 1948). Current musicologists do not deny that grand opera embraced private business norms but place these in the context of democratization and its embodiment in the "nation." Grand opera was as politicized as its predecessors and became "a subtly used tool of the state" (Fulcher 1987, 2). Fulcher doubts the evidence that a break of patronage led to opera's reliance upon markets. There was instead a subtle shift to the idea of the nation and the spectacle associated with grand opera, which sought to seduce the public. The cultural institutions "dispensed a culture calculated to project an image that would inspire and reconcile but the very vagueness of which encouraged different groups to assimilate and construe it differently" (Fulcher 1987, 202).[14] A somewhat similar thesis located in the political economy of its time is presented in terms of the anxieties unleashed by the industrial revolution and the stresses of living in a growing metropolis. It became technologically possible to produce the grand spectacle that audiences wanted and the Paris Opera "gave its audiences the opportunity to forget their mundane existence and dream vividly as they watched the theatrical illusion" (Gerhard 1998, 23).[15]

Creative practices can flourish under both market-based and patronage networks. It is useful to give this careful consideration before ruling in favor of one or the other. First, a case made in favor of state patronage on the basis of market failure may need additional scrutiny. It may not

be market failure that argues for state patronage but merely path dependence and the state's prerogatives to maintain particular institutional and
cultural practices. In other words, a case for circumscribing state patronage made purely in economic terms may find no resonance among the
deliberative processes of the state that may be predisposed toward other
practices. Part of the predisposition is historic: state patronage itself grew
out of a historic system of religious and aristocratic patronage. Gregory
the Great, pope from 590 to 604, encouraged the *Schola Cantourm* that
would later give rise to the chants that are identified by his name. The early
Renaissance owes its origins as much to the Church as it does to wealthy
patrons such as Casimo de Medici. By the fifteenth century, "merchants,
manufacturers, and financiers" supplanted the "munificent source" or religious and Church patronage in Italy (Chagy 1973, 25–26).[16] Most great
feats of ancient and medieval architecture and art had religious or aristocratic benefactors. And any case made for the quality or diversity of creative
expressions, either under patronage or market networks, might also need
additional empirical substantiation. Both markets and states have a way of
rewarding particular types of creativity over others, although markets may
favor innovation and uniqueness more than state or religious patrons do
(Cowen 1998).[17] Even though markets are embedded in cultural practices,
market-based networks tend to be less hierarchical in terms of the constraints on artists. Therefore, the degree of control over individual artists
is less while the degree of artistic freedom may be higher.

Despite the shortcomings of market systems, a new school recognizes
that political and market freedoms combined with skills rapidly reproduce
creative economies. Florida (2002) argues for the importance of three Ts—
tolerance, technology, and talent. These are key drivers, in the United Sates
and elsewhere, for the creative economy, which now accounts for up to one-
third of the U.S. workforce. Florida documents the case of various "creative
cities" in the United States where the combination of the three Ts allowed
for the creative economy to grow, especially information technology industries. Table 2.1 presents the results for four countries studied by the World
Intellectual Property Organization and shows the importance of copyright
industries to both economic output and employment. Significantly, in the
periods studied by WIPO, mostly post-1990 for the four cases, none of the
cases features negative compound annual growth rates. Nevertheless, even
these macrostatistics suggest something significant: the United States is
the only country where the ratio of copyright industries' contribution to

TABLE 2.1

Percentage Share of Copyright Industries in GNP and Employment

	Core copyright share of GNP (%)[a]	Share of total employment (%)	Total copyright share of GNP (%)[b]	Share of total employment (%)
Singapore (2001)	2.8	3.64	5.67	5.80
Canada (2002)	3.99	—	5.38	6.96 (2001)
USA (2002)	5.98	4.02	11.97	8.4
Hungary (2002)	3.96	4.15	6.69	7.1

[a] According to WIPO, core copyright industries are wholly engaged in creative activities in all aspects of the value chain from conceptualization to consumption and archiving.

[b] The total copyright industry includes core copyright as well as partial copyright industries, the latter including those in which only a portion of the value chain includes creative activities

Source: WIPO 2006.

gross national product and percentage employment is greater than 1, suggesting greater efficiency of returns to the factor, in this case labor.

Currid (2007) goes one step further to note that New York City is just as defined by the creative industries as it is by its behemoth service sectors such as banking and finance. In fact, New Yorkers themselves identify more with the "Warhol economy" than with any other sector in defining their collective identity. In this sense, creative work itself gives rise to particular cultural understandings of identity rather than being limited by prior cultural understandings. In extrapolating from this, one might even note that creativity led by markets is more likely to define cultural understandings than be defined by it, even though there could be a feedback loop between cultural policies and creativity as noted in figure 0.1.

The twentieth century raised the stature of creative work and broadened its definition, leading to the rise of a creative class or workforce sustaining itself on artistic output alone. Creative cities that sustain the entrepreneurship and imagination of the creative classes are examples of this phenomenon. Of course, it is an old trend. The Florentine Renaissance is similarly attributed to a climate of tolerance, advances in technology, and a gathering of talents. Cippolla (1990), in particular, points out the high levels of education among Florentines—estimating literacy to be around 40 percent in the age group between five and fourteen in 1338—and notes that "in Florence it was taken for granted that an artisan should be able to 'write, read, and keep accounts'" (92).[18] Even where patrons sought to control those they benefited, artists found some creative license. Incidentally, it is as true the other way round. In the context of Cosimo de Medici's patronage of the arts, Kent (2000, 68) notes: "The way in which the ruling classes draw upon culture as a source of power is so complex that it might be described plainly as a mystery."[19]

There are, nevertheless, two important cost implications of the rise of the creative classes in the twentieth century that affect our understanding of creative work. First, the idea of a creative class is new. The idea of a starving artist may be a bit of myth. Historically, most artists have sustained themselves through a variety of jobs, and the creative classes were never so expansive that they could sustain themselves on creative output alone. In the nineteenth century, patronage invariably covered a fraction of the artist's time or output and "rarely consisted of unconditional support for the artist to create" (Cummings and Katz 1987, 7). As the creative classes have multiplied, so have the pressures mounted upon patronage systems, especially state-led ones, to sustain them. In the post–World War II era, the emergence of the social-welfare state boded well for artists just as its dismemberment at the end of the twentieth century has eclipsed the livelihood of many. In this sense, Elizabeth Currid's New York represents a success story of the creative classes' being able to thrive on market means, even if this success includes many heart-breaking stories. Second, running parallel with the rise of a creative class has been the rise of costs, which has altered many creative practices and the networks that sustain them. Part of this phenomenon is the industrial and postindustrial technologies that have led to rising costs of production, distribution, and exhibition. An average Hollywood film cost $96 million in 2005 (Vogel 2007, 115). As noted earlier, Baumol and Bowen (1966) elegantly points out the cost disease in performing arts by showing that production innovations are hard to achieve in performing arts when the same number of artists must perform the same piece in a requisite amount of time that the composer or writer initially intended. While technical innovations in production can bring enhanced aesthetics or larger audiences, the cost savings are canceled through the rising costs of the inputs themselves and the lack of substitutability, as in the artists themselves. Rising costs might also apply to so-called subversive art, which might have the aura of being inexpensive.

The aesthetic analysis of Drucker (2005) points out that the progressive artist deploys the same slick techniques of production as a conservative Hollywood house. The 1990s art world was abuzz with roll-outs of high-fashion and good-looking models in live art to question societal values of femininity and sexuality.

High costs and the rise of the creative classes have led to new types of contractual forms to clear the high transaction costs. Film production houses, through the use of options contracts, hedge with writers to cancel the launch if they deem the final product too risky. An incentives contract might minimize risks by paying artists only a little money up front but paying royalties later if the sales increase.[20] In general, the rise in production costs has also led to the rise of coproductions (among opera houses, for example, or multicity tours for musical artists) and also of subcontracting relationships, where the costs are spread through various firms rather than internalized by one. Small countries hedge risk or boost film-production capacity through coproduction agreements. Along with coproduction comes the trend for outsourcing the production among various firms: TV and film production now regularly takes place in smaller firms, and only the distribution systems are concentrated among large firms (such as Sony Pictures or Telemundo) to take advantage of what are often global economies of scale within markets (Goldsmith and O'Regan 2005; Vogel 2007; Hart 2010). This mass production has also, of course, affected the quality of products by leading to the use of symbolic metaphors or formulas that are universally understood. Often the success of the Hollywood action film or, more recently, the Bollywood musical, is attributed to phenomena such as these.

Market networks are supplanting patronage networks for creative products. The increasing complexity of organizing inputs for production, especially on a global scale, has led to complex property rights. The rise of a "market-friendly" creative class is also supported by technological innovations that not only affect costs but also are transforming long-cherished ideas in the creative industries.

Technology and Costs

The effect of information technologies is fundamentally rooted in the political, economic, and cultural context of their deployment. Digital technology has shaped not just creative expressions themselves but also the cultural politics that follow. One of the main material factors spreading globalization, and widespread anxieties thereof, is technological change. Cultural policies that have come about in response to digitization include the intellectual property amendments that have arisen in the last couple decades. Also, Baumol's cost disease, referring to the rise in unit cost of creative production over time, is both counterbalanced and enhanced, depending on the context, with the proliferation of digital technologies: while marginal costs of reproducing an extra unit of CD, for example, are negligible in a digital environment, the fixed costs remain high. Digital technologies also offer avenues for production and distribution through social networks, such as Facebook, or other digital platforms, such as YouTube. User-generated content on the Internet is so far the most important creative phenomenon of the twenty-first century. Hart (2010) notes that the old analog media players from films, TV, and music now must coexist with new players, most of them involved in user-generated content. These include blogs, YouTube, file-sharing websites, and e-books.

Technologies propose change; cultural politics dispose this change in specific ways. The last chapter detailed these cultural politics. This section outlines the ways in which digitization and the fall in marginal costs shape these cultural politics and their ultimate resolution in specific cultural policies. New technologies are making existing business models obsolete. In the context of falling costs of digital reproduction and content sharing over the Internet, the *Financial Times* recently asked: "Is the technological environment about to sweep many of the media conglomerates that dominated culture and news during the 20th century?" (Brown 2009). Media conglomerates fought for various types of copyright protection to guard their revenues as digital technologies proliferated. The current business models tend to favor new forms of delivery for digitized content such as through iTunes store for music.

The development of digital technology changed the way information industries are organized. Historically, different types of media technologies evolved as distinct industry types dominated by one or more firms. The vertical dimension of figure 2.2a captures the various tasks performed by the different types of industries. Vertically integrated industries developed different pipelines for different functions needed to deliver information. Thus, entertainment industries, such as Hollywood, not only developed the content but also owned the theaters where the content was showcased.

Figure 2.2   The Information Industry

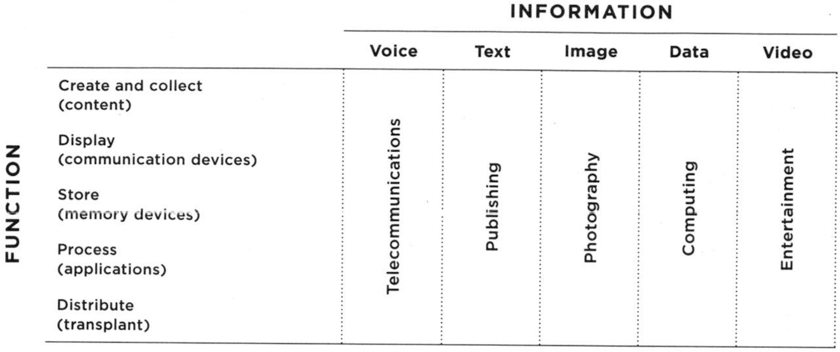

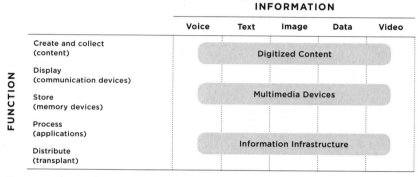

Figure 2.2a   Influence of Analog Technology

Figure 2.2b   Influence of Digital Technology

Source: Sheth and Singh (1994).

Analog technology, in other words, separated voice, text, image, data and video industries. Regulatory activities further sustained the separation. In the latter part of the twentieth century, cable television in many countries could distribute its content over high-bandwidth networks, but cable providers were not allowed to get into the telephony market.

Digital technology has undone the technological logic behind separate industries and pipelines. This, in turn, has also spurred multimedia interactive instruments and fiber-optic cables capable of carrying all types of messages at high speeds and low costs (including over the local loop, the last segment connecting a telecommunications network to a household). Earlier technology was "analogous" (therefore the term analog) to sending information in electrical waves and was time-consuming and often inefficient. New technology allows information to be encoded in streams of binary digits (digitization) that can be sent efficiently and at relatively low cost over long distances. Digitization affects all aspects of the information industry, allowing various media (voice, text, image, data, and video) to be digitized, sent over the same pipeline, and accessed by a single instrument. As shown in figure 2.2b, this offers the potential for horizontal integration of industry types.

The vertical and horizontal integration of pipelines are expanding and deepening media networks. The expansion follows as different types of vertical pipelines merge. One example is the media conglomerate Time Warner, which combines cable, film, broadband, music, and publishing. The deepening occurs through horizontal integration, allowing for a variety of functions to be performed over the same network with the use of a multimedia device. A personal computer now transmits all forms of communication and networking via one instrument.

Technological innovation is also pushing down the unit costs. Anyone who has bought a computer only to see its price halved the next season is familiar with this logic. This is a development popularly known as Moore's Law, wherein computing power is predicted to increase exponentially with little or no increase in cost (the law is named after the Intel chairman and cofounder, Gordon Moore, who first observed the effect in 1965). The logic itself is simple. First, digital technology comes with high fixed costs and minuscule marginal or reproduction costs. For example, a computer disc, once produced, can be reproduced a million times over at negligible cost. Selling one disc for $1 million is hard but a million can sell for $1 each. Success for information-age products derives in large measure from the ability to rapidly generate large demand in a short time. Given the fixed costs inherent in a product—in a software program or a film—the only way to recover these costs is to distribute them over large, often global distribution networks. This indirectly also explains the success of iTunes music store. Music companies stuck to their old model of selling music through prepackaged CDs and doubted the efficacy of selling music singles, but 10 billion songs had been downloaded from iTunes music store by February 2010. Second, superior microprocessors do increasingly complicated tasks faster and cheaper.[21] Again, generating massive demand helps to recover the costs of developing these technologies in the first place.

Declining marginal costs mean that the network is deepening and expanding faster than ever before. For example, a poor country with access to some capital can, if it has the political will, leapfrog the technological frontier and bring a variety of multimedia services to remote areas by use of inexpensive satellite-based terminals. And as technology proliferates and networks carry messages more efficiently around the globe, distance matters less and less. Regulatory barriers designed to keep "foreign" content out of markets will work in a world of traditional broadcast and film distribution but are untenable in a world where consumers can download content over the Internet or access it through content-sharing websites such as YouTube. Digital broadcast satellites and digital compression can also break down national or local barriers that affix themselves to cultural content (Feigenbaum 2010).

The implications of technological change for cultural policies are far-reaching and only partially understood. I summarize a few here. First, digital technologies have made intellectual property issues, especially copyright and trademark issues, salient in cultural-policy agendas worldwide. The early intellectual property efforts in the United States were centered on pharmaceuticals and brand-name clothing and products. This all changed in the 1990s as the Internet proliferated and it became relatively easy to copy or download products, in turn pushing copyright to the forefront of policy measures desired by entertainment industries. This becomes evident from even a cursory look at the focus on copyright and "piracy" on the homepages of the Motion Picture Association of America and the Recording Industry Association of American (mpaa.org and riaa.org). The subfield of cultural economics has largely overlooked copyright issues. At the 2008 conference of the Association of Cultural Economics, outgoing president Ruth Towse exhorted the discipline to regard copyright as cultural policy. Nevertheless, her address mostly touched upon analog-style issues such as the role of collecting societies, itself bequeathed from medieval days, in distributing royalties to performing artists in Europe (Towse 2008).[22] The move to consider copyright as cultural policy is to be applauded: it questions the patronage-driven nature of "old" cultural policies while pointing out the importance of property rights in "new," market-led ones.[23] An examination of digital technology and copyright would point toward the kinds of international politics that have resulted in intellectual property rights agreements at the WTO and the ascendance of WIPO in global governance. Music and film companies lobbied nationally and internationally for the Trade-Related Aspects of Intellectual Property Rights agreement that came out of the WTO in 1995 and the movement toward

digital rights management in the 1990s at WIPO. By 2010, content providers were aware that copyright by itself will not salvage their fortunes and,
therefore, began to focus on other aspects of the value chain.

The cost dynamics of digital technology have led to two different moves
in terms of production and distribution. On the one hand, as the costs
of producing television and films have increased, media companies have
turned to a variety of measures to share or minimize them. An example is
the complicated contracts that are contingent upon profits for performers
and technicians. Coproduction agreements also allow companies to share
costs. Council of Europe funding encourages coproduction among small
states to make viable a film industry that may not otherwise exist. On the
other hand, technology has also made it possible to produce and distribute
niche products over networks and allows an increasing number of people
to become creative producers. The only way to recover costs from a film
with $100 million production budget is to aim for global distribution and
launches. Nevertheless, such markets, commanded by media conglomerates, do not mean imminent death for independent, low-cost productions.
Independent companies can seek out low-cost and specific networks to
distribute their products. A laptop computer can generate special effects
now that at one time cost thousands of dollars (Feigenbaum 2004). A ga-
rage band can distribute its product worldwide through YouTube or its own
website; however, whether these measures are financially viable or will attract enough audiences is another question.

Despite the difficulties of generating buzz with tight marketing budgets, social media has helped several bands make it big.[24] MySpace bands
are the best examples. As of 2009, Colbie Caillat's MySpace profile page
had displayed more than 46 million times. The music majors relentless-
ly courted her and she finally signed with Universal.[25] File-sharing sites
also promote artists; the U.K.'s Arctic Monkeys is a good example. Viral
campaigns through file-sharing and social media increased the popular-
ity of the band before it ever signed a record contract. Their debut album,
Whatever People Say I Am That's What I'm Not, became the fastest-selling
album in U.K. history. Artists have also become famous with or through
music blogs, perhaps the biggest promoters of new music in the last few
years. Referred to as "buzzbands" in popular jargon, bands that have become famous through music blogs include the Arcade Fire and Clap Your
Hands Say Yeah. Local artists now use social media regularly for promotion. Even without big money and contracts, the Internet address is useful.

The Washington, D.C., artist Tom Goss circulated his song "Till the End" over YouTube to connect with gay rights groups across the United States and then went on a nationwide tour.[26]

Digital technology thus makes possible a cultural double movement: global conglomerates are paralleled by and also make possible niche producers. The so-called world music sections on most CD shelves features the big four music producers—Sony, EMI, Universal, and Warner—but as a result of the deepening of tastes, independent music producers from West Africa or India can sell their content directly or through distribution agreements with the big four. Independent record producers currently control about one-fifth of the music industry. The rationale for this cultural double movement is easy to locate. Globalization scholarship in general has focused on the increasing integration of the world alongside increasing fragmentation of ethnicities and localities. Terms such as "glocalism" or "fragmegration" capture these dynamics.[27] Political economists have also long recognized cluster and agglomerative effects, whereby dominant firms make possible the existence of small firms that complement and parallel their various supply and distribution chains.[28] Specifically, in the case of creative products, Cowen's entire thesis in *Creative Destruction: How Globalization is Changing the World's Culture* rests on the simultaneous homogenization and heterogenization of creative products. "For those convinced that technology will defeat local cultures, ask who, thirty-five years ago, would have expected a small Caribbean island to become a world leader in experimental electronic music?" On the same page he notes: "Kingston is dotted with hundreds of recording studios, and Jamaica has more record labels than does the United Kingdom" (Cowen 2002, 27).

In sum, the rise of information networks is to be located, first of all, in digital technology that has allowed for not only the vertical and horizontal integration of content pipelines but also the declining costs of its use. In other words, information networks are poised to expand globally. However, there may be many complicating externalities along the path toward deployment of digital technology. The costs may still be formidable for individuals in poor countries. The technologies may be anathema for a few elite and other groups who regard the spread of information as a threat to a status quo they favor. In other words, the extent to which networking comes about and the global effects it has cannot be measured by technological developments alone. Cultural politics intervene between technologies and the policies governing them.

Cultural Globalization: Technology and Networks

While there are various cultural-policy models at play in creative industries, the two versions I have discussed can be described as the patronage model versus the market-networks model. Subsidies and grants to artists and creative industries are examples of the patronage model, but the choice of cultural policies is seldom solely situated in economic and technological factors. These may be necessary conditions, but the sufficient conditions are located in cultural politics that provide the context for understanding the genesis of specific cultural policies. When one country chooses quotas and subsidies to favor its film industry and another chooses market incentives, it is a result not just of industry structures or economic calculations or import threats but also of the way film as a creative or symbolic product is valued in the country in question. It also points us to the kinds of deliberative or nondeliberative (cultural-policy-elite) contexts under which particular cultural policies are shaped and adopted.

Tax incentives and copyright policies are examples of the market-based model. At the heart of the creative industries of a bygone era were the lonely writers, artists, painters, poets, or composers who depended on royal or religious patronage to recoup their fixed costs (including the opportunity costs of their time) as well as the network externalities of their work. A composer with royal patronage was assured an orchestra or an opera troupe that would perform the work. Such patronage also helped to solve the problem of demand, in this case, the problem of cultivating taste.[29] Patronage went a long way toward branding the product as aesthetically superior.

Mass production and technology would undo the logic of dependence on royal patronage wherein creative work was decreed a "scarce commodity." The mass production of the paperback, for example, meant that more and more people could own and read books. The distribution of phonographs meant that the demand for listening to music both increased and intensified. As mass production took roots, distribution and retailing mechanisms became important. Hollywood's success lay in internalizing the transaction costs of production and distribution through a studio system. Commercial networks took the place of royal branding and patronage.

The legacy of the two simplified models described above is still with us. Patronage continues to exist through arts-funding organizations and religious and other institutions that support films and television programming.

Whereas in the United States, such arts-funding organizations tend to cater to niche markets, the model in Western Europe, at least until the end of the twentieth century, was broader in scope, with state-owned radio and television networks. States funded highly commercialized genres such as cinema along with artists and museums.

It needs to be emphasized that the two models presented above are simplifications. In fact, the two often operate in tandem: despite patronage in Europe, opera impresarios traveled (networked) as far as Indonesia and India to stage Western operatic works in the "colonies" (Rosselli 1984; Pitt 1997). Artists, despite royal patronage, always relied on networks and markets to earn a livelihood (Cowen 1998; Wyszomirski 2008). French films funded by the state agency CNC developed extensive commercial distribution networks, especially in Francophone countries. At another level, all creative work is hybrid work, and none of this hybridity would exist without networks (Hannerz 1992; García Canclini 1995; Kraidy 2005). On the other hand, market networks have never quite shied away from patronage, either. American mass production, especially of creative products that may be branded as cultural, fit well the purposes of the internationalist U.S. state in the twentieth century, which saw the Americanization of the world as important for its sense of purpose regarding the spread of markets and democracy worldwide (de Grazia 2005). As far back as the 1920s, Hollywood worked closely with the Pentagon to solicit the help of the American military in distributing to markets abroad (Jarvie 1992). More recently, "soft power" and "cultural diplomacy" have entered the vocabulary of royal patronage in the United States and other places (Kurlantzick 2008; Katzenstein 2005; Nye 2004).

Creative industries, inasmuch as their products can be seen to embody "cultural values," can take advantage of patronage or commercial networks or both. Yet the need to try to recover the outlay of several years' worth of work (for a novelist, for example) or the high total costs in creative commodities (iPod, for example) should not be underemphasized. Creative industries, especially as a result of technological developments, are high-fixed-cost practices. A few, such as filmmaking and some globally launched music, feature high fixed and marginal costs. The average cost of making a film (including advertising) was $96.15 million in 2005 (Vogel 2007, 115). Software, on the other hand, features negligible marginal costs but high fixed costs. Either way, the only way to recover costs is through mass distribution and consumption. In 2005, foreign markets generated 47.8 percent of $89 billion in total revenues for Hollywood (Vogel 2007, 82).

Given the cost economics of creative industries, global distribution networks are becoming important for recouping costs. New technologies are therefore facilitating new cultural politics that seek to arbitrate, on the one hand, the cultural policies of patronage versus markets, and, on the other, the broad claims regarding cultural identities (the end points of figures 0.1 and 2.1). At this point, then, the ring is ready for a clash between those who gained primarily from the patronage model of internalizing moral hazard and transaction costs versus those sectors that grew up on commercial networks. The next chapter attends to this cultural clash, mostly in the context of the United States and European Union.

3

Culture Wars

Well, we usually go to France and Belgium or perhaps Germany,
said Gabriel awkwardly.

And why do you go to France and Belgium, said Miss Ivors,
instead of visiting your own land?

Well, said Gabriel, it's partly to keep in touch with the languages
and partly for a change.

And haven't you your own language to keep in touch with—Irish?
Asked Miss Ivors.

Well, said Gabriel, if it comes to that, you know, Irish is not my
language.
                                            —James Joyce, "The Dead"

The famous French historian Fernand Braudel optimistically overestimated
the effects of intercultural exchange in noting that "no civilization can survive without mobility: all are enriched by trade and the stimulating impact
of strangers" (1963/1993, 10). In terms of trade, such exchanges feature
both stimulation and conflicts. Especially in the case of trade in creative
products, conflict is hard to resolve and often devolves into highly charged
culture wars revolving around identity issues in cultural politics.

Trade in creative products is ubiquitous and continues to grow. While
estimates vary, UNESCO reported that creative industries accounted for 7
percent of the gross domestic product worldwide at $1.3 trillion in 2002
and was expected to rise to $1.7 trillion by 2007. Cultural products may
be intangible services such as digital content or tangible goods such as
crafts. Creative goods (not services) accounted for less than 1 percent of total international trade, but their volume rose from $39.3 billion in exports
in 1994 to $57.6 billion in 2006 (UNESCO 2005; 2009, 358.).[1] Creative
industries also feature growth rates of 10–20 percent (Barrowclough and
Kozul-Wright 2008, 6–7). International tourism yielded $944 billion with
922 million visitors in 2008, compared to $440 billion and 441 million
in 1990 (UN World Tourism Organization 2005, 2009). The World Trade
Organization calculates that travel services in general account for nearly

30 percent of the total world trade in commercial services (WTO 2005b, 160). Cultural tourism, discussed in chapter 5, is a subsection of the total trade in tourism.

National elites both shape and respond to perceived threats to cultural identities as a result of creative products from international trade. These responses are increasingly reflected in international rules governing trade in creative goods and services. This chapter traces the context, controversies, and coordination mechanisms that underlie such trade, focusing chiefly on the conflict between the United States and the European Union. I first trace the growth of this trade in the rise of entertainment industries, the expansion of information networks, and the formation and liberalization of international rules governing trade in creative sectors. I then detail the defining historical case for understanding such trade, namely the audio-visual dispute of 1991 through 1993 at the General Agreement on Tariffs and Trade. Chapter 4 traces the subsequent framing of the UNESCO declaration and convention on cultural diversity from 2001 through 2005. It also describes the role of the World Trade Organization (1995 to the present), UNESCO, and the European Union.

Historical Context

As international trade grew in the world, so did the need to govern flows, including those deemed cultural. This section addresses three aspects of these governance arrangements: the rise of free trade in the nineteenth century, which benefited creative products; protections against creative-industry exports throughout the twentieth century as this trade expanded; and the shaping of international trade-policy governance since the end of the last century.

The so-called long nineteenth century, from the French Revolution of 1789 to the First World War in 1914, broke down empires, entrenched industrialization, and saw the major effects of European colonization. The growing prosperity in Western Europe and the New World and the annexation of colonies generated economic surpluses. Countries found it in their interest to trade with one another. In 1846, Britain repealed the Corn Laws that protected its agriculture but also stalled its industrial exports. In return, continental Europe tore down its protectionist barriers. Trade in creative products benefited from this free trade wave. Yet this trade preceded the nineteenth century. Goods such as Italian glassware, French silks, Belgian laces—all of which may be considered creative products—were exchanged readily. Although trade in creative products was probably quite nominal, standardized data for this trade during this era are almost nonexistent. We do know that cultural exchanges were fairly widespread in Western Europe, especially in fine and performing arts. While local schools flourished, the arts in various territories were heavily influenced by other places: the Flemish masters traveled to Italy, Handel moved to Germany and then England, and Mozart's librettist, Lorenzo Da Ponte, moved to the New World and died in New York in 1838 while teaching Italian at Columbia University (an endowed chair is named after him there). He is credited with spreading Italian culture in his adopted land (Carter 1997). Meanwhile, opera impresarios traveled all over the colonies with their companies, and European powers displayed colonial, especially Oriental, spectacles in their museums and opera houses. Post-Enlightenment thinkers elevated the cause of cultural refinement and legitimized cultural exchanges.

Printing originated in the mid-fifteenth century with the Gutenberg Bible, and book printing was widespread in Europe by the nineteenth century. The rise of book publishing in Europe led to the copying of books, especially in the United States, where the paperback became popular, and authors such as Charles Dickens began to argue for copyright protections. Intellectual property, legal protections given to artistic creations, had not been a problem when the Church controlled most literary production and was the chief patron of the arts. With the spread of printing technologies and literacy, the birth of democracies, and the strengthening of nation-states, new protections were needed. With the collapse of the Holy Roman Empire in 1816, the Church lost its control of printing. What began as royal privilege rewarding individual inventions, became intellectual property rights in the nineteenth century. The Statute of Anne in 1709 was the first modern copyright law that tried to stem book piracy and allowed writers to earn an independent living. However, piracy in United States continued.

The current international rules for patent and copyright protections can be traced back to the Paris Convention for patents in 1883 and the Berne Convention for copyrights in 1886. The World Intellectual Property Organization, founded in 1970, now administers both conventions. The twentieth century marked the birth of technologically enhanced and globally poised creative industries. Most of the resulting international governance rules in this era reflect the dominance of the "jewel in the crown" of cultural industries—Hollywood. Hollywood's moves to dominate the European market and the Europe's history of protections can be traced back to the 1920s.[2] At that time, studios began to put distribution networks in place in Europe, which allowed them to achieve economies of scale in distribution throughout Europe. The British, constituting the biggest export market for Hollywood, instituted quotas in films with the Cinematograph Films Act of 1927 (renewed in 1938).

The Second World War wiped out the film capacities of Italian and French producers. Meanwhile, the postwar world turned to designing an international institution for trade, the General Agreement on Tariffs and Trade, which came into being in 1947. As part of this agreement, which pertained to trade in general, the European countries used an infant-industry argument to keep films out of GATT provisions. They claimed their film industries were too young to compete with Hollywood and must be protected. Quotas directed at restricting imports were the orders of the day (and remain the preferred instruments of international cultural policies): France instituted import quotas, restricting the number of foreign films brought into the country. Italy and the United Kingdom tried screen-time quotas to restrict the number of times foreign films could be shown. Audio-visuals, the term for creative industries in GATT, were the only cultural product mentioned in the original 1947 GATT framework (article IV: "Special Provisions Related to Cinematograph Films"), which allowed for such quotas and screen times. GATT was entrusted with carrying out successive rounds of trade negotiations among various countries, but films were always excepted. Summing up successive GATT negotiations, Jarvie (1998, 40) notes: "In the fifty years since the GATT was negotiated, film and television issues have not made it beyond the agenda of the various 'rounds' of renegotiations" from 1947 to the 1980s. Nevertheless, the language of quotas was enacted not merely to boost infant industries in Europe but also to preserve the ability of film industries to produce representations that carried meaning in particular national contexts. While the 1946 Blum-Byrnes negotiations on film imports between the United States and France might have been over various types of quotas, they were inherently about preserving identity. Why else would France, desperate for U.S. financing and in a context that favored trade, look for exceptions for film? "At a time when many French industries were devastated by World War II and could benefit from protection, the French government sought special provisions for the film industry only" (Goff 2007, 118).

As explained in detail later, the precedence set by the Washington Agreement signed on May 26, 1946 between Secretary of State James F. Byrnes and the former head of French Popular Front government, Léon Blum, was of particular importance to the GATT agreement.[3] Two pages of this agreement pertained to the film industry and have come to be known as the Blum-Byrnes Agreement. The agreement established quotas for foreign films coming into France. In 1946, four weeks per quarter of the year were restricted for French films, and this rose to five weeks by the Paris Agreement of 1948. Article IV of GATT allowed for screen quotas; article XX(a) provides exceptions for public morals and order; and article XX(f), for preserving national treasures. Nevertheless, the tenor of GATT in general encouraged trade flows and allowed countries to export creative products to one another. Interestingly, the early rules at UNESCO, mostly crafted at the initiative of the United States, were consistent with GATT and designed to encourage flows of creative products, as in the Florence Agreement on the Importation of Educational, Scientific and Cultural Materials or in wider instruments supporting creative and cultural expressions and freedoms.[4]

GATT, as noted, had several rounds of multilateral trade renegotiations, but "audio-visual" goods were deemed nonnegotiable until GATT's Uruguay Round of trade talks, so named for the eight years of negotiations that began in Punta del Este, Uruguay, in September 1986. Two contentious issues during this round that pertained to creative products resulted in far-reaching trade agreements signed when the round closed in 1994: the General Agreement on Trade in Services and the Trade Related Aspects of Intellectual Property. The negotiation of these agreements was difficult but in the end reflected, among the various sectors covered, the growing importance of trade in creative products. At the end of the Uruguay Round the GATT charter was also revised and replaced with that of the World Trade Organization, which came into being in 1995. The newly negotiated GATS and TRIPS also took effect at this time.

GATS and TRIPS

The movement to include creative products and intellectual property as part of international trade talks began in the United States in the 1970s. Until then, the concept of trade was limited to physical or tangible products, but the United States began to argue that its comparative advantage lay in intangible products or services, such as monies earned from licensing of films or television programs around the world or royalties earned by musical artists. These efforts, spearheaded by businesses in the United States, were hardly understood in Europe initially and, in the 1980s, heavily opposed by the developing world. Service firms in the United States wanted other countries to reduce their trade barriers. Intellectual property is not traded by itself but embodied in both goods and services. Firms from the United States began to argue that it was a trade issue because piracy was costing them millions of dollars that they would have earned had they traded these products instead.

Intellectual Property

Brand-name clothing, accessory, pharmaceutical, and software firms initially pushed for intellectual property protection as part of U.S. trade interests in the 1970s. By the mid-1980s, creative industries led by film, television, and music joined the foray. Their collective efforts resulted in TRIPS. The controversial agreement was widely unacceptable to the developing world, and there remain significant points of departure between the United States and European Union on trade in copyright products.

Although intellectual property interests joined forces in the 1970s, they were mostly concerned about patents (as in pharmaceuticals), but this changed when entertainment industries such as music and film joined the coalition. This coalition succeeded in amending the U.S. Trade Act of 1974 to apply intellectual property infringements on countries where piracy was common and to put these issues into the Uruguay Round. The international Intellectual Property Committee, composed of around fifteen global firms, including multinationals such as Warner Communications, applied pressure on negotiators in the United States, Europe, and Japan for the completion of TRIPS. Lobbies such as the Motion Picture Association of America and Recording Industry Association of America supported the IPC moves.

Developing countries argued that not only was their intellectual property commonly held or in the "public domain" (thus outside the purview of this Western-style individualistic property-rights schema) but that the agreement would deny them access to crucially needed technologies. They argued that technological innovation comes from technological imitation, which could not happen if technology was protected with stringent intellectual property provisions. Finally, they argued that their creative products—whether music, ancient medicines, seeds, or plant varieties—were regularly "stolen" by Western firms. These firms then "repackaged" these products and sold them back to the developing world with intellectual property provisions attached after minimal modifications.[5]

There were also significant departures between the United States and other developed countries, especially in Europe, on cultural heritage and copyright issues. Europeans wanted to attach geographical indicators to products that would prevent other regions from marking their products with the same "geographic brand names." While so far the thinking is limited to specific indicators such as Champagne, Kalamata (olives), or Parma (cheese), it is easy to see how this could apply to cultural-heritage questions, especially folklore and music. Overall, the issue is complicated and unresolved. The second big issue is governing moral rights of authors, or *droit de suite* as it is referred to in current European legislation. Most continental European laws allow only the original artists or authors to modify or profit from artworks while U.S. law favors successive owners.[6] Thus, a production firm "owns" a film in the United States whereas in Europe the creators own the intellectual property and acquire profits from the use and sale of their work over time. European Union countries are now enforcing legislation to protect the moral rights of authors. Many in the EU are concerned that most transnational art houses like Sotheby's or Christie's will sell their art only in the United States to avoid paying profits to the original creators or their offspring.

Services

As early as the 1970s, American banking, software, and telecommunications companies lobbied to include services in trade talks. Seventy percent of the U.S. workforce was employed in the service sector, which accounted for about ten percent of the global trade or $350 billion in the early 1980s (statistics cited in Singh 2008b). The United States advocated for the inclusion of services in trade negotiations through the Organization for Economic Cooperation and Development, which was considered the rich countries' club, and received support from the European Community and Japan. These countries were also liberalizing their own service sectors. But the developing world remained opposed, resulting in a decision at the beginning of the Uruguay Round of trade talks in September 1986 that allowed services to be negotiated on parallel but separate tracks from goods. It was understood that goods negotiations and services negotiations were part of the same enterprise, but technically, goods negotiations could forge ahead if the services negotiations fell behind. A Group on Negotiation for Services began work in 1986 and was headed by the Colombian ambassador to GATT, Felipe Jaramillo, whose presence helped to get other developing countries on board.

Two things are important in understanding the position of creative products: the GATS framework as a whole and the way it pertained to particular products, specifically audio-visual. The framework for GATS evolved out of the work of the GNS, where many developing countries were full participants and which was led by an ambassador from a developing country. The rudiments of the GATS framework were in place by 1989 and rested on two elements: countries would liberalize or open their markets in selected sectors (known as positive lists) and then put in restrictions within these sectors (known as negative lists). Thus, a country could choose to open up its films sector but then use negative lists to keep certain public-policy provisions in place.[7] It would be perfectly legal for a country under this framework to restrict rules for foreign ownership or keep in place certain types of taxes or quotas favoring local firms. At face value, this was a departure from goods negotiations in GATT, which did not allow for positive and negative lists. The second pillar of GATS is the "mode of supply" or the way that the service product is consumed. Unlike a shirt that must be shipped across frontiers, a tourist can only consume another country's tourism by going there or by buying airline tickets (perhaps on the Internet) from that country's airline. GATS defines four modes of supply, which I explain here in terms of cultural products:

Mode 1. Cross-border supply: a consumer can watch a film from another country by importing the film

Mode 2. Consumption abroad: a tourist must go abroad to consume the service

Mode 3. Commercial presence: the only way to export some services is to set up a subsidiary abroad, such as a transnational arts enterprises and such cultural industries as music and film firms

Mode 4. Movement of skilled personnel: sometimes the only way to export a service is by allowing people to move across frontiers. This applies to the movement of cultural exchange programs and performers

The GATS framework allowed countries to make specific commitments toward liberalization for each of the four modes of supply for any sectors they chose, although there were pressures from the United States to commit in as many sectors as possible. In fact, the United States had wanted free trade in services in all sectors, except for those excluded through negotiations. In other words, the United States opposed positive lists and wanted to allow for negative lists only under special circumstances. As the GATS framework stands now, with positive and negative lists allowed, the United States clearly did not get its way. Thus, unlike popular misconceptions about the GATS framework, this was not a blanket liberalization foisted upon hapless developing countries. These were full participants, and by the end of the Uruguay Round many, such as India, Brazil, and Mexico, realized that they had much to gain from GATS. Eight sectors, including audio-visual (mostly films and television), were chosen during the Uruguay Round for the initial exercise in liberalization. The audio-visual negotiations, discussed in detail in the next subsection, almost brought the Uruguay Round to a halt and pitted the United States in a fierce battle with the European Community, specifically Hollywood against the French film industry.

Cultural Exceptions and Empirical Contradictions

The case analyzed here involves mostly the United States and the European Community, in particular France, during the Uruguay Round and, in recent years, the entire world in the framing of the UNESCO Convention on the Protection and Promotion of the Diversity of Cultural Expressions. As noted earlier, after the late 1940s, Western Europe successfully argued that its creative industries, especially film, needed special protections such as quotas. During the Uruguay Round of trade talks from 1986 to 1994, talk of the need for a "cultural exception" supplemented the language of quotas. This resulted in the European Union taking the now-famous MFN exemption, which allowed it to preserve its cultural-industry policies.[8]

The idea of "protecting" cultural diversity as enshrined in the UNESCO convention reflects two underlying and related economic suppositions only marginally supported by empirical data. First, vulnerable countries, especially those from the developing world, need to protect their creative industries from being marginalized by multinational conglomerates. Second, market-driven solutions may not work for the purpose of protecting "cultural diversity," especially at the international level, and thus state regulations and incentives are necessary. But even a cursory look at international trade in creative products shows two contradictory but important trends. Developed countries at the forefront of efforts to "protect" cultural diversity are also at the forefront of trade in creative products. Developing countries, jumping on the protections bandwagon in fear of losing out in such trade, are actually gaining increased shares, even though they remain marginal.[9]

Fears continue regarding flows of creative products, the foremost being that only a few countries with large multinationals benefit. Table 3.1 lists the top twenty exporting countries in cultural goods. Apart from China, India, and Mexico, the list only contains developed countries. Nevertheless, trade in cultural goods grew from $36.2 billion in 1994 to nearly $54.7 billion in 2002, an increase of 50 percent, in less than ten years (table 3.2). Hidden within and around these statistics are a few other trends that are worth pointing out. First, Canada and France rank among the top ten countries in terms of international trade in cultural products. Second, as table 3.2 shows, while the share of trade for the United States and European Union has declined, East Asia's has doubled and other parts of the developing world are seeing their shares grow as well. However, the total share for Latin America and Africa is still low. Third, these statistics do not count related activities such as information technology, advertising, and architectural services. Many of these activities are now outsourced to developing countries.[10] Fourth, the UNESCO data are based on customs figures and do not take into account royalty and license fees for television programs and films. Emerging centers of film and television production in the developing world—Argentina, Brazil, Mexico, Egypt, Senegal, South Africa, India, and China—are thus underestimated here.

Also, as tables 3.3 and 3.4 show, international trade in tourism services is enormous, at $944 billion and 922 million international tourist arrivals in 2008. Only cultural tourism, estimated to be about one-quarter of total international tourism receipts, is relevant for our purposes, but it is nevertheless helpful to discern a few trends in the tourism data. Tables

TABLE 3.1

Top Twenty Exporters of Core Cultural Goods

RANKING		COUNTRY	TOTAL EXPORTS OF CORE CULTURAL GOODS	
2002	2006		2002	2006
1	1	UNITED KINGDOM	8,549	9,754
2	3	UNITED STATES	7,648	8,643
3	4	GERMANY	5,789	5,881
4	2	CHINA	5,275	9,646
5	5	FRANCE	2,521	2,972
6	13	IRELAND	2,277	997
7	12	SINGAPORE	2,001	1,087
8	14	JAPAN	1,805	912
9	10	CANADA	1,577	1,403
10	16	AUSTRIA	1,561	798
11	8	NETHERLANDS	1,546	1,564
12	9	SPAIN	1,532	1,349
13	6	SWITZERLAND	1,384	1,801
14	7	ITALY	1,381	1,701
15	18	MEXICO	1,244	584
16	11	BELGIUM	1,130	1,155
17	20	SWEDEN	875	429
18		HUNGARY	720	81
19		HONG KONG	578	208
20		DENMARK	499	419
	15	INDIA	284	831
	17	SOUTH KOREA	388	676
	19	POLAND	209	464

Note: There seem to be some great inconsistencies for data from particular countries. However, the ascendancy of China and India in the top rankings parallels other economic trends for these countries.

Source: UNESCO 2005a, 57–59 (for 2002 data); 2009a, 352–59 (for 2006 data).

3.3 and 3.4 show the top ten tourist destinations and receipts. Only China, Hong Kong, Mexico, and Turkey make it to any of these lists from the developing world. But, again, France is among the top three recipients. It is also important to point out that while developed countries dominate

TABLE 3.2

Percentage Share of Total Exports of Core Cultural Products by Region,
1994–2002

	1994	2002
Total exports	$36.2 billion	$54.7 billion
European Union (EU 15)	54.3%	51.8%
Other Europe	6.1	6.2
North America	25	16.9
Asia	11.8	21.2
East Asia	7.6	15.6
Latin America and Caribbean	1.9	3.0
Africa	0.2	0.4
Oceania	0.6	0.6

Note: Comparable data for 2006 (as for table 3.1) from UNESCO 2009a are not available.
Source: UNESCO 2005a, 63–64.

international tourism, it is one of the biggest foreign exchange earners for many developing countries. Apart from big countries such as Argentina, Brazil, China, and India, the list includes places as diverse as Belize, Fiji, Morocco, and Mauritius.

While these are macrolevel statistics, they do indicate that there may not be enough evidence to make the claim that international markets are marginalizing creative products from the developing world. They are especially not marginalizing them from countries like France and Canada that vociferously make claims regarding their marginalization. The corollary claim that developing countries are being marginalized because only American creative products dominate the world is also not borne out by looking at the top ten cultural exporters.

The growth of creative-industry exports from the countries feeling most threatened by U.S. dominance of international markets provides a counterpoint to the claims made against the United States. However, by themselves these statistics do not delegitimize the anxieties and the cultural politics within particular countries or at the international level that follow from Hollywood's domination. Even the statistics themselves must be questioned. They are mostly based on customs receipts and do not account for the royalty payments creative industries receive. For example,

TABLE 3.3

Top Ten International Tourist Arrivals in 2008 (Millions)

France	81.9
United States	58.0
Spain	53.3
China	53.0
Italy	42.7
United Kingdom	30.2
Ukraine	25.4
Turkey	25.0
Germany	24.9
Mexico	22.6
Total top ten	417
Total world	922

Source: UN World Tourism Organization 2009, 3–5.

worldwide box-office receipts for Hollywood films were $26.7 billion in 2007, nearly three times the $9.63 billion from the domestic market.[11] International markets are no doubt of utmost importance to Hollywood, which dominates screens globally. The anxieties regarding the loss of creative expressions in many parts of the world do not then emanate from the export strength of other countries but from their import worries and what is sometimes billed as the lack of "shelf space" for their own products within their own borders. In Goff's words, "The debates are fueled by legitimate sociocultural concerns" regarding "potentially homogenizing forces of economic liberalization" (2007, 171). The rest of this chapter attends to these "legitimate sociocultural concerns," detailing how they are enacted in international disputes regarding creative products. While I leave it to others to detail whether trade in creative products is homogenizing, a couple of caveats are nevertheless importance here. First, clearly the case for cultural homogenization must be made with import rather than export statistics. Protectionist countries do suffer from some cognitive dissonance in speaking against creative-product exporting while continuing to benefit from it. Second, while Goff and others make a case for cultural homogenization, others make an equally compelling case for cultural diversity and new forms of hybridity.[12] The following sections describe the global delib-

TABLE 3.4

Top Ten International Tourism Receipts in 2008 ($ Billions)

United States	110.1
Spain	61.6
France	55.6
Italy	45.7
China	40.0
Germany	36.0
United Kingdom	40.8
Australia	24.7
Turkey	22.0
Austria	21.8
Total top ten	458.3
Total world	944

Source: UN World Tourism Organization 2009, 6.

erations within which flows of creative products become threats to cultural identity, usually conceived in national terms.

Creative Expressions and Global Deliberations

Disputes around creative expressions often fail to produce an agreement because of the symbolic importance of creativity and its connection to various forms of cultural identity, especially national identity. These disputes but must be resolved through some form of deliberation. Two things are important in a prima facie understanding of the deliberative processes involving national identities. First, as I noted earlier, the linking of creative expressions to national identity is a political process, and elite entrepreneurs often have to ward off several challenges. For example, the French constitution bars keeping any statistics on ethnic identity and languages—societal segregations that are commonly understood to constitute cultural identity in most other countries. As France remains a key global actor in framing moves to protect cultural diversity in the world, it is easy to point a finger at France's own internal affairs. For example, two days after the UNESCO cultural diversity convention, in which France was a central player, ethnic rioting broke out in France's banlieues. Although the two incidents were not related, the coincidence was ironic. Second, the case for preserving national identity is not made solely in terms of creative expressions. In Mexico, oil is viewed as national patrimony, therefore important to cultural identity; until recently, sugar played a similar role in Cuba (Ortiz Mena 2006; M. Frank 2005). Gastronomy in France or the steel worker in the United States is an important component of national identity. Nevertheless, it cannot be denied either that the representational characteristics of creative goods and services are perhaps more important than those of sugar, oil, or gastronomy.

The case I analyze here mostly involves the United States and Western Europe, in particular, France during the Uruguay Round and France and Canada thereafter. As I noted earlier, after the late 1940s, Western Europe successfully argued that creative industries, especially film, needed special protections such as quotas because of their symbolic importance. A weakened France after World War II was forced to deal with this issue in the language of quotas alone—preserving four out of thirteen weeks for French-language films. Around the time of the Uruguay Round of trade talks, from 1986 to 1994, the need for a "cultural exception" supplemented the language of quotas. This resulted in the European Union taking the now-famous MFN exemption, a technical opt-out clause from the audiovisual agreement, which allowed it to preserve its creative-industry policies. Later, the Europeans supported framing a UNESCO convention, popularly understood to support cultural diversity.

The main issue concerned the 51 percent programming quota for television that had come out of a European Commission's Television Without Frontiers directive, which came in to force in 1992 just as the Uruguay Round entered its endgame. In reality, few states implemented this quota, but the EU position was to try to enshrine it formally through GATS. In WTO's jargon, the EU sought to make a status quo binding. A related issue was the EU position that content restrictions applied to all of the 300-plus channels that were coming about as a result of satellite and cable technologies. The United States wanted to restrict 50 to 70 percent of the channels. Television programs in France and many other European states are subsidized by film box-office receipts and levies on blank videotapes used to record the programs. Given that U.S. films and television programs dominate in Europe, the MPAA also argued that it was subsidizing European television and objected to the agreement sought by the Europeans at the Uruguay Round.

These global deliberations featured a great deal of strategic posturing through coalition building and issue framing rather than trust and problem solving. They resulted in Europeans opting for an MFN exemption. Especially important to understanding the coalition building is the effort by French officials' to convince the somewhat reluctant Germans and British to go along. Meanwhile, the United States never explicitly acknowledged the symbolic importance of film to the Europeans. It also rejected a binding commitment to the status quo—a dominant market share—from the EU at the Uruguay Round, further alienating the Europeans, who framed this move as Hollywood's desire to wipe out cinema in Europe.

The audio-visual negotiations came about in a multilateral setting, and coalition building, especially within Western Europe, was important to the outcome. While Canada and such creative-industry exporters as India, Brazil, and Hong Kong were key parties, the core of the negotiation concerned the United States and the European Community. Thus the context I discuss focuses on the somewhat bilateral nature of this negotiation, the dominance of a single issue (quotas), coalition building in Europe, and the market conditions faced by European and U.S. producers. In particular, during the Uruguay Round, the French and other Europeans sought to build a case for "cultural exception" by pointing to the early history of GATT and the film quotas. The French officials invoked the Blum-Byrnes Agreement to argue for historical precedence.[13]

The history of the television industry does not involve negotiations or quotas. Radio emerged as a state enterprise in Europe in the 1920s, and when television arrived in 1950s, it, too, went under state control (Noam 1991). As such, regulation of the television market was simpler than for commercial film markets. The Television Without Frontiers directive came about just as the European TV market was being deregulated and liberalized.

Television Without Frontiers

The audio-visual dispute during the Uruguay Round centered on the 1989 Television Without Frontiers directive issued by the European Economic Community. The directive came after almost a decade of debate in Europe regarding liberalizing television while protecting domestic markets from non-European (primarily U.S.) programming. Initially the directive exposed several divisions across Western Europe and also within individual states on this issue. It is at this time that the political connection with the evolving European cultural identity began.[14] In 1982, the Hahn Report advocated the liberalization of European television broadcasting in a step toward European unification and the formation of a European identity. Subsequently, a 1984 green paper sought to remove national barriers to broadcasting through liberalization. The green paper was met with opposition from the European Broadcasting Union, which eventually got the European Parliament (always sympathetic to anti-EEC proposals) to go along. Even member states objected that broadcasting was a cultural issue beyond the scope of the EC (L'Ecuyer and Rogerson 2000). For these and other reasons, Belgium, Denmark, Italy, Spain, West Germany, and the United Kingdom also opposed the directive (Noam 1991). Difficulties also came from nations like West Germany, where broadcasting was under the purview of subnational authorities, preventing the German federal government from taking the lead at the EC level; in particular, Bavaria was a strong objector. The directive was eventually framed in the EC in 1986 and passed in 1989. This had a lot to do with the leadership of Jacques Delors at the EC. He was closely aligned with the French position on quotas, which predated the directive, and he used the quotas issue at the EU level to build European support (Levy 1999).

It is important to understand that there was no preexisting European consensus around either broadcasting issues or their connection with cultural identities. The image of a united Europe rallying around a common identity is incorrect, though the politicization of this directive to try to create a European identity may not be off the mark.[15] The rhetoric surrounding formation of European identity through TWF also masked the fact that the television content flows among the member states were almost negligible. However, the French government did encourage the establishment and launching of ARTE in 1992, a French-German channel dubbed "Tele-Maastricht," after the Treaty of Maastricht that brought about the European Union. Nevertheless, countries like the United Kingdom, with export-oriented or offensive interests in television and films, were reluctant suitors to the French position.

The crucial language in the directive that would lead to the trade dispute with the United States had to do with a proposed provision to restrict at least 51 percent of television programming to European content. The

American film and television industry's opposition to the language was swift. It lobbied heavily both within Europe and also in the U.S. Congress. A House Ways and Means Committee resolution denounced the directive. Representatives also called upon the United States trade representative, the de facto international negotiator for the United States, to institute a formal complaint with the GATT in order to protest that the directive violated both MFN and national treatment principles. Representative Bill Richardson (Democrat–New Mexico) even introduced legislation to ban the Corporation for Public Broadcasting from buying European programming. The internal European opposition and that from the United States led to a watering down of the directive. Instead of automatic quotas, nonbinding language advocating meeting quotas "where practicable and feasible" was introduced.

The contention around GATT article IV now began. Most Western European countries that originally enacted screen quotas began to phase them out, beginning with Italy in 1962. The United Kingdom phased out its quotas only in 1985. Most countries, however, maintained screen-time regulations in one form or another. Americans argued that article IV only applied to film and not to television.

The Uruguay Round

Technically, the audio-visual negotiations discussed here were part of the Uruguay Round and thus included all the signatories to the GATS framework that formed the backdrop to these talks. WTO and USTR officials note that this point is important.[16] According to them, there was an agreement in place from which most countries sought exemptions. Eighteen countries did make commitments in the audio-visual sector during the Uruguay Round, and another eleven did so later as they acceded to or joined the WTO (Roy 2008).[17] Nevertheless, the sector accounted for most of the MFN exemptions, 108 exemptions from 46 countries, and only 9 countries have made liberalization offers in this sector during the WTO's current Doha Round, launched in 2001, of which 6 already had existing commitments (Roy 2008).

NEGOTIATION CONTEXT

The audio-visual talks during the Uruguay Round hinged around the United States and the EU (the latter negotiated as one entity for its fifteen member states). Canada was also an important player. The EU often cited the audio-visual exemption in the Canada-U.S. Free Trade Agreement in 1989 and its refusal to put these issues on the NAFTA agenda in making their case. Toward the end of the talks, Japan also threw its weight toward the EU position. The EU position needs disaggregation for analysis. The important players were the EC and the French. Jacques Delors headed the EC at that time, and he undoubtedly played a major role in pushing the TWF directive on member states and reflecting the dominance of the French position in the GATT talks on audio-visual issues. According to Levy, "This point represented a high-water mark of French influence within EU audio-visual policy, and was aided by the conjunction of the Delors Presidency of the Commission and the presence of his mentor, Francois Mitterrand, in the Elysee Palace."[18] The EC can thus be viewed as a "policy entrepreneur," both reflecting as well as shaping the member-state views (Richardson 1999; Sandholtz 1992). The EC's Directorate General on Culture, closely allied with the French position, argued explicitly that without quotas U.S. content would flood Europe.[19]

The anxiety in Europe regarding Hollywood may be understood as both cultural and economic. The French, especially, articulated their cultural anxiety in making a case for cultural exception while the economic argument was made in terms of the MFN exemption. The film industry and civil-society groups in Europe also made the argument in terms of cultural identity. However, at the negotiating table, these arguments had to be translated into economic measures and concessions. The Europeans agreed to deliberate these measures in the context of cultural identity, while the United States sought to keep cultural identity off the table and to focus instead on the overriding economic instruments such as:

- Subsidies: Most production in the EU is government subsidized. The United States wanted limitations placed on this practice. But, in a contradictory move, the United States also sought access to the cultural subsidies that the French government paid domestic producers from the box office receipts.
- Levies: U.S. production studios also wanted their "fair share" of the levies raised in Europe on sales of blank videotapes. and audiotapes. These levies are collected on behalf of and redistributed to

the artists and studios under the presumption that this work is being taped from the broadcasters (studios in the United States have long sought such levies without success). U.S. studios promised to reinvest their share of these levies in Europe. According to the Rome Convention on copyright law, the EU recognizes the rights to royalty claims not just of the production studios but also the neighboring rights of artists and writers. Even though the United States is a not a signatory, its studios felt entitled to the copyright royalties. The EU countered that not only was the United States not a signatory to the convention but the levy did not even exist in the United States. U.S. negotiators were also concerned that with the advent of digital copying the studios would be major losers.

Before the actual bargaining, the main lobbies on the U.S. side included the major film, television, and music firms. Of these the MPAA, headed by Jack Valenti, and the RIAA were important. The MPAA includes all the major studios, the American Film Marketing Association, and the Motion Pictures Exporters Association.

On the European side, there were both pro- and anti-TWF coalitions. While the anti-TWF coalition was strong before 1989, the GATT negotiations in 1993 featured an increasingly strong pro-quota (and, by definition, pro-TWF) lobby. In addition to the EBU, influential national actors included the Bertelsmann Group in Germany, the BBC in the United Kingdom, and many other national and local broadcasters. Initially, apart from French government and EU Commission support, only the European Federation of Audiovisual Workers and the International Federation of Audiovisual Workers Union supported quotas.

Two market conditions, the U.S. share of the EU creative-industry market and the government-supported structure of the EU cultural industry, made both sides aggressive in protecting their interests in Europe. The subsidization structure that links cinema and television, especially in France, is of importance here and was the major U.S. objection to the TWF initiative.

Audio-visual exports accounted for the second biggest export item, after commercial aircraft, from the United States. In 1993, U.S. films, TV shows, and videocassettes netted $3.7 billion in Europe while the EU's exports to the U.S. in this area totaled $300 million (Associated Press 1993). The EU trade deficit with the United States in film and television shows reached

TABLE 3.5
Market Shares of U.S. Films in Europe (%)

	1989	1991	1993	1994
Belgium	69.5	79.6	71.8	74.7
Denmark	63.7	83.3	74	66.7
Finland	70.0	80.0	63.0	66.0
France	55.5	58.0	57.1	60.0
Germany	65.7	80.2	87.8	81.6
Greece	86.0	88.0	—	82.0
Ireland	75.0	91.5	—	—
Italy	63.1	58.6	68.1	65.0
Luxembourg	87.0	85.0	80.0	84.0
Netherlands	75.6	92.5	89.3	90.0
Portugal	81.0	85.0	61.2	—
Spain	73.0	69.0	75.5	72.3
Sweden	69.3	70.5	72.7	70.0
United Kingdom	84.0	84.0	94.2	—

Source: World Trade Organization 1998a,

$6 billion in 1998 (CNN.com 1999). By any measure, Americans dominate the European market. Table 3.5 shows the U.S. share of the film markets in Europe. The U.S. share is low in France and Italy, both countries with a sizable film industry, but still reaches 58.2 percent and 59.4 percent, respectively, in 1992—meaning that the share of the domestic product was far smaller. French films, for instance, only captured 34.5 percent of the market in 1997 (Lange 1998). Importantly, the U.S. share of the total film market in France's reluctant partners, Germany and the United Kingdom, was 82.8 percent and 90.6 percent, respectively, in 1992. American films also pulled in 69 percent of the audiences in those countries in 1991, up from 46 percent in 1980. Among television programs, 40 percent of the "telefilms" shown on European channels were American (Goff 2000, 557).

European governments' support for the continent's audio-visual industry through an elaborate system of taxation, levies, and subsidies accounts for the other side of market conditions. Table 3.6 gives the total percentage of public support for films and video in Europe for 1994. Almost two-thirds of the production of the film and video industries is financed through state

TABLE 3.6

European Public Support for Film and Video, 1994 (%)

	SUPPORT PRODUCTION	SUPPORT DISTRIBUTION
Germany	77.54	10.20
Austria	94.22	5.78
Belgium	96.28	3.72
Denmark	94.17	2.28
Spain	92.14	2.93
Finland	85.25	11.72
France	40.47	6.59
Greece	91.53	8.47
Ireland	100.00	—
Italy	42.10	26.32
Netherlands	98.60	1.40
Portugal	86.12	6.16
Sweden	94.72	3.73
United Kingdom	100.00	—
Total EU	62.51	10.59

Source: World Trade Organization 1998a, 16.

support, rising to 100 percent in the United Kingdom and Ireland. On the other hand, there is very little support for distribution (the EU total was 10.59 percent). Most distribution channels are local and national. This is an important fact, as American producers possess considerable clout here through their transnational distribution networks.

In France, a large part of the subsidies for audio-visual programs in cinema and television come from total cinema revenues, thus the U.S. objection that its cinema receipts were subsidizing the very broadcasting that was crafted as a protectionist measure. The total tax is not broken down by taxes on French, EU, or U.S. content. However, Hollywood films continue to dominate box offices in France, contributing a majority of the revenue. France levies a 11 percent TSA or "special seat tax" on every ticket sold. Cocq and Messerlin (2005, 30) shows that the subsidy structure benefits television producers at the expense of films. Between 1986 and 2001, the TSA grew by 122 percent, but only 36 percent of the tax revenues from broadcasters went to cinema.

Market conditions conferred advantages to both sides. Americans were already entrenched in the European market; thus, their main interest in eliminating quotas was to increase their share of in this market. They could even find solace in the fact that most national governments in Europe were not implementing the TWF quotas (Levy 1999; L'Ecuyer and Rogerson 2000). Most of the film and television industry in Europe is supported by the state, and so the decided advantage for the European side was its ability to call on the beneficiaries for support. At one point in the GATT talks, on September 23, 1993, for example, 4,000 European film personnel (actors, directors, producers, writers) took out full-page advertisements in the major European papers in support of the EU position. The European side in many ways had more to lose from dismantling the quotas or its public support mechanisms.

DELIBERATION PROCESS

The deliberation context defined above—lack of trust between the coalitions, the underlying market conditions, and cultural framing—made reaching a cooperative agreement at the Uruguay Round unattractive to the Europeans and, arguably, the United States. The Europeans sought to convince the Americans that they should either accept the quotas in the final agreement or let them take the MFN exemption on audio-visual services, which they carefully referred to as the "cultural exception." Neither alternative was attractive to the Americans in trying to better their position. However, the United States would dominate the market regardless of the agreement. In that sense, the Europeans had more at stake in the deliberations.

The agenda-setting tactic the Europeans deployed centered on cultural identity. It relied on two interrelated points. One was to emphasize the importance of the ("aesthetically superior") audio-visual industry to European identity and unity, and the second was to increasingly call attention to the harmful effects of the ("aesthetically inferior") American industry. In every statement, the loss to French or European identity was directly evoked. France's former culture minister Jack Lang, an important force behind the TWF directive and EU's GATT position, declared: "The soul of France cannot be sold for a few pieces of silver."[20] European officials warned of such phenomena as a "wall to wall Dallas" in Europe, in reference to the popular TV program from the United States. France was reportedly fighting a *"guerre des images"*—a war of images or representations (Goff 2000, 553).

Increasingly vitriolic rhetoric, in reality, was thus window dressing for the hardened EU position on audio-visual. If effective, it would decrease the American market size in Europe.

The U.S. negotiators avoided the identity frame in negotiations: in the actual bargaining, the U.S. side used careful language, respectful even of the cultural identity issue.[21] French officials argued that the U.S. negotiating teams never quite understood how important symbolic representations like film are to French identity.[22] For example, U.S. domestic interests, especially the MPAA, lambasted the European position (even during the TWF framing exercise) on culture, calling it a mere front for hiding their weaker commercial position, which may have escalated the crisis. A statement from Jack Valenti, former president of the MPAA is illustrative: "The American movie is dominant in the world, not because of patent or formula or subsidy or artificial enticements. We are dominant because what we create here beguiles and entertains viewers on every continent, with an enchantment no other country in the world has been able to duplicate."[23]

The Europeans countered with careful framing moves that strengthened the coalition in support of the quotas. They critiqued the position of the U.S. creative industry as Hollywood's will to dominate. The faces people saw in the media speaking for this issue were well known throughout Europe. Goff (2000) presents a comprehensive analysis of the way elites in Europe used the dispute to endow meaning to their borders, helping to create a European identity. From the negotiation side, this framing exercise began to serve as a glue for creative industry lobbies in EU. The framing exercise helped to build a sense of European cultural identity through the need for quotas, although in practice the so-called European identity played a poor cousin to national identities, which states promoted. In the French case, the two were sometimes confused.[24] The European Commission as well as French officials now regularly espouse the historical links between states and culture in Europe. One of them noted: "The culture is the state. The culture is the soul of the nation."[25]

By any measure, the framing of the creative industry issue as a threat to European identity paid off. As shown earlier, the lobbies for TWF had been weak. By 1993, a coalition of creative-industry interests was quite visible in Europe, including creative industries that depended on the state for their production costs. The industries also had the additional advantage of putting well-known faces (film stars, directors, music stars) in front of the public. In the closing days of the talks, French TV and film producers published a paper on what Europe would lose from the agreement. French and Italian producers also held a joint press conference on the issue. It was at this time that Japan joined in favor of the cultural exemption.

With powerful domestic lobbies such as the MPAA and RIAA on the U.S. side, their collective voice matched that of the Europeans. Those who participated in the talks regularly note Hollywood's access to U.S. government.[26] If the Europeans framed the issue as that of identity and culture, the American lobby was consistent in framing it as trade. One of them notes: "We were sensitive to the culture issue but a trade barrier is a trade barrier. The way to work through it was through trade promotion and not restriction."[27]

In terms of tactics, the Americans also consistently focused on the issues involved because there was no easy resolution to the ideology underlying these issues on the European side.[28] This may have even resulted in occasional contradictory moves, such as the time that the American side demanded a fair share of the subsidies to producers while at the same time trying to argue for their elimination. The preference ordering of these moves (for example, "If not quota elimination, then we want our fair share") was not quite clear, thus resulting in the contradiction. The Europeans picked on moves like this, evoking the cultural "America wants to rob us" angle. However, the American insistence on issues over ideologies may have paid off and cannot be underestimated. One American negotiator notes that they were close to an agreement on an unrestricted digital environment in Europe but Hollywood did not come along as it was fearful of illegal copying and distribution.[29] One European negotiator notes that Europeans also proposed a freeze on the level of subsidies but that the Americans studios felt that it was not enough.[30]

Negotiations on audio-visual continued between USTR Mickey Kantor and the EU's Leon Brittan into the final hours of the Uruguay Round, but the Americans rejected the deal that EU offered, which was too close to status quo. At six A.M. on December 14, just before the deadline for negotiations under the U.S. president's fast track authority were to expire, Brittan offered to bind the television quota at 49 percent—meaning it would not be increased in the future—and also offered to continue the negotiations later on for box-office-receipt taxes in France and those on blank video and audio tapes (Preeg 1995, 172). Kantor called President Clinton—it was midnight in Washington—and the president called the head of a major studio in Hollywood to let him know the deal Europeans had offered.[31] The president then called back Kantor, who told Brittan that the Americans were rejecting the EU proposal.

Conclusion

Just as creative-industry exports have continued to grow, so have efforts increased in cultural politics to frame them or value them in cultural-identity terms. While such valuation can lead to conflict-laden international deliberation, the fact that a deal was almost reached at the end of the Uruguay Round is often missed in analyses of creative-industry deliberations. As it happened, the quotas issue in the end carried the day. The Europeans offered to sign an audio-visual agreement only if the quotas issue was addressed in it. The issue had symbolic importance: by European calculations, American acquiescence meant a de jure acknowledgment of the European position on the cultural exception. Mickey Kantor, instead of signing something that lobbies in the United States opposed, walked away from it, and the Europeans took the MFN exemption from GATS in audio-visual.[32] Deviation from MFN allowed the EU to discriminate against U.S. audio-visual products. However, as I explain in the next chapter, the cultural politics of European and national cultural identities resurfaced soon after the Uruguay Round.

4

UNESCO and the Europeans

Europe is proud of its cultural diversity. Language, literature,
theatre, visual arts, architecture, crafts, the cinema and broadcasting
may belong to a specific country or region, but they represent part
of Europe's common cultural heritage. The European Union aims
to preserve and support this diversity and to help make it accessible
to others.

—European Union, Europa Culture Portal

The European position on linking cultural identity with its creative industries has hardened since the end of the Uruguay Round. This stance has
run in parallel with other coalition-building and culture-framing moves.
Most importantly, Canada and France led an international coalition to
switch the cultural identity issue over to UNESCO by drafting a Declaration on Cultural Diversity in 2001 and the Convention on the Protection
and Promotion of the Diversity of Cultural Expressions, sometimes known
as the Universal Convention on Cultural Diversity in 2005. UNESCO is
also more receptive to cultural-identity moves than the WTO, whose mandate is limited to trade issues. The Canadian and French stance was also
hardened by moves to include the liberalization of creative industries in
(failed) negotiations on the Multilateral Agreement on Investment through
the OECD from 1995 through 1999. This chapter explains these outcomes
and other related moves in terms of cultural deliberations as hard-edged as
those outlined in the last chapter. The latter part of the chapter also details
cultural politics within the European Union.

A brief historical note on Canada is necessary to show its alignment
with EU moves. Canada was concerned after it lost a high-profile case on
magazines against the United States at the WTO's newly constituted Dispute Settlement Body. In 1997, the WTO ruled against Canada's content

regulations on advertising for U.S. magazines sold in Canada (called split-run magazines). Canada had imposed a tax on such magazines, arguing that they collected a disproportionate share of advertising. (The similarity between this tax and the French TSA comes to mind.) The WTO treated the periodical as a good and the tax was deemed a protectionist measure. The United States made its case in 1996 on the basis of a few Canadian import bans and postal discriminations. The Canadians tried to make a case on the basis of protecting cultural identities but failed. The Canadians also noted that 80 percent of the magazines sold in Canada were of foreign, mostly U.S. origin and that more than 450 U.S. titles were available (WTO 1996c). Both the WTO panel and the appellate body found Canada's measures to be in violation of its GATT commitments (WTO 1997a, 1997b). This prompted the Canadians to start seriously conferring with their colleagues across the Atlantic.

Another important impetus for the hardening of the cultural-diversity coalition was the WTO mandate to have ongoing services negotiations in particular sectors and to launch a services round. The GATS 2000 negotiations, now part of the Doha Round of trade talks, were launched in January 2000 in keeping with the in-built mandate of the Uruguay Round. By June 30, 2002, member states submitted "requests" for liberalization in various service sectors of other member states. These requests do not go through the WTO. Only member states making and receiving requests see them. The period between requests and offers entails bilateral negotiations between members. "Offers" for liberalization were to be tabled by March 31, 2003, when the negotiation process was to become multilateral again. Offers were sent directly to the WTO, and twenty-six of them, including one from the EU for its fifteen member states, were received by June 2003. Because of MFN, any commitment offer that a member state makes to another applies to all the member states.

Not surprisingly, the EU made no requests or offers in audio-visual services. While it continues to push for telecommunications liberalization, the medium for the content, it deftly tries to keep actual content issues out of the WTO; the move to shift the venue to UNESCO must be seen in this context. The institutional capacity of the EC's Directorate General on Culture has been strengthened, and the French, more or less, continue to dominate the debates. The European trade commissioner at that time, Pascal Lamy, a Frenchman, supported the Directorate General on Culture in its tasks (Lamy 2002, chap. 8). His appointment as director general of the WTO in 2005 and reappointment for another term in April 2009 did not bode well for keeping the audio-visual issue at the top of the WTO agenda.

In terms of market coalitions, the U.S. side has been less aggressive in arguing for liberalization while domestic lobbies in Europe are increasingly mobilized and seeking linkages with other international lobbies. There may be two reasons for the U.S. position.[1] First, Hollywood's influence in the Bush administration was not that strong, and the Obama administration is unlikely to push such a potentially divisive issue through the WTO. Second, the MPAA and the RIAA are now far more concerned with piracy issues than with creative-industry liberalization. In fact, in terms of piracy, they may even have common cause with the Europeans.[2] For a while, global mergers and acquisitions in creative industries, especially the merger of the French entertainment giant and the Hollywood studio that was to create Vivendi-Universal, were seen as another reason that both the United States and the Europeans might be muted on this issue but the opposite happened. Vivendi chief Jean-Marie Messier's American sympathies were reviled in France, and when the merger came apart because of financial difficulties, it was celebrated and Messier was removed from Vivendi in early 2003.

Lobbies within Europe continue to coalesce around keeping creative industries out of trade negotiations even while individual states, such as the United Kingdom, go along reluctantly with the EU position. The European Broadcasting Union has come full circle since it opposed moves toward broadcasting liberalization in Europe in the mid-1980s. It is now the most important voice in Europe in trying to preserve broadcasting plurality (that is, national programming) and, therefore, is zealously opposed to international liberalization of cultural industries. The EBU is not threatened by the spillovers of national programming into other markets. As noted earlier, the flows of broadcasting content from one national market to another in Europe are limited. The EBU is thus more concerned with keeping other international, mostly U.S. programming out of the European market. Meanwhile, the French cinema lobbies, whose officials continue to insist that they were taken by surprise on the audio-visual issue at the Uruguay Round, have strengthened their coalitional ranks. Within France, the powerful organization ARP represents the collective voice of the French actors, directors, and producers. In Brussels, the lobbying organization Eurocinema presents European (mostly French) cinema.

Four important moves by Western Europe, one at the WTO and three in other forums, reflecting the evolution of European preferences in creative industries from cultural exception to cultural diversity, are outlined below. They are detailed in a nonchronological fashion for analytical clarity.

Audio-visual at the WTO

Although nearly half of the total requests in services received by the commission from the countries at the Doha Round were in audio-visual, the EU categorically now states that it will not make any offers in audio-visual. (Health, education and social services, utilities, along with audio-visual, were the other sectors excluded.) By June 2005, of the sixty-one initial offers in services, twenty-six countries had made offers in audio-visual. However, the EU did make offers in other sectors, including movement of skilled personnel, transport, financial services, telecommunications, postal services, computer services, distribution, environmental services, construction, news agencies and entertainment, and tourism. Thus, the EU's moves for the creative industry are now about keeping this issue off of the WTO agenda altogether. Lobbying within the EU is so far advocating for the continuation of the MFN exemption and not negotiating at all on audio-visual services.

Before any requests or offers, the United States, Switzerland, and Brazil circulated proposals submitted to the WTO to spur debate and possible solutions to the issue of trade rather than culture.[3] French politicians critiqued Switzerland's proposal in particular, which would entail drafting a sectoral annex on audiovisual—to admit the special nature of culture while also allowing for trade liberalization—for being insensitive to European concerns. The U.S. proposal dealt mainly with overall subsidies issues while the Brazilian one dealt with ways "to promote the progressive liberalization of the sector in a way that creates opportunities of effective market access for exports of developing countries in this sector without affecting the margin of flexibility of governments to achieve their cultural policies objectives as they find appropriate" (WTO 2001b). Interestingly, Brazil had supported the EU moves during the Uruguay Round.

At this point, digital transmissions, through multimedia convergence, raise an interesting threat to the EU's stance in creative industries; these transmissions make keeping creative products out of any territory a moot point. However, the EU's approach to digital convergence or flows is to deal with it via existing WTO instruments exclusive of an audio-visual agreement. For example, on the question of piracy of creative products, both sides of the Atlantic are cooperating and forcing agreements similar to TRIPS plus in the bilaterals they strike with other nations, especially developing countries. At the end of 2004, the French cultural minister and the chief executive of the MPAA issued a declaration to crack down on piracy and "the threat that it poses to creativity, cultural diversity and, ultimately, consumer choice."[4] In February 2005, the European Commission also tabled a paper at the WTO that sought to address the broader issue of convergence by seeking clarification on the channel of communication, thus pertaining to WTO's telecommunications accord rather than dealing with content issues. "In essence, the EC wanted a definition that allowed it to exclude cultural content, while pursuing its own interests in telecommunications" (Kelsey 2007, 21). At the level of the WTO, the EU's preferred approach is to deal with audio-visual issues via TRIPS and the telecommunications agreements. Within the EU, the EC looked at the experience of the U.K. regulator Oftel (now Ofcom) with regulating cultural content through convergence of technologies and treating all pipelines as similar.

Observers also point out that France is now comfortable with the MFN exemption on audio-visual in the WTO.[5] At the domestic level, this allows the French to speak of the so-called cultural exception. In Brussels, it makes the task of the Directorate General on Trade easier in that it does not have to get into a bureaucratic turf war with the Directorate General on Culture on this issue.

Strengthening of Television Without Frontiers

In the meantime, the EC has put into place several mechanisms to monitor as well strengthen the TWF directive. In doing so, it brings further clout to its opposition to negotiating this issue at the WTO. TWF was amended in 1997 to include language to allow for at least 10 percent of programming time to be filled up with content created by independent producers who are not themselves broadcasters.[6] There are pressures in Europe to delete the qualifier "where practicable and feasible" around the 51 percent quotas and make the rule binding. A report from the EC on the state of TWF seems to show that most member states are meeting the quota requirements, especially among the publicly owned broadcasters (Commission of the European Communities 2002). In a move to strengthen control over new and independent broadcasters the report notes: "Only some of the minority channels in certain Member States are presenting difficulties. In this regard, the Commission would remind the member states concerned of the need for increased control and monitoring of these channels and the importance of ensuring, where practicable and appropriate means, that these television broadcasters meet the proportions laid down by Articles 4 and 5 of the Directive, in line with the principle of progressive improvement" (Commission of the European Communities 2002).

Despite the impetus given to TWF for European programming, it remains a "national" exercise. Cocq and Messerlin point out that only 12 percent of channels are European (as opposed to national) broadcasters and they collect less than 2 percent of total advertising and less than 0.7 percent of broadcasting revenues (Cocq and Messerlin 2005, 23). Although France remains at the forefront of these issues, it has also found its hand weakening at the EU: "The French want a stricter quota system and the Germans want it abolished on constitutional grounds. British officials say they would rather not have it but can live with it, provided the 'wherever applicable' get-out clause is maintained" (*Financial Times* 2002).

The Failed Multilateral Agreement on Investment

The Uruguay Round delivered a weak agreement on Trade-Related Investment Measures that would have sought to curtail domestic production and import or export requirements on foreign producers. The Organization for Economic Cooperation and Development, the rich-countries club accounting for 85 percent of the $3 trillion of foreign direct investment in 1996, then sought to produce the Multilateral Agreement on Investment through negotiations that lasted between 1995 and 1998.[7] Many causes are cited for its failure; most prominent were the withdrawal of U.S. support in the face of a weak agreement and opposition from labor and environmental groups.[8] Sometimes the French opposition to inclusion of creative industries is mentioned as well.

France's withdrawal from negotiations in 1998 was specifically attributed to the inclusion of creative industries. Until late 1996, it was unclear whether creative industries would be excluded from MAI. At this time,

France proposed a clause that sought an exception for preserving cultural and linguistic diversity. As tabled, the specific clause attached to the May 1997 draft text read: "Nothing in this Agreement shall be construed to prevent any Contracting Party to take any measure to regulate investment of foreign companies and the conditions of activity of these companies, in the framework of policies designed to promote cultural and linguistic diversity."[9] While a few European members may have favored exempting creative industries from MAI, "the concept of a general clause was not acceptable to some delegations" (UNCTAD 1999, 15). These members proposed drawing up a list of exceptions that would include creative industries (a negative list approach) or allowing members to make whatever commitments they wanted in specific aspects of cultural industries (a positive list approach). By then the creative-industries issue featured divisions between the EC Directorates General on Culture and Trade in Brussels. DG-Trade was taking the lead in MAI.

Nevertheless, an article Jack Lang, the culture minister, wrote in *Le Monde* in spring 1998 became "a lightning rod" for French politicians and media.[10] Lang played on a popular film title to speak of MAI as a threatening friend (Lang 1998). This served to galvanize creative industries in France and may account for the French halt on MAI negotiations in spring 1998. At that time, at least, the Canadians were not that concerned with the inclusion of creative industries in MAI, although Canadian creative industries and organizations had begun to make assessments of MAI's implications for themselves.[11]

While the failure of MAI in general obviated the need for any measures whatsoever, the French and Canadians became concerned about the impending GATS 2000 negotiations that were due to start as per the "built-in" agenda of the Uruguay Round.[12] The stage set ripe for moves at UNESCO.

UNESCO:
Developing an International Norm on Cultural Diversity

France and Canada joined in developing an international norm on "cultural diversity," which sought national-level protections for creative industries. The norm strengthened their claims regarding the differential and special nature of creative industries. It linked these claims inextricably with cultural identity and diversity issues. Canada's culture minister, Sheila Copps, took the lead in June 1998 toward establishing the International Network on Cultural Policy, in which France is a lead player. INCP now brings together culture ministers from fifty-six countries to exchange views on cultural policies. France and Canada took the lead in getting UNESCO to adopt, on November 2, 2001, a Universal Declaration on Cultural Diversity, which recognizes the cultural specificity of cultural industries in particular countries. Interestingly, both the INCP and UNESCO websites also underscore the importance of this declaration to the events of September 11, 2001, even though planning for the declaration started at least two years before that.[13]

The UNESCO declaration notes in the beginning that "culture is at the heart of contemporary debates about identity, social cohesion, and the development of the knowledge-based economy" and "that the process of globalization, facilitated by the rapid development of new information and communication technologies, though representing a challenge for cultural diversity, creates the conditions for renewed dialogue among cultures and civilizations" (UNESCO 2001, 2). It then defines twelve articles dealing with cultural diversity and setting the agenda away from commercial cultural industry-type considerations. This is apparent in links made in the articles to pluralism, human rights, creativity, and international solidarity. Articles 8 and 9, listed under "Cultural Diversity and Creativity" are particularly significant in this regard:

ARTICLE 8—

CULTURAL GOODS AND SERVICES: COMMODITIES OF A UNIQUE KIND

In the face of present-day economic and technological change, opening up vast prospects for creation and innovation, particular attention must be paid to the diversity of the supply of creative work, to due recognition to the rights of authors and artists and to the specificity of cultural goods and services which, as vectors of identity, values and meaning, must not be treated as mere commodities or consumer goods.

ARTICLE 9—

CULTURAL POLICIES AS CATALYSTS OF CREATIVITY

While ensuring the free circulation of ideas and works, cultural policies must create conditions conducive to the production and dissemination of diversified cultural goods through cultural industries that have the means to assert themselves at the local and global level. It is for each State, with due regard to international obligations, to define its cultural policy and to implement it through the means it considers fit, whether by operational support or appropriate regulations.

(UNESCO 2001, 3–4)

The declaration came after considerable framing activity among INCP and EU officials. The frame used was "cultural diversity" rather than "cultural exception." On October 26, 1999, the Council of the European Union, in preparation for the Seattle WTO Ministerial, declared that "the Community and the Member States maintain the possibility to preserve and develop their capacity to define and implement their cultural and audiovisual policies for the purpose of preserving cultural diversity." This was followed on December 7, 2000, by the Declaration on Cultural Diversity by the Council of Europe. The cultural ministers of the International Organization of the Francophonie adopted a similar declaration on June 15, 2001. The INCP Working Group on Cultural Diversity and Globalization met in Lucerne, Switzerland, on September 24 through 26, 2001, to finalize the plans for framing of such an instrument via UNESCO.[14]

Along the way, the cultural diversity frame began to be linked to the biodiversity frame in an effort to provide international legal rationale to the logic of cultural diversity. INCP meetings were crucial in this regard. The INCP made an explicit connection with the 1992 Convention on Biological Diversity framed in Rio de Jeneiro. Now moves were afoot to go to the next level of international law to convert the Declaration into an International Convention on Cultural Diversity. On September 3, 2002, at the World Summit on Sustainable Development in Johannesburg, Jacques Chirac, speaking at a roundtable on "Biodiversity, Cultural Diversity and Ethics," noted: "One response which France proposes is for the international community to adopt a world convention on cultural diversity. This would be the counterpart to the Convention on Biological Diversity. It would lend the weight of international law to the principles couched in the declaration just adopted by UNESCO." He also noted that, "There is nothing more foreign to the human spirit than evolution towards a uniform civilization, just as there is nothing more hostile to the movement of life than a reduction in biodiversity" (Délégation Permanente de France 2002, annex 1). In November 2002, at a UNESCO meeting in Istanbul attended by representatives of 110 countries including 72 culture ministers, a declaration was adopted to support an International Convention on Cultural Diversity and to begin work on a draft.

The EU, the French, and the INCP then concentrated their efforts toward getting UNESCO to adopt a resolution to begin work on a Universal Convention on Cultural Diversity at the thirty-second General Conference of the UNESCO. UNESCO is headquartered in Paris, and this gave the French easy access to UNESCO deliberations and excluded the United States, which was not even a UNESCO member. However, the United States rejoined UNESCO at the thirty-second conference. This move is viewed either as motivated by societal pressures within the United States or as the U.S. response to the crafting of the UNESCO convention and attempts to shift the focus away from the WTO, of which the United States was a member (Americans for UNESCO 2004; Kelsey 2007; Singh 2010b). The United States had left UNESCO during the Reagan administration over a previous culture war with the developing countries. Meanwhile, the INCP had already drafted such a convention, which was presented at its sixth annual Ministerial Meeting in late 2004 (INCP 2003). Apart from delinking "culture" from commercial considerations and linking it with international human rights and biodiversity conventions, the draft convention courts developing countries by proposing a fund for capacity building for cultural industries in such countries.[15]

In working toward a UNESCO convention, a number of international organizations, academics, and think tanks were courted by a network of the INCP, the EU, and lobbying groups. Developing countries, most of which have content and creative-industry protections in place, were viewed as key players. South Korea is an important example. UNCTAD, in cooperation with UNESCO, convened an Expert Meeting on Audiovisual Services to help bring developing countries on board (UNCTAD 2002). While not seeking to exempt audiovisual services, the meeting concluded that "a sector specific solution such as an annex, protocol or similar specific instrument could be developed" during the GATS negotiations (UNCTAD 2002, 1). Conferences sponsored by groups like EBU, FERA, Eurocinema, and BSAC are being organized all over Europe to court public and intellectual support.

The INCP was also instrumental in creating a parallel nongovernmental network of international culture-industry workers and artists that in September 2000 coalesced into the International Network for Cultural Diversity. Representatives, who would later form the INCD, were at the failed

WTO Seattle Ministerial in December 1999 in an effort to bring cultural issues to the meetings and also to organize protests against them. INCD, currently headquartered in the Canadian Conference for the Arts, is the leading arts-advocacy group in Canada. INCD and INCP annual meetings and agendas run parallel to each other. The INCD had drafted an International Convention on Cultural Diversity, which was similar to that of the INCP in its aims and philosophy except that it was more emphatic in keeping audio-visual negotiations out of the WTO. While Canada and France frame the INCD as a global network of nongovernmental organizations, the imprint of the Canadian and French governments was ubiquitous: "The official side has kept a tight reign on the 'grass-root' input through funding its liaison office and various research initiatives, holding the INCD meetings concurrently with its own, and providing consultants or staff that develop themes, suggest speakers, write background papers and summary reports and proselytize" (Acheson and Maule 2004, 246).

The program for drafting a convention was presented at the thirty-second General Conference of UNESCO in September and October 2003. UNESCO appointed a fifteen-member committee of independent experts to study the issue further. After several UNESCO meetings and drafting session, a preliminary draft was presented at the third session of UNESCO's Intergovernmental Meeting of the Experts (May 25–June 4, 2005). The draft was then presented at the thirty-third General Conference in October 2005 and passed with 148 votes in favor and two against, from the United States and Israel. It is known as the Convention on the Protection and Promotion of the Diversity of Cultural Expressions (UNESCO 2005b). The preamble to the text starts by "affirming that cultural diversity is a defining characteristic of humanity." Its thirty-five articles affirm the rights of nations to formulate cultural policies that promote cultural diversity and protect indigenous cultures. Article 20 establishes the relationship to other international treaties: "mutual supportiveness" is mentioned as the underlying principle, but the convention cannot be subordinated to other treaties. In other words, if there was to be a trade versus cultural protection on the future, it would have to be resolved in the spirit of mutual supportiveness without subordinating the UNESCO convention. However, article 20.2 then notes something that dilutes the precedence of the convention and may mean that WTO instruments may supersede (if the EU was to make an audio-visual commitment): "Nothing in this Convention shall be interpreted as modifying rights and obligations of the Parties under any other treaties to which they are parties"

(UNESCO 2005b). Furthermore, as the convention's dispute-settlement mechanism is not that strong, offering only a form of arbitration, the WTO dispute-settlement process may still favor parties against those that have not taken a commitment in audio-visual.

The UNESCO convention also recognizes that the link between creativity and culture is indirect. Article 4, "Definitions," provides the specific connections:

For the purposes of this Convention, it is understood that:

1. Cultural diversity

"Cultural diversity" refers to the manifold ways in which the cultures of groups and societies find expression. These expressions are passed on within and among groups and societies.

Cultural diversity is made manifest not only through the varied ways in which the cultural heritage of humanity is expressed, augmented and transmitted through the variety of cultural expressions, but also through diverse modes of artistic creation, production, dissemination, distribution and enjoyment, whatever the means and technologies used.

2. Cultural content

"Cultural content" refers to the symbolic meaning, artistic dimension and cultural values that originate from or express cultural identities.

3. Cultural expressions

"Cultural expressions" are those expressions that result from the creativity of individuals, groups and societies, and that have cultural content.

4. Cultural activities, goods and services

"Cultural activities, goods and services" refers to those activities, goods and services, which at the time they are considered as a specific attribute, use or purpose, embody or convey cultural expressions, irrespective of the commercial value they may have. Cultural activities may be an end in themselves, or they may contribute to the production of cultural goods and services.

5. Cultural industries

"Cultural industries" refers to industries producing and distributing cultural goods or services as defined in paragraph 4 above.

6. Cultural policies and measures

"Cultural policies and measures" refers to those policies and measures relating to culture, whether at the local, national, regional or international level that are either focused on culture as such or are designed to have a direct effect on cultural expressions of individuals, groups or societies, including on the creation, production, dissemination, distribution of and access to cultural activities, goods and services.

7. Protection

"Protection" means the adoption of measures aimed at the preservation, safeguarding and enhancement of the diversity of cultural expressions.

"Protect" means to adopt such measures.

8. Interculturality

"Interculturality" refers to the existence and equitable interaction of diverse cultures and the possibility of generating shared cultural expressions through dialogue and mutual respect.[16]

The process from the creative to the cultural in the UNESCO text is devoid of the kinds of cultural politics and negotiations outlined above. UNESCO's portal on the convention goes a step further in linking creative expressions with culture and identity and legitimizing the role of national cultural policies in regulating creative industries:[17]

The Convention seeks to strengthen the five inseparable links of the same chain: creation, production, distribution/dissemination, access and enjoyment of cultural expressions, as conveyed by cultural activities, goods and services.

In particular, the Convention aims to:

• reaffirm the sovereign right of States to draw up cultural policies
• recognize the specific nature of cultural goods and services as vehicles of identity, values and meaning
• strengthen international cooperation and solidarity so as to favour the cultural expressions of all countries

The politics of the UNESCO convention depended heavily on the use of particular tactics. Moving the venue to UNESCO, framing the issue as cultural diversity, and finding support for it through coalition building were important in this regard. In particular, France used its influence with Francophone countries to support its cause: subsidies given by the CNC to Francophone countries for cultural industries—especially cinema—are one example of this. But multilateral coordination has not ended there; European officials courted several other developing countries. Finally, France has had to coordinate its position within the multilateral EU context.

Meanwhile, pressure from the United States did lead to the dilution of several provisions in the draft convention, especially article 20 on the mutual supportiveness of international treaties and the salience of obligations under other treaties.[18] Nevertheless, it continues to assert that the very framing of the convention is not legitimate and that the convention is about trade and not culture. In one of the first instances where U.S. officials addressed questions about the convention, a press briefing held by the State Department in April 2005, officials noted that because nonstate actors initially drafted the convention, it was not legitimate. On June 3, 2005, when the draft—which had been then been amended and redrafted at an intergovernmental session—was presented at UNESCO and was being applauded, the American delegation—led by Robert Martin—staged a walkout and issued a press release that noted: "Because it is about trade, this convention clearly exceeds the mandate of UNESCO. . . . What we have done here in the past week has undermined the spirit of consensus that normally characterizes the work of UNESCO. It will surely weaken UNESCO's reputation as a responsible, thoughtful international organization." Soon after, on June 30, 2005, the United States, along with a select group of powerful states (including China, Hong Kong, Japan, Mexico and Taiwan—territories with significant cultural exports), presented a communication at the WTO's Council for Trade in Services. Among other things, they noted:

> We express great concern over efforts by key participants in the negotiations to create an a priori exclusion for such an important sector. . . .
> We urge all Members to consider carefully the broad economic benefits from including audiovisual commitments in their efforts. Above all, trade in audiovisual services results in cultural exchange, the best way to promote cultural diversity.
>
> (WTO 2005a)

The EU's framing of cultural diversity seems to have been successful in linking creative industries to cultural identity, but the position is neither monolithic nor immune to future opposition.[19] The United Kingdom, with sizable creative-industry exports and an affinity toward formal cooperation with U.S. cultural industries, will be reluctant to endorse the European position. Former prime minister Tony Blair specifically included creative industries in speaking of the "Third Way" that transcends simple divides between government and industry. In 1997, Blair also established the Creative Industries Taskforce with a primarily economic mandate. While creating indirect government incentives for creative industries, the Blair government also allowed the newly constituted Department of Culture, Media, and Sport, earlier known as the Department of Cultural Heritage, to directly fund these programs, which evolved into thinking about "Creative Britain" (DCMS 2001).[20] While speaking of creative expressions and industries, the DCMS also avoided, to a large extent, linking creativity with culture, focusing instead on the economic potential of these industries. The UK Department of Trade and Industry released a ninety-six-page report on its own position on services within the EU context as the EU was framing its offer for the WTO (2002). The report notes that while the United Kingdom's audio-visual imports outweigh its exports, the latter are significant: "The UK is the world second largest exporter of TV programs" and its music industry has "experienced phenomenal growth." It goes on to note that the United Kingdom "takes a liberalized approach to foreign investment and ownership throughout the audio-visual sectors; although this is not he case across the EU or Council of Europe" (2002, 23–25). Significantly audio-visual was included in the lists for liberalization. In deference to the French position, one DTI official notes: "You can lock up your culture or promote it. UK's approach is to promote it."[21] However, the United Kingdom subsidizes its film and broadcasting industries heavily, and that might tilt the balance in going along with the EU/French position. Furthermore, the EU has sizable export interests in sectors such as music and, as pointed out earlier, even France and the United States share an interest in the intellectual-property concerns underlying audio-visual. Thus, WTO officials also see the moves on cultural diversity as "delay tactics."[22] Developing countries such as India, Brazil, China, Mexico, and Taiwan and the territory of Hong Kong are exporters of cultural goods; they remain reluctant to go in with the cultural-diversity frame and may account for UNCTAD's lukewarm support on this issue.[23] In the meantime, the UNESCO convention was ratified on March 18, 2007.

Emergent Cultural Policies in the EU

The TWF initiative and the UNESCO convention have helped EU crystallize the importance as well as the scope of cultural policies coming from

Brussels. These initiatives are themselves part of macrolevel thinking regarding incipient notions of European identity that came to the fore in the 1990s and have attracted varying and often contradictory moves among the cultural policy elite. Within these may be discerned "a congeries of spheres of authority (SOAs) that are subject to considerable flux and not necessarily coterminous with a division of territorial space" (Rosenau 1997, 39). It is in this sense that we may also understand territoriality and cultural identity as a continually contested space featuring an interplay of cognitive, emotional, technological, and organizational aspects. In Anderson's account (1983), imagined national identities in Europe were propelled by the printing press's giving access to works in European vernaculars, which allowed national identities such as French, German, and English to emerge.[24]

The idea of national identity in Europe has always been contested by the idea of Europe from above and regional identity from below. More recently, networks of identity have emerged that intersect or transcend all three levels.[25] Several notions of European identity have existed historically. A set of collective experiences is often evoked through references to mythology, such as the image of the goddess Europa; to Christian civilization; to shared historic events, such as the European Enlightenment; or to difference, as in the Turkish threat felt in Europe since the fourteenth century and the contemporaneous fears of Islam.[26] At the local level, deeply felt identities from local affiliations, dubbed primordial by some, have never gone away and continue to reemerge in places such as Catalonia, Wales, Scotland, Walloon, or Flanders.[27]

Despite these challenges to national identity, it remains the foreground or prism through which emergent notions of cultural identity must be judged in Europe. Anthony Smith has been forthright in affirming European identity as political while cultural identity remains national or local. In fact, most EU programs are political, economic, and bureaucratic in character, and cultural symbols have often played a secondary, though not necessarily unimportant, role (McNamara 2010). The idea of a European Union pushed forward by the Eurocrats in Brussels foreshadows the cultural or democratic deficit in Europe. At cultural and historical levels, even the idea of Europe is often traced to national-level longings for an enlightened Europe that resembles Paris or ideas of European purity that can be traced to Germanic thought (R. Frank 2002).

Moves toward European cultural policies can be understood from the foreground of overlapping and multilayered identities in Europe and are informed both by national anxieties and entrepreneurial answers in Brussels. Before the TWF initiative, the idea of a European Union as framed by explicitly enunciated cultural policies was tame. Before the Treaty of Maastricht in 1993, the EU lacked any jurisdictional competence in making cultural policies, instead relying on its legal competence to fund small programs such as European Cultural Capital and the European Youth Orchestra (Gordon 2007, 14–15; Obuljen 2005). Outside of the European Community context, the forty-seven-country Strasbourg-based Council of Europe, founded in 1949, has cared for a democratic and cultural integration of Europe, but its capacity and mandate to bring these about has been limited. Its most remarkable achievements are in the area of human rights, but a common cultural heritage in Europe has been a part of its agenda. It convened the first conference of the Council of Cultural Ministers in Oslo in 1976, and since 1985 it has initiated national cultural-policy reviews, which have, in turn, served as data inputs for policymaking in Brussels and national capitals.

But it was TWF and the audio-visual moves at the Uruguay Round that galvanized the EU into clarifying its competencies for cultural policy. Specifically, article 128 of the 1993 Treaty of Maastricht, drafted in parallel to the debates at the Uruguay Round, allowed the EU to make cultural policy but only via consensual voting on program and budgets and respect for national and subnational levels of competencies in culture, as in the case of German *Länder*.[28] Article 128 was rewritten as article 151 in the 1997 Treaty of Amsterdam. Since 1993, the framing of cultural competencies has continued to dovetail with the global context of EU policy objectives. The strengthening of the TWF directive and the moves in UNESCO are examples. Although the UNESCO charter was signed individually by EU nation-states, unlike WTO agreements where the EU signs together as one entity, considerable coordination took place via Brussels.

EU leaders now regularly cite culture as a force for European unity, unlike the early EEC statements that mostly focused on economic and political objectives. The growing ascendance of these issues at various levels of policymaking (local, national, and global) is further encouraged by the importance of creative countries worldwide. Estimates cite 1.3 million people employed in creative industries in the United Kingdom and 5.8 million in the EU.[29] In 2006, the EU integrated its various culture and media programs in creating a new Education, Audiovisual, and Culture Executive Agency. In 2007 it began to allocate its structural funds, used historically for training and capacity building with poorer EU countries, within the framework of its Cohesion Policy, which includes cultural objectives (Gordon 2007, 14–16).

Cultural identity in Europe remains a contested term, and its location and dimensions with the EU objectives have not yet crystallized. While ascribing varying levels of importance to cultural policy in the EU, most analysts acknowledge that it is a relatively new arena of policymaking. Dewey notes: "Culture is now seen by many as a force for identity, a force for cohesion, and a force that fosters the democratic participation of European citizens" (2007, 4). Nevertheless, a report trying to project scenarios of EU cultural policy into 2015 notes: "Cultural policies in Europe are not only a marginal political field in the EU's range of competencies, but also a vague terrain in terms of relevant research and theorization" (Raunig 2005, 14).

Conclusion

The culture or commerce debate among policymakers and scholars that enveloped creative products is settling in favor of recognizing both dimensions in these products. Whether a product remains labeled as creative or cultural is a result of deliberative and negotiation-based politics.

Analyses of the creative economy, and policies that grow from them, tend to favor the aesthetic and economic aspects of creative expressions. The lobbying organization Americans for the Arts urged the Obama administration to include the arts in any stimulus package to jumpstart the economy. Robert Lynch, president of Americans for the Arts noted: "We wanted to make sure arts were not left out of the recovery. The artist's a paycheck is every bit as important as the steelworker's paycheck or the autoworker's paycheck" (Pogrebin 2009). Considering the arts as a profession does not negate their aesthetic content. If anything, analyses of the creative economy have favored creative freedoms and incentives, likening the creative ethos to independence (Florida 2002; Currid 2007). This does not negate the formulation of cultural policies: if anything, recognition of the creative economy boosted the sector's standing in the United Kingdom since the Blair government. In the United States, the recording, film, and broadcasting industries have long argued that they are growth drivers; the MPAA frequently reminds lawmakers that films are a top export for the United States. Hollywood has had a special relationship with the U.S. government, from support from the during World War II to pushing for its interests through the Uruguay Round and, more recently, through public-diplomacy moves. Arguments for recognizing and increasing American soft power—values and identity— through the spread of creative expressions have been especially visible since September 11. Soft-power proponents in the U.S. State Department tacitly recognize what their counterparts in the Commerce Department and the office of the U.S. trade representative must sideline: that creative products can be used to mobilize cultural identities.

The explicit "protectionist" case for creative products, made by many countries at the WTO and at UNESCO, often begins with equating creative and cultural products. Historically, either state and religious patronage of the arts upheld particular cultural identities or art itself served state purposes. It is, therefore, not surprising that most countries where the creative and the cultural are often equated do not feature independent arts agencies, such as the Arts Council in the United Kingdom or the NEA in the United States. Instead, funding is provided directly from ministries of culture.

The idea that the creative and the cultural are linked is philosophically, theoretically, and empirically sound; the idea that all creativity is cultural is not. Nevertheless, at the level of international politics this distinction does not often get made even if it is implicitly acknowledged. Recently, Tania Voon (2007) has argued that a good case for protecting some cultural products can and should be made by further tweaking the GATS framework to allow for "cultural" cautions such as those allowed by the old GATT principles for morality, heritage, and screen quotas (the latter in article IV of GATT, itself a reflection of the Blum-Byrnes agreement). In a creative and policy-oriented chapter entitled "Improving the Existing WTO Agreements," Voon looks for microlevel areas where it might be possible to bring greater coherence to WTO rules rather than proposing an ambitious overhaul. Greater alignment of rules would allow for the protection and promotion of cultural diversity without being unnecessarily restrictive to trade. She notes that the screen-quotas clause can be incorporated into GATS, but with a standstill and rollback agreement so that it freezes existing quotas. She also proposes an annex along the lines of those in air transport, telecommunications, and financial services. The annex would note valid escape routes for countries through subsidies (limited to financial, not taxation measures), MFN exemptions, and screen quotas, and certain privileges for developing countries. If the annex was clear, Voon conjectures that a "bottom-up" or positive-list approach, the currency at GATS at present, would be unnecessary. Instead, all creative products would be subject to national treatment and market access. In my opinion, it is going to take more than an annex such as this for WTO members to accept such a top-down, negative-list approach. The positive-list approach was perhaps the most significant victory of the anti-U.S. services coalition during the Uruguay Round. when the developing world found support from the European Community (Singh 2008).

I once heard a U.S. trade negotiator note that when he was looking for compromise and agreement on difficult political issues, he would ask the lawyers to leave the room. Similarly, the green light (or the WTO's green room processes) for negotiating any changes in the audio-visual framework will not come from the perceived efficacy of the microlevel legal measures that Voon outlines but, at least initially, from the political willingness of the most hard-line members to start negotiating audiovisual again at the WTO. Proposals that tried to make audio-visual a part of the GATS 2000 or, later, the Doha Round agenda, have therefore been broadly unsuccessful. In particular, the communication from Switzerland proposed middle-of-the-road solutions such as a cultural diversity safeguard, clarification on subsidies, exceptions for public morals, and the like (WTO 2001c). French officials lambasted the proposal when it was released. The failure of the proposal was not in the efficacy of its measure but in its suggestion that it might be politically feasible to negotiate audio-visual issues.

My concerns are rooted in the underlying politics of creative products, where it is hard to disentangle the argument regarding the special nature of these products from knee-jerk reactions to U.S. dominance and the international coalitional politics that call attention to them. If the political opposition could be overcome, the measures countries such as Switzerland suggest would be practical and feasible. In the heavily watched dispute between the United States and China at the WTO over the distribution of audiovisual services, the United States argued that the government control of distribution in China unfairly restricted U.S. publishing and entertainment products. Here one can see how clarifications on government procurement and subsidies would have allowed China to preserve its own cultural industries while not being overly trade restrictive (USTR 2007). China nevertheless argued that in regulating distribution it was preserving Chinese morals and heritage. It lost its case before a WTO panel in August 2009 but appealed the ruling in September 2009 (*Financial Times* 2009a).

However, my point is this: China is confident in the strength of its own cultural industries but, despite this strength, wants to restrict U.S. cultural products. Getting countries like China to agree to Switzerland's proposal will take political pressure.

The most fraught deliberations have concerned the entertainment industries. Not many countries are concerned that their fine or performing arts are dying because of globalization. In fact, government grants, subsidies, and other measures such as taxation are hardly ever questioned in international politics. There are also a few creative products for which countries readily make commitments. Chapter 6 will detail the case of tourism. Other products with design, aesthetic, and readily acknowledged commercial aspects include architecture, advertising, and videogames. Countries have made GATS commitments in many of these subsectors. Films and music are another story. There is still room here for balancing the creative and the cultural.

5

Cultural Patrons in the Developing World

Okeke interpreted wisely to the spirits and leaders of Umuofia:
"The white man says he is happy you have come to him with your
grievances, like friends. He will be happy if you leave the matter in
his hands."

"We cannot leave the matter in his hands because he does not
understand our customs, just as we do not understand his. We say
he is foolish because he does not know our ways, and perhaps he says
we are foolish because we do not know his. Let him go away."

—Chinua Achebe, *Things Fall Apart*

How are creative products in the developing world prioritized? How are
these products linked to evolving notions of cultural identity in the developing world? In the immediate postcolonial era, creative products were
marginalized in policymaking. Cultural ministries, if they existed, were
at the bottom of power hierarchies and possessed few resources. This has
all changed now: the contribution of creative industries to economic development is now apparent both in their prioritization for policymaking,
nationally and internationally, and in the growing scholarship in this area.
Concurrently, the debates at the international level are also reflected in the
developing world. For example, are existing cultural identities and diversity
in the developing world threatened with flows of creative products from
the developed world? Often these flows are posited as threatening cultural
expressions and representations in the developing world.

This chapter attends to the questions posed above. In particular, it
questions the intellectual and empirical bases of various claims about
the politics of cultural identity and diversity regarding creative expressions and products in the developing world. Conceptually, I argue that
cultural identity or diversity viewed from the perspective of the nation-
state is problematic. Politically, of course, nation-states, make this claim
themselves in protecting their self-interest globally. Cultural identity,

measured territorially within the confines of the nation-state, becomes a political label that, in part, masks the interactive and hybrid features of cultures. Empirically, as the last two chapters showed, nation-states at the forefront of the movement protecting (national) cultural identities and diversity are, in fact, top exporters of cultural products, something that is not apparent in the mercantilist position taken by these states with respect to international trade in cultural products. Furthermore, these states often make their claims on the behalf of developing countries. The chapter explores the position of developing countries explicitly taking advantage of the globalization of culture to promote both their creative and cultural distinctiveness and their exports. It specifically examines the way developing countries are prioritizing their creative industries and taking advantage of international commercial networks. These "cultural voices," I conclude, are growing economically and socially and cannot be dismissed as playing second fiddle to those from the developed world. I also acknowledge the problems many countries in the developing world, especially in sub-Saharan Africa, face in mobilizing their creative industries while adding their weight to the coalitional partners arguing against the onslaught of Hollywood or U.S. "cultural" content in their societies and markets.

Emergent Cultural Identities and Voices

The idea of protecting a cultural identity implicitly assumes some kind of a territorial boundary, most prominently that of the nation-state, placed around creative products. The idea of territorially bound cultures is increasingly hard to sustain in the face of global networks enabling rapid flows of representations and other forms of cultural knowledge. Creative representations and knowledge can be repositories of cultural identity and memories—in other words, collective ways of life—and cultural policies are often aimed at enhancing these processes. Placing territorial protections around ways of life is hard but is nevertheless supported historically by various regulations and narratives. Nevertheless, UNCTAD's *Creative Economy Report 2008* acknowledges up front the tension between creativity, culture, and globalization: "Globalization and connectivity are new realities that have brought profound changes in lifestyles worldwide. This is reshaping the overall pattern of cultural production, consumption and trade in a world filled with images, sounds, texts and symbols" (UNCTAD 2008). As I argue, the clear alternative to territorial boundaries seems to be networks that facilitate flows of creative products.

Nation-states epitomize territorial thinking about a way of life. The modern view of the nation-state privileges states over nations, legitimizing the former's authority. In Western Europe, the spread of the printing press favored local languages and cultural reproduction and distribution in these languages (Anderson 1983; Deibert 1997). However, the imprint of the state legitimized this way of thinking in the post-Westphalian world. In Ruggie's terms, territorial epistemes are viewed from the single fixed-point perspective of the nation-state (Ruggie 1993).

The idea of a nation-state was always problematic in postcolonial development; the territories of former colonies were often constructed by the colonizing powers. Although the authority of the state was contested within Europe, too, this contestation was marked by competition among rival organizational forms; in the postcolonial world, nations were weakened under colonial rule, allowing the states to command authority, though often without popular acceptance.[1] Building the nation-state took on heightened significance in these societies, with the state leading the way toward the promised land. However, soon the promises came undone. Postcolonial states were sovereign then in the international legal sense of recognition but not the Rousseauian sense of embodiment of the general will. Even those states that found legitimacy in nationalist movements found that the consensus to rule that they inherited quickly dissolved into ethnic or national conflicts leading to dictatorship or populism around Asia, Africa, and Latin America.

The so-called postcolonial literature and other narratives provide a glimpse into the evolving cultural identities of these societies in the context of the nation-state.[2] While it is hard to generalize, the novel often represents fragmented lives that seek a creative voice not stifled by the existing power relations or co-opted into them. The following passage from Tsitsi Dungarembga's *Nervous Conditions* (1988: 179) is illustrative of this in the case of colonial Rhodesia:

> It would be a marvelous opportunity, she said sarcastically, to forget. To forget who you were, what you were and why you were that. The process she said, was called assimilation, and that was what was intended for the precocious few who might prove a nuisance if left to themselves, whereas

the others—well really, who cared about the others? So they made a little space into which you were assimilated, and a honorary space in which you could join them and they could make sure that you behaved yourself.

Even in cases where the hope of finding this voice is vested in the state, the effort is ultimately futile.[3]

Eternal questions of our eternal debates. We all agreed that much dismantling was needed to introduce modernity within our traditions. Torn between the past and the present, we deplored the 'hard sweat' that would be inevitable. We counted the possible losses. But we knew that nothing would be as before. We were full of nostalgia but were resolutely progressive.

(Ba 1980, 19)

Paulo Freire's answer to this lies in the process of consciousness awakening (Freire 1970/2000), as Ba's and Dungarembga's protagonists realize.[4] Freire offers the concept of dialogic praxis, which entails a combination of thought, action, and transformation. The oppressed of the developing world can be liberated only through this pedagogy, which that enables them to find their "cultural voice": Freire thus offers a way out of cultural paralyses or silence. "In order for the oppressed to be able to wage the struggle for their liberation, they must perceive the reality of their oppression not as a closed world from which there is no exit, but as a limiting situation they can transform" (Friere 1970/2000, 49).

Cultures do not need protection from interventions—they need voices. Cultural identity in the developing world is represented as well as facilitated by several interventions. Colonialism and the postcolonial state are themselves broadly contextualized in the intervention of modernity upon tradition, a theme intensely and continuously portrayed in postcolonial representations. Nestor García Canclini's book *Hybrid Cultures* investigates the hypothesis that "the *uncertainty* about the meaning and value of modernity derives not only from what separates nations, ethnic groups, and classes, but also from the sociocultural hybrids in which the traditional and the modern are mixed" (1995, 2). In another essay he notes that the cultural-policy debates were dominated by the state and "analyzed whether the many groups, ethnic communities, and regions were sufficiently represented in each national heritage, excessively reduced their local specificities to politico-cultural abstractions in the interest of social control or legitimate a certain form of nationalism" (2000, 303).

As we move from modernity to the current era of globalization, the crucial link is provided by the interventions brought about by technology and information networks. In both cases the intervention is external, but whereas modernity was thrust upon colonial societies, information networks specifically, or globalization in general, provide a way for these societies to interact with the outside world.[5] While the organizational forms in which technology is introduced to developing countries, for example, transnational enterprises, may be top-down, the zones of autonomy provided to actors on the ground to shape outcomes in their favor are broadened. Even when networks accrue regulative power to those who govern them, they may still allow for serendipitous, subversive, or autonomous outcomes, such as the formation of new epistemes in the cultural sense, discovery of markets in the economic sense, or exercises in global solidarity in the social sense. Because networking is interactive, it influences the formation of both identities and interests that in turn influence collective memory and cultural representations.[6] Keck and Sikkink (1998, 16) note that the primary function of networks is persuasion and socialization and note several instances where global social movements present collective epistemes (e.g., violence against women) as a result of networked interactions.

However, the question of preponderant power in networks cannot be ignored. Radical constructivists such as Castells show how various forms of identity are arising in different parts of the world depending on the sociohistorical context and the dominant production structure (1997). Here, the primary function performed by networks is that of sustaining and coordinating global financial, production, and distribution flows. Labor, on the other hand, is fragmented (Castells 1996, 475). Social movements here can challenge dominant structures using subordinate networks through "conscious, purposive social action" but this is not a fait accompli (Castells 1998, 380). In the end, networked capitalism, in replacing industrial capitalism, creates fragmented and multiple social identities, including feminist ones.[7]

As previously noted, cultural complexity arises out of the clash of modernity and tradition as out of various forms of networked interaction. Between the structures of power understood in radical worldviews and the liberal notions of agency, Appadurai (1996, 2000, 2004) introduces global "scapes," embodying networked interactions that simultaneously include existing meaning and production systems around the world while allowing for various forms of imaginary capacities to arise, especially from below. Culture then becomes "a dialogue between aspirations and sedimented traditions" (2004, 84). Global imaginaries allow for both "politics of recognition" (Charles Taylor's term [1994]) and a "capacity to aspire": "As the imagination as a social force itself works across national lines to produce locality as a spatial fact and a sensibility, we see the beginnings of social forms without either the predatory mobility of unregulated capital or the predatory stability of many states" (Appadurai 2000, 7).

Notice that in the immediate postcolonial world, the cultural voice (which in this chapter I take to be analogous to the capacity to aspire) sought to find its institutional resolve in the newly founded nation-state. In the globalizing world, this voice arises through networked interactions that encompass, though may not necessarily marginalize, the state. In fact, inasmuch as networked interactions in the developing world may be weak, the cultural voice allows the state to step in and shape cultural meanings and the rules for their production. Furthermore, even though networks may be extraterritorial, many institutionalized interactions continue to be dominated by nation-states. Into such a confluence of territoriality and extraterritoriality, in which cultural memories, meanings, and identities are continually renegotiated, the search for global rules to govern cultural policies has entered the new millennium featuring both state and nonstate actors.

Cultural Policies in the Developing World

In the immediate postcolonial era, the quest for modernization molded the developing world's creative expressions and resultant cultural policies. The state assumed a paternalistic role, but a combination of its domination over society and its lack of resources to effectively encourage creative expressions may have even resulted in a creative stagnation. This section examines these changes in contrast to the current changes underway as a result of globalization. I examine three major themes here, dealing with the changing role of the state, the deepening of international networks, and the emerging confidence of creative and cultural voices in the developing world.

State: Dominance to Prioritization

The postcolonial state lacked the legitimacy, resources, and imagination to play an effective role in cultural policymaking. The consensus around economic development emphasized agriculture and industry, often associated with import substitution industrialization policies, and cultural policy had little role to play in these efforts, which became known as modernization policies. If anything, while the colonial-era movements often evoked cultural history and heritage for solidarity, the postcolonial state viewed culture as more or less traditional. National cultural identity was important for the purposes of nation-state building but it was not linked to creative expressions and products in the national imagination. Ministries or departments in charge of culture also often dealt with the science and technology portfolios; the latter would provide a more "modern," direction for culture. At the international level, this was reflected in UNESCO: the United Nations Educational, Scientific, and Cultural Organization.

The postcolonial state inherited the legitimacy attached to being at the forefront of modernization efforts in the developing world, but its primary resources were directed toward agriculture and industry (Lerner 1958).[8] As such, the consensus among cultural policy specialists is that creative products received "a comparatively low priority, when pitted against the needs of a developing economy, a backward industry" (Vatsayan 1972). In communist states such as China and Cuba, a focus on culture was also seen as decadent and bourgeois.

However, analysts seem to have missed one cultural product that was emphasized the developing countries: development communication, which prioritized communication media for economic development. In its early formulations, development-communication models posited that radio, television, and newspapers would free the minds of traditional societies and peoples.[9] The implicit cultural policy in terms of identity, then, was to "modernize" people and make them shed traditional ways of thinking. This was consistent with most writings of the period in seeing the state as the vehicle that would deliver the developing world from traditional cultures, which were perceived as backward.[10] Furthermore, the state sought to use these communication technologies for its own propagandistic purposes and controlled the flow of content.

The international counterpart of the concerns raised in development-communication debates resulted in calls for a New World Information and

Communication Order at UNESCO in 1976. Developing countries argued that there was great asymmetry in news and media content flows in which they were continually beholden to the developed world. Empirical studies confirmed these trends and led theoretically to concepts regarding media imperialism and cultural dependency. The influential MacBride commission report—*Many Voices, One World*—advocated self-reliant national communication infrastructures. In questioning Western media institutions, the developing world received ideological support from the USSR and its allies. These information wars are posited as the chief reason for the U.S. decision to leave UNESCO in 1984 (it rejoined in 2003).[11]

With respect to cultural organizations or infrastructure such as production studios and museums, government agencies were ill-equipped to deal with cultural heritage, promotion, or exchanges. Few developing countries singled out creative industries for prioritization, with the exception of a few state-sponsored programs here and there and impetus given to cultural tourism in a few places. Rudolph's summary of cultural policies in India could be taken to apply to many other parts of the developing world: "Government's reluctance to respect the autonomy of cultural organizations created to promote the values and interests of the arts (and history) is in part a reflection of its paternalism" (1983, 12). The state used its pulpit to speak about modernization and the value of the nation-state, but, being resource constrained, it it could not emphasize implementing policies to help the existing cultural sectors.

Several societal and international factors are now converging to change the role of the state in cultural policymaking, and states are beginning to prioritize creative products. In terms of societal acceptance, the state, except for a few exceptions, was discredited in the developing world for not delivering on the economic growth or modernization it promised. These goals themselves were considerably questioned. Societal unrest and dissatisfaction resulted in populism and dictatorship in many parts of the developing world in the 1970s. The domestic compact around state-led identity began to break down just as the state began to move away from playing a dirigiste role in the economy. Meanwhile, at the international level, as the last chapter showed, creative-industry issues were already receiving attention at the GATT/WTO, and cultural identity had always been part of UNESCO's agenda, which got a boost in the mid-1990s from efforts to frame a declaration and subsequently a Convention on the Protection and Promotion of the Diversity of Cultural Expressions.

Two changes resulted from the weakening of the state and new pressures upon it to pay attention to cultural-identity issues. First, cultural issues began to be prioritized at the state level in myriad ways, not all of which were about nation-building efforts. The newly emergent ministries of culture all over the developing world are symbolic of this importance. Culture is no longer relegated to tradition and the ministries lumped in with those of science and technology or information and broadcasting. If anything, culture ministries are becoming aware of both heritage issues and the economic importance of such creative industries as media and tourism, which elevates the linkages between culture and other ministries rather than relegating it to a secondary role. Second, this prioritization began in the context of market-driven measures to which the developing world was turning as a result of the failure of past economic strategies and pressures from multiple quarters in the developed world. The market-driven mechanisms will be discussed in the next section, but I turn to prioritization here, which ranges from explicit policy and regulatory instruments to recognition and construction of subnational and transnational identities by the state.

Many states are now moving toward either prioritizing cultural industries as a whole at the forefront of their development efforts or singling out priority sectors. The following examples are instructive, even if not all-encompassing.

- China's tenth Five-Year Plan (2001–6) made creative industries a salient feature of the export driven economy and the eleventh plan (2006–11) pushes this further. Each major city has developed blueprints for giving incentives to creative sectors. Shenzen, supported by the ministry of culture and other government departments, organized the fifth China International Cultural Industry Fair in May 2009, which each year showcases China's creative industries. many of which work with foreign collaboration. Other cities, such as Nanjing, have similar initiatives now. Cultural policies cover both traditional and nontraditional sectors. Videogames and animation are booming, and China's leading game developer, Shanda, was recently listed on Nasdaq. Priorities for traditional projects included plans for 1,000 new museums by 2015. The Olympic Games in Beijing in 2008, preparations for which began a decade ago, were viewed as providing the global context for China's sure-footedness in cultural policy. The spectacular opening ceremonies at the Olympiad in Beijing, staged by the film director Zhang Yimou, the choreographer Zhang Jigang, and the composer Tan Dun, presented a culturally confident China to an estimated global TV audience of two to four billion people. Said one cultural policy official in Beijing: "Now China considers cultural industries as highest in the chain of industries, even more than autos."[12] In order to push these measures, the state realizes that academics and industry must work together and is setting up various institutes around the country to assist cultural industries.

• The Indian government has now boosted the hapless department of culture and sports in the ministry of education. Culture now has its own ministry. Mission Culture was launched in 2005 to develop India's cultural policies and preserve its tangible and intangible cultural heritage. The government earmarked 500 million rupees for the next five years. The sum is paltry, and India's democratic system being what it is, state incentives are often haphazardly designed and implemented and lack the kind of streamlining that a more centralized system, like China's, is able to effect. But the Indian government is cognizant of the "soft power" of its cultural exports and is working toward promoting it through international cultural networks and tourism (Johnson 2006).[13] As in China, creative industries are also being prioritized as the central government finally recognizes India's film sector as an "industry" and provides it tax exemption from exports. Indian businesses in general and the software industry in particular see several opportunities in global creative industries, including animation and videogames.

• A number of countries have provided a combination of taxes, quota, and subsidies to revive film industries that almost died out for political or competitive reasons. These include vibrant film industries in Argentina, Mexico, and Korea. Meanwhile, South Africa is emerging as a major site for film production in Africa, displacing Dakar, with *Tsotsi* winning the Oscar for best foreign film of 2005 and *Yesterday* nominated for the same award. Many of the film collaborations are with Hollywood. Even tiny Uruguay has capitalized on the different types of locations it offers to jumpstart local production firms and partner with international ones. The case of Uruguay is detailed later in this chapter.

• Cash-strapped developing countries are realizing, in varying degrees, the enormous potential of tourism. These range from big cruise ships in Belize to high-end tourism in Mauritius. Travel services now account for nearly 10 percent of global trade and, as noted earlier, a number of small economies now count on tourism as a major source of export revenues. (See next chapter for further details on cultural tourism.)

- Many international organizations are prioritizing creative industries and providing assistance to the developing world in terms of documentation, analysis, and capacity building. Apart from UNESCO, creative-industry programs now exist in UNCTAD, UNDP, the World Bank, and the WIPO. Projects have ranged from developing a crafts industry in Mozambique to boosting media and broadcasting capacity in Uruguay.

While the measures noted above are a form of explicit prioritization, less formal measures include appeals to cultural identity and rights issues in general. Indigenous groups all over Latin America are "calling for the multiethnic, pluricultural, and multilingual nature of Latin American societies" (Davis 2003, 328). Not only are these states responding but also many indigenous leaders are now becoming prominent in Latin American politics. Africa is also coming together in myriad ways. Nelson Mandela's and Thabo Mbeki's calls for an African renaissance in speaking of an incipient cultural identity must be understood in this context. They are referring to other historical trends in which Africa was coming together culturally. For example, while African filmmakers had made their mark, African cinema was not distinguished as a genre until recently (Willemen 1992).

The Chinese state is beginning to cautiously re-explore its cultural identity after burying it under the Cultural Revolution and communism in the past. While official transcripts still decry bourgeois values and culture, the state is also eager to project a multicultural and international identity. Words inscribed at the Capital Museum in Beijing, opened to the public in May 2006 following an architectural collaboration between the French and the Chinese, are apt: "Today Beijing aims to develop into an international metropolis with a harmonic integration between traditional and modern cultures."[14] Its public diplomacy has also widened in the last few years to court allies and the Chinese diaspora. Kurlantzick writes in the *Charm Offensive* (2007, 61) that "China has developed more sophisticated tools of influence, which it deploys across the world." These include "tools related to Chinese culture and arts and language and ethnicity."

International Networks: Top-Down to Interactive

The state's role in cultural politics is being redefined and organized just as international networks grow in importance. International networks existed before and featured all three types of actors mentioned here: states, market players, and civil-society organizations. However, the relative influence of these actors has changed, as has the way they interact with one another. On the one hand, the rules framed at the WTO and UNESCO feature state actors speaking for or against creative product flows. On the other hand, international creative-product flows continue to increase even though international rules seem to favor protectionism, given the lack of support for audio-visual liberalizations at the WTO (see chapter 3).

The framing of GATS involved developing countries as full-fledged actors, but a quick analysis reveals its weaknesses as a state-driven agreement. Many of the provisions in the agreement reflected joint problem solving by developing countries, and by the time the agreement was signed in 1994, they viewed it positively in terms of their international trade. Nevertheless, while the developing countries' share of global trade in creative products continues to rise, they have not seriously considered using features of the GATS agreement in their favor. There are several reasons for this, chiefly concerning state centrality in the agreement. At the international level, the highly publicized dispute between the EU and the United States has worked against the developing world's interests. While the U.S. position receives lukewarm support from India, China, and Mexico at the WTO, most developing countries, fearing repercussions from the EU, are either shy of making commitments (Brazil) or are threatened by the EU not to do so or risk having their bilateral aid or import restrictions cut for creative industries; rumors abound in Geneva that Francophone Africa often hears such remonstrations from France and Latin Americans from Iberian countries.

At the domestic level, most developing countries have not carried out any kind of discussions with creative industries, even where there are obvious benefits. A carefully planned cultural-tourism policy would involve the stakeholders in deliberations that would lead to sustainable tourism while also showcasing other creative industries in the country. While even the smallest economies have made some careful commitments in specific sectors, this is not the case with tourism. Most developing countries profess ignorance of GATS mechanisms, but the truth may be that consultations with the highly varied tourism industry entail significant transaction costs. Furthermore, many of the developing countries are beholden to traditional agriculture and manufacturing interests, leaving little political space for new service providers to lobby for their interests (Singh 2005, 2008b). I found this to be the case with Belize and Costa Rica. Both economies boast significant revenues from tourism but whereas Costa Rica has moved toward making limited commitments in tourism (hotels, travel services), Belize remains blissfully ignorant of such measures. Belize's trade policy in particular is more or less beholden to its inefficient banana producers, who remain fearful of the end to preferential treatment from the EU. Trade in tourism products in Belize remains quite open, though, so that Belize would have nothing to lose by making commitments at the WTO. My research also showed that Colombia initially showcased protectionist moves in creative industries even though its music and broadcasting industries garner significant revenues from exports (Singh 2008c).

While trade in creative products continues to grow, the cultural-diversity convention at UNESCO is counterintuitive at best and completely off the mark at worst. Cultural diversity is left for states to define, but it is not clear which states, apart from France and Canada, the main drivers of the agreement, face overwhelming pressures from their creative industries to protect them from international trade. In fact, GATS allows countries to make commitments that leave regulatory provisions in place to protect their cultural industries.[15] The convention also glosses over international trade features on which even countries like Canada and United States are united. These pertain to their growing exports in creative products (see tables 3.1 and 3.2) and support for intellectual-property enforcement through the WTO. No mention is made of the thriving cultural-tourism industries in these countries. If design, advertising, fashion, and other creative industries are included, the export advantage of these countries becomes greater.[16]

International civil society networks do exist but are fragmented or find that to be effective they must either work through state-driven international organizations or through cultural-industry networks. The International Network for Cultural Diversity, set up since 1998, is a case in point. Consisting of cultural activists it is "dedicated to countering the homogenizing effects of globalization on culture" (www.incd.net/about). It boasts 500 members from seventy countries but was set up with Canadian government funding to frame a declaration and convention in cultural diversity at UNESCO and to put a civil society face on it. This is not unusual: politics are often about someone paying the transaction costs of collective action. The problem is that INCD's dominant episteme and sense of purpose were dictated before it was set up. Beyond cultural ministries in developing countries, few civil society or creative producers were involved or consulted. Trade officials in developing countries also opposed the convention.

Another example may be taken from the networks of artists in Africa. FEPACI (the Pan-African Federation of Cineastes), founded in 1967, has been instrumental in furthering the cause of African cinema and giving it a concrete identity, but it often relies on funding from government bodies, as at the April 2006 Africa Film Summit in Johannesburg. One of FEPACI's purposes has been to cut the umbilical cord of funding from Europe. The biannual film festival, FESPACO, held in Ouagadougou, Burkina Faso, has more or less languished and is viewed as only promoting Francophone directors through French government funding. Recently, there have been moves among pan-African film-industry officials to look beyond French patronage for funding and sustainability.

If the grassroots creative products from the developing world are coming of age, it is because of the success of commercial networks. Here are a few examples:

- Two billion people around the world now watch Latin American telenovelas, and the cultural establishments backing them have now challenged U.S. network television's dominance. Other countries are mimicking the telenovela model. India and Brazil might collaborate in the future. The Spanish-language U.S. network Univision paid $105 million in 2004 for telenovela imports (Martinez 2005). Korean soaps are popular in East Asia.
- Chinese, Indian. Korean, Argentinean, Brazilian, South African films are now seen as success stories, not despite but because of global commercial networks. Many of them feature several types of collaborations among artists and also may be financed internationally. Hollywood connections have also boosted South Africa's film industry, displacing Senegal and its ties to Paris as the center of film production in Africa. The Cannes film festival is also beginning to feature financiers for international cinema productions along with its traditional function of bringing together film distributors (Paillard 2006). Bollywood now considers South Asian diasporic markets as

a major source of revenue. Mukherjee (2005, 240) cites an estimate from the Electronic Software Exports Promotion Council, which noted that India exported $74 million in television content in 2001. The growing popularity of Indian cinema among diasporic audiences and beyond is another important feature. The *Financial Times* noted that Germany now plays Bollywood films during prime time and some of the DVD releases sell more than 100,000 copies (Yuk 2006). UNESCO (2005, 46) estimates that exports accounted for nearly 25 percent of the $900 million in revenues for the Indian film industry. All these figures are modest, India accounting for less than 1 percent of global film industry revenues, but the Indian film industry is expected to grow from $1.25 billion in 2005 to over $10 billion by 2010 according to one industry study cited by *Financial Times* (Yuk 2006). As table 3.1 shows, India can count itself among the top 20 cultural goods exporters, chiefly because of film exports. India exports 30 percent of its films to nearly ninety-five countries, which generates 60 to 70 percent of the revenues for these films (Roy 2008, 345).

• The world-music movement pushed by commercial networks has introduced artists to global markets. Lebanon and Egypt are emerging as major centers of Arab female singers and Bamako, Mali, is contending with South Africa as another center of music production in sub-Saharan Africa (Mellor 2005). This last fact is especially instructive: the music industry in sub-Saharan Africa is mostly commercially driven and, arguably, more sustainable than the African film industry.

• Zimbabwe has used heritage goods to emerge as one of the biggest exporters of cultural products from Africa, with total exports of $27 million in 2002 (UNESCO, 2005, 59). Heritage goods include arts and crafts.

• I have mentioned many examples of cultural tourism, and a perusal of data from the UN World Tourism Organization (2005, 2009) reveals the importance of this activity for the developing world. The next chapter details the specific case of cultural tourism.

Creative Voices: Distinctiveness and Confidence

A cultural voice, for Freire, is developed only when there is dialogic communication and both the oppressors and the oppressed apprehend the reality of oppression, epitomized by his calls for consciousness awakening (Freire 2000). Freire speaks of "cultural voices" in the context of oppressed classes; in this book, creative voices speak to the same notion of nonoppression.[17] Both the redefinition of the state and the proliferation of international commercial networks are leading to distinctiveness and confidence in creative voices from the developing world.[18] This marks the third phase of creative voices (following patronage from, first, states and, then, international organizations) from the developing world in the quest for modernization and subsequent calls for cultural diversity.

The paternalistic postcolonial state marked out modernization as the right cultural aspiration for the developing world. This modernization was historically specific only in terms of implicitly accepting that its own history was irrelevant, but both the elite and policy understandings in the developing and developed worlds legitimized it. Calls for diversity from UNESCO seek to reclaim the histories that were lost in the struggle to modernize. In this, these attempts are sincere. But they are equally paternalistic in terms of the developed-world patrons who push for particular frameworks of diversity.

The creative voices coming through on the international commercial networks rely less on some primeval notion on authentic diversity than on hybridity and innovation (García Canclini 1995). They serve to illustrate not just the complexity of cultures and their transnational linkages but, more importantly, a distinctiveness that is confident of borrowing from genres around the world and more or less unafraid of commercial processes.[19] Browne (2008, 95) notes that "the African film producer has not copied the American producer although he may have been influenced by the Western world in making films in the first place."

Again, a few examples might be illustrative and speak to the list of the commercial networks above:

- The Hindi-language or Mumbai-based Bollywood film, problematic and commercial as that label might be, now reveals a change in content to reflect diasporic interests. While the musical melodrama is distinctive, it initially developed in response to Indian and Western traditions of storytelling. It continues to be influenced by several forces that include changing storylines to reflect diasporic audiences and explicit collaborations with screenwriting academies abroad for production purposes.

- Telenovelas were themselves fashioned on U.S. soap operas, but over time they became "distinct from the soap operas of the United States" in emphasizing the struggles of "poverty, class conflict, and institutional instability, something U.S. soaps ignore" (Martinez 2005).
- Music is perhaps the most hybrid and syncretic cultural form, but even then distinctions are not hard to make. South Africa's kwaito (featured recently in the film *Tsotsi*) combines African rhythms with hip-hop and house music. Most music stars from Mali and Senegal (Ali Farka Touré, Yossou N'Dour, Salif Keïta) now collaborate with artists abroad, especially from the West. Beyond this lies the confidence of these voices in destabilizing existing power relations. Salif Keïta, an albino, has explicitly challenged Malian cultural notions that viewed albinos as bearers of evil (Trofimov 2006). Even as religious conservatives decry the rise of sexy female singers in the Arab world, these singers are widely viewed as destabilizing traditional roles and liberating women from them (Mellor 2005).

A broad force is also shaping awareness in the developing world that its peoples have a story that stands on its own and that is up to the people to narrate that story through various representations and media. It is this force that guides the creative energies of Bollywood or Bamako, Mali. At the grassroots level, cultural-identity and rights movements are questioning their marginalization from political discussions and often use cultural expressions such as language, crafts, and folklore to make their case. The rise of rights movements in Latin America for indigenous people and people of African descent are cases in point (Davis 2004). Cultural identity is a powerful trope for the elite to use to awaken these populations. The Colombian minister of culture, Paula Morena, who is of African descent, tells the story of her conversation in the remote region of Bunenaventura, with a group of rappers, who in reference to their geographic location note that "nothing has happened here and nothing will happen."[20] She notes that in response to conversations such as these, the current national plan on culture in Colombia includes policies on language, memory, and history.

The owners of the new creative voices in and from the developing world are aware of the power structures that they confront but are craftily using global imaginaries to both borrow from and add to the distinctiveness of their cultural products. This is done with a certain chutzpah, as in manufacturing "authenticity" to sell to tourists, or with sincerity in the syncretic voices of world's music genres. The new creative voices sometimes work with the state and at other times work at cross-purposes with it. Either way, the distinctiveness and confidence of these creative voices come through. This distinctiveness and the political purposes it serves help to connect oppressed past and present opportunities. However, awareness of creative-industry networks that are not driven by patronage is still missing at the state level and also to some extent in agencies such as UNESCO and UNCTAD, which are trying to build capacities in these countries.

Developing World and Market Networks

Global rules and frameworks provide opportunities to benefit the creative industries of developing countries, but to take advantage, these countries must be in a position to calculate their interests carefully and, where possible, arrange for their own creative industries to establish the nature of the relationship with the global frame.

The two main networks of support for creative products—state-driven patronage and commercial networks—present particular problems in the context of the developing world. A developing country's participation in the WTO's GATS framework is an apt indicator of its ability to take advantage of global commercial networks. In order to do so, developing countries need to make specific and legally binding commitments in GATS across the four modes of supply in every subsector important to the creative economy. The four modes of supply were described in chapter 3, and table 5.1 lists the creative industry subsectors for GATS. The relevant subsectors, apart from audio-visual, include tourism, advertising, and architectural services. Table 5.2 gives the number of countries that have made some form of market liberalization in these sectors. While such macrolevel data are not helpful in understanding the underlying politics, a few things do become apparent. The highly politicized audio-visual sector has the fewest commitments, but the proportion of states with commitments in other subsectors is healthy, given that there are 153 members of the WTO. As the following discussion shows, creative industries' ability to take meaningful advantage of commercial networks varies across the developing world according to the type of state involvement and also the nature of the creative industries' involvement in the policymaking process. The frequent critique

TABLE 5.1

Partial List of Creative Sectors in WTO Services
Sectoral Classification List

SECTORS AND SUBSECTORS	CORRESPONDING CPC*
1. Business services	**Section B**
A. Professional Services	
d. Architectural services	8671
F. Other Business Services	
a. Advertising services	871
p. Photographic services	875
r. Printing, publishing	88442
2. Communication services	
D. Audiovisual services	
a. Motion picture and video tape production and distribution services	9611
b. Motion picture projection service	9612
c. Radio and television services	9613
d. Radio and television transmission services	7524
e. Sound recording	n.a.
f. Other	
9. Tourism and travel-related services	
a. Hotels and restaurants (incl. catering)	641-643
b. Travel agencies and tour operators services	7471
c. Tourist guides services	7472
10. Recreational, cultural, and sporting services	
(other than audiovisual services)	
a. Entertainment services (including theater, live bands, and circus services)	9619
b. News agency services	962
c. Libraries, archives, museums, and other other cultural services	963
d. Sporting and other recreational services	964

Note: This is a partial list. Technically, sectors such as telecommunications and distribution are related to the creative sector. However, the subsectors listed above include some degree of aesthetic or imaginative content important for creative products.

*CPC: Central Product Classification, United Nations Statistics Division

Source: World Trade Organization, Services Sectoral Classification List: Note by the Secretariat, MTN/GNS/W120, July 10, 1991.

TABLE 5.2
Number of Countries Making Market Commitments
in Creative Industry Subsectors

SUBSECTOR	NUMBER OF COUNTRIES
Professional services (including architectural services)	94
Other business services (including advertising, photography, printing, publishing)	90
Audio-visual	29
Tourism	131
Recreational, cultural, and sporting	46

Source: World Trade Organization Services Database. Available at http://tsdb.wto.org/default.aspx. Accessed March 15, 2009.

that globalization will affect creative industries adversely obtains only to the extent that these industries operate in ignorance or are marginalized in policymaking at national and international levels.

The following analysis briefly compares a few cases from Latin America and Asia; they help to show why and how Latin America moved most notably toward taking advantage of the commercial potential in making tourism commitments in GATS while Asian countries covered a range of sectors, including audio-visual.

Latin America

The two ends of the spectrum of market-network commitments are provided by Argentina and Belize, and an in-between case, especially relevant for contextualizing Belize, is provided by another small economy, Costa Rica. Belize made no commitments in any of the sectors or subsectors that might be termed creative, while Costa Rica made commitments in tourism and travel-related services. Argentina's commitments at the Uruguay Round were held to be quite "generous" compared not just to similar countries such as Brazil and Chile but also to the rest of the world (Bouzas and Soltz 2005). Interestingly, Argentina publicly committed to an agriculture-led liberalization strategy in 1989, in line with its membership in the Cairns group and parting from developing-world leaders such as Brazil and India, which had begun to throw their weight behind the emerging GATS framework.

Argentina made GATS commitments in 37.4 percent of all the subsectors (WTO 1994a).[21] The Services Sectoral Classification provides for 12 sectors that can be further subdivided into 155 in each of the fours modes of supply, for a total of 620. Many of the commitments of importance to creative industries were in business services—including architecture and advertising—but pressures from domestic business groups allowed for only limited commitments in mode 4, pertaining to movement of personnel (for an explanation of the four modes of supply, see chapter 3, pages 53–54). Argentina's commitments apply to senior managers. In other words, Argentina makes no market-access or national-treatment restrictions on architectural or advertising firms coming from outside, but they must hire local personnel except for senior managers that may be brought in from outside. In its well-organized travel and tourism industry, Argentina followed the pattern of the business services.[22] The subsectors covered include hotels, restaurants, travel agencies, tour operators, and tourist guides. In audio-visual, there are no commitments.

Several factors related to international and domestic pressures help explain the pattern of Argentina's commitments. First, the leadership of the Economy Ministry in handling the trade talks was important; it consulted with the private sector and also researched domestic regulations with a variety of government departments and other agencies in drawing up the offer. Second, the consistency among the various modes came from the Economy Ministry's disposal to make a "clean offer." Third, in terms of audio-visual, Argentina was constrained both by the domestic incentives given in the 1980s to jump start the film industry in the post-dictatorship era, as well as purported pressures from Western Europe; Latin American countries, which rely on Spanish and Portuguese markets were told that they would find their exports hurt if they made audio-visual commitments.[23]

Belize, on the other hand, made no commitments in any of the creative industries, including tourism, which accounts for a majority of the country's foreign-exchange earnings (WTO 1994b).[24] The five-person Ministry of International Trade concentrates mostly on protecting Belize's historic sugar, citrus, and banana exports, which are given preferential treatment by Europe. In fact Belize's trade strategy is pretty much tied in with its diplomatic mission in Brussels rather than Geneva, where there is no trade official, although there is a mission to other UN agencies. Trade officials note that the tourism industry is too splintered and disorganized to understand that it is exporting tourism services. However, tourism-industry organizations seem to be fairly well networked, at least in the Caribbean Common Market, and they note that they are seldom consulted for trade talks, even in the national commission set up to deal with trade matters. Industry officials also note that they lack the capacity to make GATS commitments. However, Belize did make commitments to GATS in general, including those for liberalizing its medical-services market, especially neurosurgery (supposedly to thumb its nose at the United States, which was pressuring it to make commitments) and also in telecommunications.

Costa Rica's creative-industry commitments look similar to those of Argentina, except that they are less "generous" (WTO 1994c). The mode 4 commitments are even more restrictive, including licensing requirements. The travel and tourism commitments include interesting domestic regulatory provisions that guard Costa Rica's commitment to eco-friendly tourism: "The 200-metre strip along the Atlantic and Pacific Coasts of the Republic, the 'land maritime zone'" is protected from foreign commercial establishments (WTO 1994c).

The Costa Rica Ministry of International Trade, COMEX, boasts a team of international trade lawyers who understand the country's current and future competitive trade advantages well. They work closely with CINDE, Costa Rica's trade and investment promotion authority, which earned its good reputation by attracting a $300 million Intel venture in 1996. As a result, the software industry has also taken off in the country, and while its foray into creative electronic industry is limited, the country can build on this base. Unlike Belize, Costa Rica, with its mixture of well-crafted trade politics and presidential authority (Belize has a parliamentary system), has moved beyond the stranglehold of its traditional agricultural interests, which were centered on coffee exports.

Asia

A number of Asian countries, especially in the Asia Pacific region, boast strong creative industries in entertainment and electronic media, and thus of the seventeen commitments in audio-visual at the Uruguay Round, seven came from Asia: Japan, Korea, Hong Kong, Thailand, Malaysia, Singapore, and India. China would sign on later with its accession in 2001. And New Zealand, a non-Asian but geographically proximate country, made one of the most liberal commitments in audio-visual. Here the China, India and Malaysia cases are analyzed briefly, but it is important to remember the objections of the United States, which was joined by China, Hong Kong, Japan, Mexico, and Taiwan, as I discuss in chapter 4.

China and India illustrate the case of trying to take advantage of audio-visual commitments. Although, India's commitments in 1994 at GATS were timid and minimal, it has since moved independently toward liberalization in the audio-visual sector (WTO 1994d). Similarly, while China did not make commitments in 1994 as it moved toward eventual WTO accession, it did undertake these commitments at accession in 2001 (WTO 2002). Although Chinese officials regularly claim that China is a net importer in cultural products, this is not borne out by data. China's export strategy may be characterized as quite comprehensive and strategic in creative-industry exports.[25]

China was mostly responding to pressures from the United States, especially the MPAA, in making its WTO commitments, but it did manage to safeguard some provisions, again revealing the tailored nature of GATS, that cover existing Chinese laws while maintaining China's creative-industry interests (WTO 2002). Commercial presence is allowed for market access only, joint ventures are allowed, and China reserves the right to examine the content of these products. Foreign service providers are also allowed to construct or renovate theaters but cannot hold more than 49 percent equity (although China has more than 20,000 theaters, only a few in major cities have state-of-the-art facilities). Land remains state-owned, therefore all types of market access are only allowed on leased lands. Under U.S. pressure, China raised its initial ceiling of ten imported films each year to twenty. The number is small and applies to both U.S. and non-U.S. films. Because most U.S. studios count on less than 10 percent of their films for a majority of their revenues, even if U.S. films only capture fifteen of the twenty films allowed in the quota, these can still provide a big market for Hollywood. Nevertheless, as noted in the last chapter, China recently lost a case at the WTO involving the distribution of films over state-led networks. The U.S. argued that the networks were trade restrictive while China tried to maintain them in the name of cultural identity and morality. China has now appealed the WTO panel's decision.

China's creative-industry strategy also has strong domestic roots and is crafted to take advantage of globalization processes. As noted earlier,

China's tenth Five Year Plan (2001–6) made creative industries a salient feature of the export-driven economy and the eleventh plan (2006–11) pushes this further. Each major city has developed blueprints for giving incentives to creative sectors.

While India did not support the U.S. opposition to the UNESCO convention at the WTO in June 2005, it is prioritizing creative-industry exports.[26] However, at the end of the Uruguay Round, India did align itself with the U.S. position and tacitly continues to do by further liberalizing its audio-visual sector. In 1994, its commitments were quite timid. No mode 1 or 2 commitments were undertaken, and mode 4 personnel were restricted to senior managers and executives. Most crucially, mode 3 commitments for commercial presence were tempered with many restrictions: one hundred titles through representative offices for market access, and notifications to the Ministry of Information and Broadcasting on the merits of the film in several categories to receive national treatment. However, these restrictions were lifted in 2002.

One study notes the success that Indian audio-visual policy has in striking "a balance between preserving the rich cultural heritage of the nation and increasing the efficiency and global competitiveness of the sector through privatization and foreign investment" (Mukherjee 2005, 238). It provides several instances of the policy, from the rather restrictive audio-visual commitments made in 1994 to the unilateral liberalization commitments made thereafter. Mukherjee (2005, 240) cites an estimate from the Electronic Software Exports Promotion Council that noted that India exported $74 million in television content in 2001. The growing popularity of Indian cinema among diasporic and more general audiences is another important feature. The *Financial Times* notes that Germany now plays Bollywood films during prime time and some of the DVD releases sell more than 100,000 copies (Yuk 2006). UNESCO (2005, 46) estimates that exports accounted for nearly 25 percent of the $900 million in revenues for the Indian film industry. All these figures are modest, India accounting for less than 1 percent of global film-industry revenues, but, as noted earlier, the Indian film industry is expected to grow from $1.25 billion in 2005 to over $10 billion by 2010 according to an industry study cited by the *Financial Times*.

In India's case, the creative industries of export significance, film and television in particular, are privately owned. Although the market structure is fragmented and reveals many players, the firms are thriving and growing more organized; the film industry is now networking with India's powerful trade associations in general but also with specific ones like those for software. The industry is also networking globally; for example, India is emerging as a major outsourcing center for animation. The film industry, mostly organized around individual firms, is also hopeful of the type of international financing that some television production attracts to lift its production profile. Recently, Hollywood majors such as Warner, Disney, Viacom, and Sony Pictures have set up production studios in India (Leahy 2009). Interestingly, in 2008 the Indian corporation Reliance acquired 50 percent of Dreamworks for $500 million from to create a joint venture. Unlike in China, the government's role in India for creative industries has been more facilitative, streamlining policies and providing incentives, rather than dirigiste. As noted earlier, the Indian government has now divorced the department of culture and sports from the Ministry of Education; culture and tourism now have a ministry. However, as in China, creative industries are prioritized by the central government's finally recognizing India's vast film production as an industry and providing it tax exemption from exports.

Malaysia does not rank among the top creative-industry exporters but its commitments in audio-visual in particular and GATS in general reflect its strategic thinking in becoming a knowledge economy (*Financial Times* 2009b). Its exports in creative-industry products are still modest: of its $216 million in exports in 2004, $93 million were in books, $71 in recorded media, and only $32 million in audio-visual (UNESCO 2005, 59).[27] However, more than 60 percent of the Malaysian economy is now driven by services, and this may explain why Malaysia has made forty-five service-related requests for liberalization in the Doha Round in the WTO while only receiving fourteen (Cheen 2005). In addition to tourism, Malaysia is moving toward export of creative-industry professionals, especially in architectural and advertising services. Several professional organizations were created by the state to promote exports and work closely with the Ministry of International Trade and Industry. Malaysian GATS strategy is also directed toward producing coherence in otherwise fragmented sectors like tourism (the opposite of Belize's strategy).

In sum, the global rules developing in UNESCO and the WTO only provide a partial story of commerce in creative-industry products. Where countries have significant creative-industry exports, with either export-based coalitions or a lack of import-protection coalitions, these countries have not hesitated to make audio-visual commitments at WTO. In passing, I have also mentioned cultural tourism and other related creative industries; they help to show that creative-product exports may be higher than those estimated by using only what constitute core cultural products.[28]

Market liberalization of creative industries is interesting in that the country carrying out the liberalization is inviting other countries into its territory. But a closer look at these liberalizations reveals another story. First, GATS commitments often call for calculation of "national" interests or comparative advantage in particular sectors. Argentina's commitments in architecture, Costa Rica's in tourism, and China's or India's in film reveal the way these countries are trying to take advantage of global commercial networks to jumpstart their creative industries. Second, there is no one-size-fits-all. GATS commitments can be tailored specifically to a country's interest.[29] Often, existing cultural policies can be preserved or strategized. However, as Belize shows, many countries also fail to take advantage of the GATS framework. Belize's tourism sector remains splintered and weak despite the country's potential for cultural and eco-tourism, including UNESCO heritage sites such as coral reefs. Conversely, Costa Rica has boosted its nature-based tourism by carefully liberalizing its tourism industry. In general, making GATS commitments is also a way for a country to take an inventory of its policies and align them with the national interest. In the recent bilateral trade negotiations with the United States, the Colombian Ministry of Culture heavily opposed liberalization in audio-visual until, in consultation with trade officials, it realized that it stood to gain from growing exports of music, publishing, and audio-visual content (Singh 2008c).

Challenge for the Future

This chapter has traced the rise of creative industries and cultural voices in the developing world at various levels, including national and international networks. The dominance of cultural voices in political decision-making processes, however, is a necessary but not a sufficient condition for providing impetus to creative industries. Pierre Sauvé (2006, 16) notes

> For most developing countries, structural difficulties represent daunting obstacles to cultural production and diffusion. This ranges from factors as diverse as the paucity of disposable income to spend on non-essential

consumption, literacy, problem of secure and reliable access to electrici-
ty, particularly in rural areas, the low availability of consumer equipment
(TVs, DVD players) as well as a general dearth of producers, broadcasters
and distributors facilities.

This section briefly documents a few key challenges for the developing
world as various countries strategically position their creative industries for
the future. I emphasize infrastructural capacities in the developing world,
leaving the analysis of consumption and broader infrastructural capacities
to other texts.

The supply and demand of creative products entails a value chain, as
depicted in figure 5.1. Developing countries encounter problems all along
the way, though the barriers to entry in particular stages may be small. A
recent UNCTAD report (2008, 44) notes, for example, that in Africa the
"value chain is simple (primary inputs combined to produce outputs sold
directly to consumers)." Despite the presence of well-known musicians all
over sub-Saharan Africa, only seven African countries have an established
live-performance industry, with venues and equipment: Congo, Democratic
Republic of Congo, Tanzania, Kenya, South Africa, Mali, and Senegal. The
renowned Senegalese musician Youssou N'Dour, associated with the Wolof
polyrhythmic mbalax style, has set up his own performance establishment
(Thiosanne) and a recording studio (Xippi) in Dakar. However, only South
Africa and Zimbabwe possess a well-established recording industry. Nearly
all music is pirated in Africa, and it is thus hard for musicians to earn royalties from local sales.[30] In contrast, Latin America, which accounts for 5 percent of world music sales, "has an established live music practice, a local and
national broadcasting system, a domestic recording industry and in some
instances access to international markets" (Cunningham et al. 2008, 75).[31]

Figure 5.1   Analytical Model of the "Cultural Production Chain" or
            "Culture Cycle"

Source: UNESCO Institute for Statistics (2007), 24.

In general, the infrastructural capacity for content production in key creative industries such as film, broadcasting, and music is severely lacking in most developing countries. Only China, India, Mexico, and Thailand have the capacity to produce enough television content for a primetime schedule (Sauvé 2006, 55). In countries such as Senegal, over 95 percent of television content is foreign (Sauvé 2006, 58). There are, of course, exceptions. Telenovelas from Latin American and the video-production industry in Nigeria provide a glimpse into how production capacity can be boosted in small countries.

Financing is hard. Few countries provide direct financing for content creation. Most developing countries feature a patchwork of financing relationships ranging from direct tax incentives to direct funding. Partnership with international firms can be one way of ensuring funding. Successful cases in the film industries of China and South Africa have come about through international partnerships, especially with Hollywood. In India's case, most financing came from funds raised from family-owned film studios. India's classic *Mughal-e-Azam*, released in 1961, took over a decade in production because of financing shortfalls. The National Film Development Corporation provided small funds to "art" cinema, to support directors. These films were notable in either highlighting social atrocities and violence or in commemorating a glorious past. Either way, they projected a secular and progressive Indian identity and a state that backed such ideals. More recently, Sony, Disney, and Viacom have treaded the lucrative domestic market in India by cofinancing small-budget Bollywood films. In 2008, Warner financed a blockbuster, *From Chandni Chowk to China*, and planned to produce six more in 2009 (Leahy 2009).

In South Africa, the initiative to connect with foreign investors has come from the government's National Film and Video Foundation, which has an aggressive development program. Recent award-winning films such as *Yesterday* and *Tsotsi* speak to the success of NFVF. Securing financing and marketing for South African films is NFVF's key objective and highlights a networked approach in which public and private, domestic and international agencies play a role. The "Indaba Charter" adopted by NFVF and film stakeholders in South Africa in 2005 is clear in mobilizing a network approach and breaking the "dependency syndrome" of overreliance on the government (Department of Arts and Culture and NFVF 2007, 7). NFVF has also raised the profile of its films through participation at international film festivals such as Cannes and Berlin, where it regularly partners with

Trade and Investment South Africa, the semi-autonomous investment-promotion vehicle. NFVF also backs South Africa's efforts to provide leadership for African cinema in general. South Africa now hosts the PanAfrican Federation of Filmmakers, responsible for the FESPACO film festival in Ougadougou. As noted earlier, FESPACO was a French-run show for Francophone cinema; the shift to South Africa is significant. West African film-industry professionals have long accepted yet bemoaned French funding and control of their fledgling film industry. They are skeptical of South African moves but equally fatigued from pulling at the patronage strings of French agencies.[32] These tensions were quite visible at the 2006 Africa Film Summit held in Tshawane, South Africa, and hosted by the country's Department of Arts and Culture and NFVF. Policymakers and film-industry professionals agreed that while African film had managed to survive, not much had changed in the last fifty years in terms of production, distribution, and exhibition.[33] While many professionals decried the loss of African identity and values through commercialization, other saw tremendous opportunities in global market networks and the diffusion of technology, especially the way the video-based Nollywood—nicknamed "vrai cinéma africain"—has grown in the last decade.[34] Nevertheless, "The Tshwane Declaration" at the end of the summit, in noting pan-African strategies, also called for using the WTO framework more effectively for the protection of local production (Department of Arts and Culture and NFVF 2007, 5).

An intermediate step in the development of a creative-content industry is a variety of offshoring practices, most notably offering location shootings for studios in developed countries. Small countries like Uruguay have capitalized on their advertising and design agencies to attract filmmakers from the United States, Europe, Australia, and even New Zealand, the latter itself aggressive with its own location-shooting agenda. Uruguay's Metropolis Films, a small advertising firm founded in 1991, worked aggressively to attract Hollywood's *Miami Vice* to shoot its Cuba scenes in the city of Persepolis. Now with offices in Buenos Aires and Puerto Rico, Metropolis showcases places resembling Manhattan, the Italian countryside, the wild West, the Swiss Alps, and Paris—and films can be shot in Uruguay for a fraction of the cost they would incur in the actual locations.[35] An official at Metropolis films also spoke to his studio's expertise in the informal contractual relationships that govern economics in the film industry in general.[36] "In the audio-visual sector, nowadays a big word is trust. For example, financial contracts and arrangements at locations," and Metropolis

Films capitalizes on its reputation in these contractual arrangements.[37] In general, what a small developing country like Uruguay can offer foreign firms is apparent from a brochure produced by Metropolis Films:

- Make Metropolis Films your door to South America
- Spanish, English and German-speaking crews
- Full availability of equipment
- Great variety of locations
- Quick quotes with no hidden extras
- Large variety of casting backgrounds from Europe, Africa and Latin America

This brief discussion is merely suggestive of possibilities. It does not take away from the variety of problems gripping creative industries in the developing world. Nor does the presence of networks diminish the importance of appropriate domestic and international incentives and policies. The UNCTAD *Creative Economy Report* (2008, 13) summarizes the case:

Developing countries can further integrate into the global economy by nurturing their creative capacities and enhancing the competitiveness of their creative goods and services in world markets, provided that appropriate public policies are in place at the national level and market imbalances can be redressed at the international level.

Burkina Faso, home of FESPACO, provides an interesting case. Its film industry has generally produced two to three films per year since 1971 and was completely dependent on foreign funding.[38] The latter created an elite set of filmmakers but not a general capacity for film production. Meanwhile, film distribution remained tied to either a French or a U.S. firm. Digital technology has had a two-pronged effect: the number of cinemas declined from fifty in 2001 to nineteen in 2004 as film viewing moved indoors; at the same time, new technologies offer filmmakers cost-effective opportunities that they lacked earlier. Such famous directors as Gaston Kaboré, Dani Kouyaté, S. Pierre Yameogo, and Fanta Régina Nacro have created their own studios. Meanwhile, the government has provided incentives for film, including regional distribution incentives and tightening copyright laws. However Hoefert de Turégano's summation of Burkina Faso's film industry (2008, 126) is equally apt for similar countries:

This brings us back to the question of what form the film industry in Burkina Faso will take. Burkina has a rich film culture, it has a budding local production scene, it is grappling with the problems of distribution and exhibition, it is not neglecting the importance of film education and training, it has the best African film festival in the world, and it has a government that is working to create a structured, legal context for the film and audiovisual sector, in sum, many factors working in its favour. Whether these advantages can be translated into economic success remains to be seen.

Conclusion

A creative voice from the developing world is emancipatory when it can communicate, rise above existing power structures, and posit its distinctiveness. State-driven and paternalistic cultural policies and international rules, such as those at the WTO and UNESCO, do not let developing countries escape imposed identities. Strangely enough, grassroots expressions from the developing world have not shied away from using commercial networks and processes.[39] For example, a recent volume on South African identities notes that commercial processes influence but do not dominate identity formation (Nuttail and Michael 2001). It is, therefore, important to make this argument in the context of global anthropologies that locate agency, imagination, and voice in the complex networking mechanisms that surround sites of cultural production.[40] The anthropologist Charles Kleymeyer is suspicious of global media in their power to effect negative stereotypes and the alienation felt at the grassroots among poor societies that do not hear their stories told from within. Nevertheless, his notion of a cultural energy in grassroots cultural expressions goes beyond the cultural politics of identity to speak to a "capacity to aspire" among groups:

> Cultural energy helps people to reach deep down and find strength and resolve they were not sure they had. When the gospel choir bursts into song, when the panpipes blend with the high valley wind, when the actor triumphs over adversity with a clap of hands, when the drum rhythms roll, people feel inspired, affirmed, bonded to other members of their group, and capable of going to the edge of their dream and beyond.
>
> (Kleymeyer 1994, 200)

The critique of market-driven processes from critical theorists and cultural studies scholars is that markets commodify culture, forcing cultural products to deepen and expand capitalistic processes through consumption.[41] Marxists, on the other hand, view commodification as part of the new international division of cultural labor (Miller and Yúdice 2002). There is also considerable uneasiness and frustration among creative producers when considering markets as an alternative. The South African filmmaker Lawrence Dworkin notes: "If South Africa ever enjoyed a hint of an original and distinct film identity it has now been fully smothered by a plethora of no name brand schlock. The exploitation of South Africa's film resources by an unholy alliance of foreign interests with a small and powerful clique of local entrepreneurs, hardly likely to even understand the notion of a 'film identity', has left us with a very poor legacy indeed."[42] It is beyond the scope of this chapter to resolve this ideological divide in assaying film aesthetics in terms of markets versus patronage systems, but, quite clearly, both put forward varying degrees of oppression and production opportunities. The evidence provided in this chapter shows that oppression can happen regardless of consumption and production processes and liberation can take place through all kinds of networked exchanges, including commercial ones.

This chapter is merely a start in thinking of cultural policies and creative voices in the developing world. It provides a few guidelines, but its scope is such that it generalizes across contexts. Further work is needed to deepen our understanding of creative agency in particular contexts. I have presented success stories as well as challenges and dire situations. Nevertheless, international networks and the deliberative activities thereof are a starting point for thinking of creative voices. They do not, however, end the stifling of these voices. There are plenty of global commercial rules and processes that bind the developing world: the intellectual property agreements from the WTO and the increasing theft of cultural heritage and properties are examples. Similarly, there are a myriad of local or national cultural practices that remain quite oppressive. To celebrate culture for culture's sake, whether at the grassroots level or globally, is to think that the ties that bind us as groups are always emancipatory. Cultures have power to enslave and to emancipate—their dualism is quite apparent in the developing world.

6

Culture by Any Other Name

We ask how recollections are to be located. And we answer: with the
help of landmarks that we carry within ourselves, for it suffices to
look around ourselves, to think about others, and to locate ourselves
within the social framework in order to retrieve them.

—Maurice Halbwachs, *On Collective Memory*

To the anxieties of globalization articulated through national cultural
policies, tourism offers two counterpoints: first, the general trend toward
protection and, second, questioning the boundaries of culture in cultural
policies. While some countries restrict imports of creative products in the
name of preserving "indigenous" cultures, in the tourism field these same
countries want to encourage international flows. In chapter 3, I noted that
few countries liberalized their audio-visual sectors. Tourism, on the other
hand, remains a sector in which countries have made the most commitments toward liberalization. Specifically, only 29 WTO members have
committed to liberalization in "audio-visual services," the chief instrument
liberalizing creative product flows, but 128 have agreed to liberalization
in tourism and travel services.[1] According to UNESCO statistics, in 2006
$56.85 billion in cultural products were exported (UNESCO 2009a, 358).[2]
That same year, the tourism industry generated $733 billion, nearly thir-
teen times as much (UNWTO 2006, 3–4).

Despite the plausible reasons for encouraging tourism but not creative-
industry flows, the contradiction in how a threat to culture is constituted is
obvious. At face value it seems that the 922 million international tourists
in 2008 are judged as less threatening to the shelf life of a culture than a
few billion dollars worth of film imports. Putting films and tourism on the

spectrum "blurs the distinctions between the movement of people and the movement of images" (McDowell, Steinberg, and Tomasello 2008, 102). Urry (2002) points out that mass mobility of people through tourism accounts for transformation in social identity. In terms of protecting "indigenous" cultures, foreign images and people are important to changing identities and, arguably, need to be studied alongside native identity. The critique that showcasing heritage to foreigners is different from importing foreign images for domestic audiences falls apart when we realize that even when showcasing heritage to foreign tourists, countries continually construct and reconstruct a past in present terms. In fact, tourism is often the "portal" through which countries present their cultural heritage (OECD 2009; UNCTAD 2008). In other words, the presentations to cultural tourists are always hybrid, and the ability to "protect" and "preserve" a "culture" as a result of tourism is a moot point.[3] At another level, there would be no such thing as xenophobia if foreigners did not threaten some sense of a cultural identity.

A second and related contradiction concerns the definition of a cultural product and the calculations of power that inform this definition. A few products thus become salient to notions of cultural identity while others are marginalized. While this process is largely political, what is called "cultural" is also continually enlarged through the related phenomena of popular culture, mass media, and electronic information flows. Creative industries such as film and music are highly interactive and hybrid, in most cases reducing the ability of a cultural elite to use them to trace any myth of origin or purity. Despite national labels for music or cinema, these artforms showcase a multiplicity of influences that cannot be contained within the nation-state context. Global homogenized popular culture also defies the ability of these elites to re-create canonical, pure, or authentic cultural traditions. Cultural tourism, narrowly understood as related to the cultural heritage of a country, then begins to fall apart when creative industries enter the picture. In general, creative industries unmask the nation-state by exposing the tenuous fault lines in the construction of heritage in nationalistic terms.

Globalization and Issues in Growth of Tourism

Tourism receipts have consistently grown, and many countries continue to make a variety of commitments to ensure that this continues. A note on the importance of tourism helps to place the role of cultural tourism in a broad context. Tourism is the biggest industry in the world both in terms of its contribution to GNP and the number of people employed in it. An estimate from the World Travel and Tourism Council shows that the contribution of travel and tourism to GDP will rise from 10.3 percent in 2006 to 10.9 percent in 2016. The industry accounted for 234 million jobs in 2006, or 8.7 percent of worldwide employment (cited in OECD 2008, 2).

Tourism industry also generates significant linkages with other industries either as a demander of inputs (food, construction) or as supplier of inputs because the goods demanded by tourists are also demanded by other industries, such as finance and wholesale and retail trade. In particular, a viable tourism strategy for a country needs to examine five major constraints: transportation and infrastructure, accommodation, utilities and information infrastructure, marketing and promotion activities, and education and training (Grosso et al. 2007).

In creative industries such as film and television, attention is regularly accorded to the necessary hardware, such as studios, equipment, distribution theaters, museums, and the like.[4] This is the case with tourism as well. Without hotels, restaurants, transportation, and other infrastructure any form of tourism will be limited. Subsets of tourism, such as cultural tourism, also depend on this hardware. In the context of the commodification of tourism, Edensor (1998, 7) notes that there is an important link between "heterogeneous tourist spaces" such as hotels and restaurants and the "enclaves" or monuments and heritage sites: "Contemporary tourist processes produce distinct forms of tourist space on a global stage. Tourist space is liable to be commodified in particular ways, and its organization provides a distinctive material character, replete with hotels, highways, tours and other infrastructural facilities, which often contrasts with adjacent, nontourist space."

There is another important sense in which tourism has externalities. As noted before, tourism is the portal through which other creative industries, especially cultural heritage, are presented or elevated in rank. Commercial advertising, especially from ministries of culture, often invites tourists to experience culture heritage through festivals, monuments, parks and natural environments, museums, and cultural districts or cities. More generally, UNCTAD (2008, 23) notes that "the cultural ambience and traditions of different locations can be an attraction for Tourists." OECD (2009, 17) is more assertive in underlining the mutually beneficial relationship of culture and tourism: "Culture is increasingly an important element of the tourism product, which also creates distinctiveness in a crowded global marketplace. At the same time, tourism provides an important means of enhancing culture and creating income which can support and strengthen cultural heritage, cultural production and creativity."

Tourism is now one of the main sources of export revenues and hard currency for several developing countries. In 2008, international tourist arrivals totaled 922 million, accounting for $944 billion in receipts (UN-WTO 2009, 3–5). Although the developing world accounted for less than 20 percent of the arrivals and receipts, international organizations such as the World Trade Organization, UNESCO, UNCTAD, WIPO, and the United Nations World Tourism Organization are working with the developing world to promote cultural policies—often linked to creative industries such as tourism—in some form or another. In many countries the ministries of culture and tourism are the same. Most of these cultural policies seek promotion and growth, but the problems of tourism are regularly reported and include environmental effects, security concerns, and natural disasters, such as the 2004 tsunami. Increasingly, attention is also being paid to sex trafficking and the sexual exploitation of children.

As tables 3.3 and 3.4 show, international trade in tourism services is enormous. From the developing world, only China, Mexico, and Turkey are among the top ten destinations. However, it is important to point out that while developed countries dominate international tourism, it is one of the biggest foreign-exchange earners for a host of developing countries. Apart from big countries such as Argentina, Brazil, China, and India, the list includes places as diverse as Belize, Fiji, Morocco, and Mauritius.[5] Admittedly, not all tourism is international or cultural, yet these statistics show the importance of this activity in calculating trade in cultural products. Canada is one of the biggest promoters in the WTO of liberalized tourism markets.

Cultural Tourism and Identity

Tourism is about identity, about understanding ourselves in different places. Cultural tourism, which deals specifically with various types of group identities, is a subset of tourism. Both types of tourism, at the international level discussed here, are encouraged through information and transportation flows. It is a fitting metaphor—quantitatively, critically, and analytically—for globalization that the tourism industry is the largest in the world, generating nearly one trillion dollars in receipts from international tourists alone.

There are many reasons for tourism, ranging from boredom to curiosity, leisure to sports, and a tourist may travel through a wide range of destinations including historic sites, natural wonders, cruise ships, or amusement parks. UNWTO estimates that almost 40 percent of all tourism is cultural. Based on these estimates, the OECD calculates that there were 359 million international cultural tourists in 2007 (see table 6.1). A survey of 8,000 tourists at twenty European locations found that only 20–30 percent identified themselves as cultural tourists, but larger percentages partook of cultural activities such as visits to museums or monuments. Broadly defined, almost all tourism has a cultural component, if not in the curiosity of the tourists then at least in the way they understand their own identity in relation to their tourist activities or the way that local populations might themselves relate to the tourist sites in question.[6] The throngs that line up in U.S. amusement parks are very much a part of cultural traditions and cultural commodifications in the current era.[7] The opening ceremonies of the Olympic Games in Beijing in August 2009, directed by filmmaker Zhang Yimou, showcased sports and cultural heritage and were informed by the genius of creative industries including design and architecture. Going to Paris as a whole may be understood as a cultural experience that, while different from a U.S. amusement park, offers its own set of commodifications, regardless of the different aesthetic or amusement experiences the two places might provide.

Understanding tourism at the level of identity, individual or collective, helps to explain both the creative and constitutive aspects of cultural tourism

TABLE 6.1

International Cultural Tourism Data

YEAR	TOTAL INTERNATIONAL ARRIVALS (MILLIONS)	PERCENTAGE CULTURAL TRIPS (%)	TOTAL NUMBER OF CULTURAL TRIPS (MILLIONS)
1996	538	37	199
2007	898	40	359

Source: OECD (2009, 21), from UNWTO estimates.

and also the motivations of the tourist to travel. Despite the proliferation of survey data, the causes of tourism at a deeper and abstract level are complex. They also help to connect tourism with individual and group anxieties. Why does the tourist travel: longing, desire, fantasy, curiosity, restlessness, escape? Consider the following passage that opens Alain de Botton's *The Art of Travel* (2003, 8–9) as he ponders a newly arrived travel brochure in London under a dreary December sky:

> The longing provoked by the brochure was an example, at once touching and bathetic, of how projects (and even whole lives) might be influenced by the simplest and most unexamined images of happiness; of how a lengthy and ruinously expensive journey might be set into motion by nothing more than the sight of a photograph of a palm tree gently inclining in a tropical breeze.
>
> I resolved to travel to the island of Barbados.

Such travel decisions, intermeshed in creative representations and media flows, speak to the push and pull or, in economist's parlance, demand and supply of travel and tourism. They reveal the enormously creative enterprise underlying the beckoning of distant lands and the search for meaningful and creative experiences. The flows of representations that guide such creative practices are hard to miss in a media-inundated world. The promises of palm tries compete with those of tigers in India or the Machu Picchu trails in Peru. Immediately after the passage above, de Botton notes: "If our lives are dominated by a search for happiness, then perhaps few activities reveal as much about the dynamics of this quest—in all its ardor and paradoxes—than our travels" (9).

Anxieties and fears over flows of creative expressions often lead to the political protection of cultural identity. In the case of tourism, anxieties of identity lead to a desire to travel and experience different cultures. Self-actualization through travel then comes replete with references, often disparaging, to the "other" found in exotic places, from whom the tourist derives her sense of worth. I will return to this point shortly.

That tourism comes replete with media representations is obvious. Even if the producers of a representation seek a tight rein over the interpretations, the social meanings it gives birth to will always feature some contestation from audience reception. In cultural tourism, a prepackaged heritage is presented within, for example, the confines of ancient city walls and a regulated set of images. The opening of the Beijing Olympics in parallels the earlier opening of the Forbidden City. But it is not just communist authorities who regulate cultural tourism to present a particular "national" spectacle.

These definitions allow a resolution of the contradiction between imported films and foreign tourists mentioned in the introduction. The GATS instruments and the UNESCO convention (see chapters 3 and 4) both speak to the many ways that the liberalization of commodified creative expressions is difficult, yet tourism is the opposite: countries, with rare exceptions, welcome foreign tourists, and the expectation is that host societies and countries can manage the show to present culture in particular ways.[8] In this sense Bhutan and the United States have something in common in terms of the consistency of their international cultural policies. Bhutan restricts both foreign creative products as well as foreigners because it fears that the show cannot be managed, allowing a mere 2,000 tourists per year. The United States encourages both tourists and expressions, though it need hardly be afraid, at least in terms revenue economics. Less than 1 percent of box office receipts in the United States are from foreign films, while over 50 million tourists arrive on U.S. soil each year.

The tourist's perceived loss of freedom and increased anxiety, evidenced in cultural narratives, is precisely what gives a host territory the confidence to think that its "culture" is not threatened by tourism. Despite seemingly rude or intrusive tourists, the hosts may still cherish the notion that their lifestyle remains intact. The host country is on stage, the tourist is merely a spectator, and the show belongs to those "staging patrimony" as García Canclini calls it (1995, chapter 4). It is in this sense that García Canclini views a museum as "the ceremonial headquarters of the patrimony," presenting a "ritualized system of social action" (1995, 115). Objects in a museum have been chosen and re-presented in the sanitized context of the nation-state, often divorcing them from their original contexts or meanings. Parades of tourists visiting these museums serve to further legitimize the collection and reinforce the showcased ideas of heritage. Halbwachs (1992, 47) is apt:

> We preserve memories of each epoch in our lives, and these are continually reproduced; through them, by a continual relationship a sense of our identity is reproduced. But precisely because these memories are repetitions, because they are successively engaged in very different systems

of notions, at different periods of our lives, they have lost the form and appearance they once had.

A cultural tourist is presented a reinterpreted and constructed past according to the precepts of those who participate in the exercise. For example, despite the recent proliferation of private museums, most museums are run by public agencies and thus the displays privilege the nation-state. In analyzing the conservative backlash against exhibits that might be deemed unpatriotic at the Smithsonian, the historian Michael Kammen (2006, 285) writes that "it is a public institution located in the nation's capital, subject to the political whims and whiles of Congress." Public choice economists also note that bureaucrats have "an incentive to adopt a more cautious (i.e. conservationist) stance" and tend to shy away from presenting anything that might be judged controversial as "deterioration of heritage" (Rizzo 2006, 1003).

Despite institutional attempts to present a prepackaged past, tourists engage with the interpretations presented to them according to their own expectations, imaginaries, and socialization. Edensor (1998, 202) notes that "sites of international tourism are exemplary points of dialogue and negotiation between tourists and locals. Hybrid narratives are articulated alongside somewhat serially reproduced, culturally situated stories, and new cultural forms and practices may emerge out of the interchange of knowledge and ideas." Of paramount importance here is the tourist "gaze," which disciplines those presenting the spectacle to tourists and guides the further presentation of the spectacle (Urry 2002; Edensor 1998).

The seemingly iron-clad nature of national patrimony, as it is presented by the cultural elite and bureaucrats, is thus not so secure for myriad reasons; a half dozen are presented here.[9] First, while the cultural tourist might experience a loss of familiar cultural cues, she may not find the given interpretation entirely convincing and will interpret it according to her own cultural imaginary. Goffman (1959, 244) notes the dramaturgical clues inherent in any society, which may be challenged while visiting another: "Reports by Western travelers are filled with instances in which their dramaturgical sense was offended or surprised, and if we are to generalize to other cultures we must consider these instances as well as more favorable ones." Second, thanks to media and information technologies, the cultural tourist can easily come across other interpretations. In electronic and mediated environments, the hierarchies producing patrimony are often challenged and contested. During the Beijing Olympic opening ceremonies, a number of editorials in global newspapers, while admiring the precision and grand scale of the spectacle, often comparing it to the grandeur of the Tang dynasty, also called attention to the goose-stepping soldiers who hoisted the Chinese and Olympics flags. Third, creative industries that intersect popular cultures further weaken the hierarchies of power. What is so Chinese about the hundreds of t-shirt or curio vendors at every tourist stop along the Great Wall? If they have a right to stay there, then why not the Starbucks inside the Forbidden City in Beijing or the McDonald's next to the Spanish Steps in Rome?[10] Popular cultures, notes García Canclini (1995, 137–38), "constitute their own patrimony," and their proliferation via electronic media "generates more fluid interactions between the cultured and the popular, the traditional and the modern." Fourth, appeals to historic authenticity are considerably weakened when technologies continually reproduce the authentic. In fact, as Walter Benjamin's seminal essay "The Work of Art in the Age of Mechanical Reproduction" informs us, the authentic and unique value of any artwork must be judged against its reproduction and ubiquity (Benjamin 1935/1969). A digitally remastered recording or even a recording purified of any type of weakness can provide a more "pure" or "authentic" music experience than going to a concert.[11] Fifth, all cultures consciously or subconsciously manufacture and reproduce cultural "authenticity" to appeal to tourists. While the cultural elite often deride the "O Sole Mio"–singing gondoliers in Venice, other less obvious cases abound: for example, the lighting of national monuments at night or festivals and carnivals organized to attract tourists. Nevertheless, the gondoliers are often posited as destroying local cultural heritage while the Montreux Jazz Festival, full of "imported" artists, is posited as preserving it. Cipolla (1980, 86–87) notes that in the early sixteenth century there may have been as many as 12,000 prostitutes in Venice and that visitors "could buy at little expense a booklet containing the 'tariff of all prostitutes in which one finds the price and the qualities of the courtesans of Venice.'" Despite the difficulty of calculating the number of sex workers historically, he notes that there may have been anywhere from 10,000 to 40,000 of them in Rome in the sixteenth and seventeenth centuries, and even the official census of 1600 listed 604 female sex workers out of a total population of 30,000 females: "For a holy city, the percentage looks high, especially if one considers that the figures refer only to those prostitutes who were officially recognized as such" (1980, 87). When the cultural elite decry the present state of Venice to invoke the past, what kind of a past is being invoked? Clearly, claims to historical authenticity in the construction of a city's representation are always exclusionary and dependent on those making the decisions.

Finally, one must not forget the experiment with freedom that might propel the tourist to go abroad in the first place. This especially might be an impetus to indulge in activities such as gambling or sex tourism (McDowell, Steinberg, and Tomasello 2008, 115). Sexual excitement in general, even if sexual acts are not performed, is often noted among the primary causes and consequences of tourism (Gmelch 2004).[12] Implicit in positing other places as zones of sexual plenitude is the belief that one's own home culture might offer a more respectable or repressed, sexuality. For example, in showing the connection between sexual domination and Orientalism, Said (1978, 309) notes that "the associations between the Orient and sex is remarkably persistent. The Middle East is resistant, as any virgin would be, but the male scholar wins the prize by bursting open, penetrating through the Gordian knot despite 'the taxing task.'" Felski (1995, 138) adds: "For white women as for white men, it seems that the exotic is intimately linked to the erotic, as racial and cultural difference is woven in to the very heart of sexual fantasy." All travel becomes a sexual fantasy that includes domination.[13] It is in this context that I now present the peculiar case of sex tourism through the lens of cultural policies. While the case sits on the margins of cultural policies, it illustrates how cultural policies are deliberately constructed, especially the power hierarchies that inform this definition. From the perspective of both the cultural tourist and the host society, the silence on implicit cultural policies promoting sex work merely serves to temporarily disguise rather than obliterate the boundaries of culture in cultural tourism.

Sex Work and Cultural Policies

This chapter now examines the links between globalization and sex work from the perspective of national and international cultural policies affecting tourism. The implicit policies promoting sex work not only are cultural in their substance but also point to the governmental and bureaucratic (mis-)understanding of culture. Many developing countries are increasingly prioritizing tourism assets to take advantage of globalization processes and generate economic growth. These policies highlight, promote, and maintain cultural assets, whether through cultural heritage preservation or by boosting creative industries such as film, television, and the performing arts. However, many issues lie at the margins of cultural-tourism policy, and sex work is one of them. While a few countries have legalized sex work, most treat it as an industry that must not speak its name, even though unofficially it is neither discouraged nor acknowledged. An exception is Greece, which in September 2006 agued to the European Union that its budget deficit as percentage of national income was less than previously assumed. Greece's claim was based on expanding its national income to include sex work (Hope and Parker 2006).

The sex industry, at its core, is a service industry.[14] Thus, I place sex tourism in two contexts important for understanding contemporary cultural policies: one expands the notion of cultural policies, and the other notes their origins and effects, though the two areas are not mutually exclusive. Both contexts expose the constructed link between creative work and the superimposition of cultural boundaries around such work.[15]

Sex tourism does pose particular challenges to connecting creative work to culture or identity. It speaks to the silences in cultural policy. The international tourist in Bangkok who pays for sex to a Thai sex worker speaks to the economic value of sex work as well its creative and cultural values: the tourist could have had sex in his country of origin but went to Bangkok because the creative and cultural contexts of Bangkok matter.[16] As more and more industries are understood as creative and cultural and their effects documented, where do we place the sex industry?[17] The sex industry points us to the limits of cultural policies in terms of expanding the scope of cultural industries and also in documenting their effects. Officials do not want to name it; neither do they do much to stop it. A recent article on the sex trade in Thailand sums up the situation aptly: "The rulers of the land of the free (as 'Thailand' literally means) have always been of two minds about the fact that their country's great source of tourist revenue (the 'one night in Bangkok' mystique) is also its great source of shame" (Iyer 2005).

Creativity and economics have a symbiotic but conflicted relationship that grows even more complex when we think of sex tourism in the context of globalization. As we saw in chapter 2, most textbooks in cultural economics begin with discussions of the valuation and scope of cultural industries. A valuation of sex work, however, is difficult and involves mapping both economic and human-rights aspects. I am mindful of public-health, trafficking, and human-rights issues involved, but I concentrate on making explicit the promotion of sex tourism through cultural policies.[18] However, highlighting the cultural policies governing sex work points out the institutional incentives and support surrounding the industry; at least, it makes apparent the difficulty of cutting through institutional layers to address human-rights concerns.

Regardless of the specific valuation, sex tourism clearly fits into the expanding notion of creative industries, which includes well-known ones such as performing arts, cultural goods such music and film, and now cultural tourism.[19] Sex work, historically, has also involved some mastery over a range of performing arts, especially singing and dancing, including Japanese geisha or *devdasis* in India. *Devdasis* lived in temples; they were "married" to gods and performed religious services. Apart from their position as sex workers, they were entrusted with learning the classical dance *bharatanatayam*.[20] Postcolonial India outlawed *devdasi* practices, clearly a divorce between the high art of *bhartanatayam* and the unnamed art of sex work. *Bhartanatayam* became India's secular national dance.

In mapping sex work as a creative industry several interconnected linkages become important for understanding the underlying political economy of cultural policies. First, the sex tourist may view herself as a cultural tourist responding to a portfolio of choices that include sex. Second, the location of sex industries is important and, at least for the international tourist, often means global cities known for their cultural heritage, such as Amsterdam, Paris, and Bangkok. Cultural-policy literature has recently accorded importance to the rise of sexual creative industries—which are broader than but do intersect with other creative industries—in particular locations. Florida (2002) speaks to the three factors that give rise to such creative industries—talent, tolerance, and technology. The fit of sexual politics with Florida's "three Ts" has already attracted attention on one particular count: Florida uses the "Bohemian index," including tolerance of gay life, as a way of measuring tolerance. Florida's intention is to show that relatively tolerant societies generate high rates of economic growth as well. What can we make of explicit or implicit "tolerance" of sex workers in official policies? Consideration of human rights and sex trafficking may very well negate the image of tolerance. Brennan's problematization of such locations in poor regions also instructs us on the limits of Florida's analysis. Brennan (2004, 16) notes that "the sex trade becomes a focal point of a place, and the social and economic relations of that place are filtered through the nightly (and daily) selling of sex to foreigners. In contrast, the sex trade in red-light districts in the developed world—such as Frankfurt, Rome, or New York—by no means defines social and economic life outside these districts." In the town of Sousa in the Dominican Republic and in Bangkok, sex tourism is a major source of revenue for the local economy but raises questions and problems that need acknowledgment and deep understanding.

The rise of sex tourism is hard to understand without noting the increasing scope and intensity of globalization and the fantasies that tourism generates. Much has been written on the Orientalist nature of travel to putatively "exotic" places. In Said's *Orientalism*, the East—now often seen as the entire developing world—is assigned an inferior position and is in need of the benefits of the "white man's burden"—the task of civilization. Said also argues that the fantasy of domination is played out in sexual terms.

Michel Houellebecq's novel *Platform* presents a horrifying journey into international division of ethnic labor centered on sex work. The protagonist, Michel Renault, a bureaucrat from the French Ministry of Culture, sets up a global sex-tourism industry and at one point makes the following presentation to an investor:

> "Therefore," I went on, "you have several hundred million westerners who have everything they could want but no longer manage to obtain sexual satisfaction. They spend their lives looking without finding it, and they are completely miserable. On the other hand, you have several billion people who have nothing, who are starving, who die young, who live in conditions unfit for human habitation, and who have nothing left to sell except their bodies and their unspoiled sexuality. It's simple, really simple to understand: it's an ideal trading opportunity. The money you could make is almost unimaginable, vastly more than from computers or biotechnology, more than the media industry; there isn't a single economic sector that's comparable.
>
> (Houellebecq 2004, 173)

Sex Workers in Thailand

There is no shortage of references to the sex industry in Thailand.[21] In 1993, the Thai government reproached the London-based publisher of the

Longman Dictionary of English Language and Culture for describing Bangkok as a city "where there are a lot of prostitutes" because the entry would "project a negative image of Thailand . . . [and] erode the good moral standards of Thais" (Vanaspong 2002, 139): quite obviously a cultural ranking that would rattle the purveyors of patrimony. Nevertheless, Thailand's reputation as a hot spot for sex tourism has persisted, and the country has been in the headlines whenever issues like human trafficking and the sexual exploitation of children make the news.

Two issues arise from my mapping of the Thai sex industry: first, the political economy of the sex industry and the role it plays in the Thai economy; second, the difficulty of understanding the sex industry in terms of formal and informal state cultural policies.

THE CULTURAL ECONOMY OF SEX WORK

Though the Thai government took issue with Bangkok being characterized as a place with a lot of prostitutes, the reality is that commercial sex work is a well-known industry in Thailand that serves both local and international clients. While the supply factors, as one might expect, are rooted in poverty, demand is much more complicated and must account for transnational fantasies, corruption, international encounters, and cultural policies.

There are varying estimates of how many people are engaged in the Thai commercial sex industry—in brothels, in independent sex work, and through the many venues that enable indirect sex work. The numbers vary from 60,000 or 75,000 (a 1992 figure from the Communicable Diseases Control Department [CDCD] of the Thai Ministry Public Health), to 400,000, according to the Foundation for Women (Skrobanek 2003). A 1997 figure from the Ministry of Public Health put it at 64,886, of which 90 percent were Burmese (Lim 1998).

Cultural policies concerning tourism and entertainment establishments are directly related to the bars that attract foreign visitors, whether businessmen, military personnel, expatriates, or tourists. Many sex workers in Thailand do not work in brothels but in indirect places like karaoke bars, massage parlors, dance clubs, and go-go bars. These businesses offer entertainment, drinks, and other services besides sex. So women working at bars and serving drinks may get some income from that work and earn additional income for sex work. "Sex isn't sold everywhere in Bangkok, but it's available in enough places and enough kinds of places at a low enough price to confirm the First World view that the whole city is an erotic theme park" (Bishop and Robinson 1998, 7). Some of the venues for indirect sex work explicitly target white foreign (*farang*) men as well as men from Japan, Malaysia, India, China, and other parts of the world. Sex tourism is one sector of the overall commercial sex industry in Thailand that receives a good deal of attention worldwide, though it should be noted that Thai men make up the majority of the clients in the Thai commercial sex industry. "While foreign-oriented bars are not typical of sex work in Thailand because they comprise only a small portion of the industry, they are its most visible portion to foreigners" (Steinfatt 2002, 29).

The sex industry in Thailand might amount to one-sixth of its total economy. Starting with a figure of 200,000 sex workers, Boonchalaski and Guest (1998, 133) estimate that 1.2 million people are connected to the sex industry, which includes two staff members for every sex worker in the various establishments and four family members who benefit from each worker's remittances. Furthermore, hotels and restaurants benefit from the sex industry as well. They also report a survey that noted average remittances from a sex worker to be $150 per month. Lim (1998, 12) notes that $300 million annually was remitted by Thai sex workers to their families. Lim also reports that the Thai underground economy amounts to between $33 and $44 billion per year, of which sex work accounts for two-thirds. The underground economy itself amounts to 15 to 18 percent of the GDP; in other words, I estimate that sex work accounts for 10 to 12 percent of Thai GDP.

The potential to make enough money to support their families attracts many women to the commercial sex industry, but what attracts so many foreign men to Thailand? Putting it crudely, surely price does not account for demand alone as the cost of hotels and airfares make it comparable to sex bought even in affluent economies. In cultural-economy terms, the formation of tastes is equally important. The foreigners choose to travel far from home to fulfill their fantasies. Brennan's analysis is succinct: "Sexscapes link the practices of sex work to the forces of globalized economy" (2004, 16). Brennan's use of the term "sexscape" builds on Appadurai's notion of "scapes" or globalized interconnections, real and imagined (Appadurai 1996).

The connection between sex tourism and cultural tourism is easy to find as sex workers are both presented and perceived in cultural terms—each sex worker's identity is imagined as part of some hypothetical collective. It is often noted that the sex industry in Thailand is rather different from the sex industry in the West. Thai women are described as tender and nurturing, offering companionship to their clients, not just sex. "Men feel particularly cherished by what they experience as the compliance, eagerness to please and considerateness of Thai women" (Seabrook 2001, 3). Western sex workers, by contrast, are viewed as more mechanistic and functional. The image of the Thai sex worker as a subservient caretaker and exotic beauty points to the Orientalist and racist undertones of Thailand's commercial sex industry. In Davidson's study of prostitution, sex tourists interviewed "reproduced the classic racist opposition between the 'primitive', who exists in some 'state of nature', and the 'civilized', constrained by powerful legal and moral codes, in their (mis)understandings of their host cultures" (1998, 178).

Brennan (2004) and Seabrook (2001) note that Western clients who idealize "exotic" or "Oriental" women rarely see themselves as racist. They argue that overtly racist responses do not surface until the Western client becomes angry with a woman who explains her need to support her family. The client may feel as though he has been cheated or betrayed because the sex worker is concerned with more than their one-on-one relationship. In essence, there is little understanding that the family is the only source of social security for Thais and that the sex worker's world does not revolve around her client. Davidson (1998) concludes that white Western tourists perceive their own whiteness as giving them status that makes them sexually desirable to "Third World" women and girls. It is in this sense that Brennan (2004, 33) refers to the proliferation of sex-tourist destinations in the developing world as sexscapes, where sex tourists can live out racialized sexual fantasies that "often arise out of associations between nationality and race which are rooted in colonial racist discourses, and, more recently, are fueled by media depictions and Internet discussions and photos."

Another factor of importance in sex-trade demand (or as a pull factor for female labor) is the role of beach resorts in Thailand, which have proliferated since the 1950s, when they were used as rest and recuperation locations for soldiers involved in the various wars in Vietnam.[22] Bishop and Robinson (1998, 31) note that the New Yorker's "Letter from Bangkok" series, which has run periodically since the mid-1950s, while not explicitly mentioning sex work did refer to it indirectly. For example, they quote a 1967 letter: "Bangkok has become the liveliest, the loudest, and probably the most licentious city in Southeast Asia. New restaurants, bars, night clubs, and so-called 'massage parlors' are opening every week" (1998, 35). Seabook (2001, 70) estimates that by 1970 U.S. soldiers were spending close to $20 million per year during R&R in Thailand.

Western cultural representations are sensitive to Bangkok's place in the imaginaries of the military. The racist fantasies of the sexscape and the role of military personnel is portrayed in the musical *Miss Saigon*. In this late-twentieth-century retelling of the Madame Butterfly/Miss Crysanthemum "Oriental" sex fantasy, an American GI becomes separated from his Vietnamese sex-worker mistress, who eventually finds her way to Bangkok. Years later, the GI, Chris, returns with his white American wife to reclaim his son from Miss Saigon, who shoots herself in her Bangkok brothel.

Sex tourism in Thailand does perpetuate Orientalist and racist stereotypes, but commercial sex workers are not necessarily unaware of these stereotypes.[23] However, they are more concerned with their ability to provide for their families. The effects of sex work on the Thai economy are significant, and many Thais are economically dependent on the commercial sex industry. Millions of people in all areas of the service sector derive a significant portion of their income from expenditures of those supported by the sex sector. Steinfatt (2002) argues that the rich and middle class would have little to lose from the removal of commercial sex from the Thai economy, but that such a removal would have an enormous effect on the poor.

CULTURAL POLICIES AND INSTITUTIONAL PROMOTION OF SEX WORK

The illegality of prostitution and the state's tacit approval of the commercial sex industry highlight a gap between explicit and implicit policies in Thailand. Before 1960, prostitution was legal in Thailand. The Contagious Disease Act of 1908 required brothels and prostitutes to register and pay specific fees to the government (Ghosh 2002). The Prostitution Suppression Act of 1960 made the trade illegal in Thailand. However, the Entertainment Places Act passed six years later regulated nightclubs, dance halls, bars, massage parlors, baths, and places "which have women to attend male customers" (Seabrook 2001, 7). This 1966 act set the stage for an agreement with the U.S. military to allow American soldiers stationed in Vietnam to come to Thailand for rest and recreation. Officially, sex work is illegal in Thailand, but the Entertainment Places Act in effect legalized the existence of places that promote commercial sex.

For foreign men interested in visiting Thailand, there are countless tourist agencies and websites that provide photographs of attractive women who will act as escorts or girlfriends. Hotels have contract arrangements with escort services, and they enforce certain standards of behavior and appearance for the escorts. In more provincial hotels, arrangements between customers and women are made through coffee shops, nightclubs, or karaoke bars. Just as soldiers came to Thailand for rest and recreation during the Vietnam War, many firms and industries with large workforces of single men provide holidays in Thailand (Hamilton 1997). Vanaspong (2002, 140) explains that prostitution draws millions of dollars every year and has become an integral part of Thailand's image around the world: "Tourists and expatriate men are inundated with information about where to buy women, cheap gems and Thai silk. It becomes part of the shopping trip."

A quick Internet search using the words "Thailand escort" in Google brought up approximately 2,870,000 results.[24] For example, the "About Thailand Info" website includes an "Entertainment and Sports in Thailand" page with links to "Nightlife" and "Escorts and Guides"; the latter provides links for the kinds of adult-entertainment, escort, and sex services available to foreign visitors. The "Escort and Guides" page includes links to twenty different websites for escort/sex services. One of these links is for Bangkok Intimate, a site featuring women who work only part-time as escorts and whose primary occupations are as students, office girls, shop assistants, and waitresses. The seemingly endless number of websites such as these indicate the significant number of businesses involved in sex tourism. These websites are not targeting Thai men but the foreign men who may visit Thailand as sex tourists.

While the website of the Tourism Authority of Thailand does not refer specifically to entertainment establishments that cater to foreign tourists, such as Bangkok's famous Patpong area, neither does TAT take serious steps to deter sex tourism. There is thus no official acknowledgment that the lucrative tourist industry is linked to sex workers, though oblique references can be found. In many Thai tourism promotional materials, whether websites or brochures, "nightlife" is simply a euphemism for commercial sex.

In linking sex work to cultural policy and tourism, I remain mindful of the sensitive challenges posed by this work. Human trafficking, HIV/AIDS, racism, and dehumanization are, sadly, overwhelming problems. In providing an ethnography of the sex trade in Bangkok, Seabrook (2001, 36) notes: "Some of the short-term tourists are extremely insensitive to the women, and have little imaginative understanding of the people whose lives touch theirs. . . . Most say they come here 'for the pussy', 'fuck and forget 'em', 'because there's no complications', 'because the women are a good lay', 'they know how to make you feel like a man', 'they're professionals, even those who aren't.' " While a case can be made to shut down sex work on the basis of dehumanization, this would be a facile solution indeed. Charges of trafficking, dehumanization, and racism are made against many industries. The answer lies in reform and the monitoring of abusive practices, not in shutting down the industry altogether. I am, therefore, also careful in not equating all sex work with trafficking.

Conclusion

This chapter has dealt with two contradictions. The first deals with protecting against "foreign" creative expressions while welcoming tourists. States are concerned about flows of creative expressions and equate their proliferation with market-driven networks around the world. They hesitate to make liberalization commitments at the WTO because these would ostensibly strengthen markets and weaken local cultures. However, states do not hesitate to make tourism commitments. I have underlined a possible "cultural" reason for this contradiction. States may actually think that they can control the presentation of cultural heritage to tourists but think they lack control over other creative expressions coming into their territories. There are many reasons for both the myopia and the duplicity among states that hold this view. Furthermore, as chapter 5 pointed out, many states making commitments to open tourism have not really thought them through and have not consulted their local industries in doing so. Again, this is merely the continuation of patriarchal practices fostered through states rather than careful reasoning applied to best practices for promoting a cultural-tourism industry. In time, as cultural-tourism industries grow and coalesce, they will either pressure states to attend to their needs or come to bypass the state altogether.

The second contradiction presented in this chapter concerns sex work in states such as Thailand. Sex work is both promoted and demanded in cultural terms, but no tourism official or expert would dare call sex work a cultural industry or admit that the cultural identity of any place is linked to sex work. This is, of course, not a plea to make sex work part of cultural policies in all states but to point out the cognitive dissonance within a few states when they choose to call an industry explicitly "cultural." Despite its being the oldest profession, sex work, as practiced today, carries stigmas and problems associated with human rights, trafficking, and public health. A useful place to start documenting the position of sex work is in naming it as cultural and then enunciating the explicit and implicit policies that affect it. Bishop and Robinson (1998, 4) write that the sex industry is "a topic usually off limits to social discourse" in Thailand. By naming it, we are able to account for the laws that govern sex work, in particular the 1966 Entertainment Places Act, which implicitly encouraged sex work even while it remained technically illegal. Furthermore, four government institutions, in particular, can be named as regulating or being cognizant of sex work: tourism officials who promote sex work through coded language that is well understood inside and outside of Thailand; public-health officials providing services and maintaining data on sex workers and sexual practices; the Ministry of Interior police force that regulates places of entertainment; and police officials who overlook sex work, mostly in return for sexual favors or bribes.

It is also important to note how globalization affects cultural tourism and the sex industry. First, tourism itself is both a cause and an effect of globalization and partly arises out of anxieties about the self. Even the choice of Bangkok as an R&R location for American soldiers during the Vietnam War can be understood in this context. Second, technological media such as the Internet and air travel to "exotic" places underlie the growth of tourism and sex industries. Third, all tourism at some level can be linked to sexual stimulation: the racialized fantasies regarding "Oriental" sex workers are themselves to be understood in the context of global imaginaries.

The Creative Voice and Cultural Policy

"I have never doubted the truth of signs, Adso; they are the only things man has with which to orient himself in the world. What I did not understand is the relation among signs . . . I behaved stubbornly, pursuing a semblance of order, when I should have known well that there is no order in the universe."

"But in imagining an erroneous order you still found something . . ."

"What you say is very fine, Adso, and I thank you. The order that our mind imagines is like a net, or like a ladder, built to attain something. But afterward you must throw the ladder away, because you discover that, even if it was useful, it was meaningless. . . . The only truths that are useful are instruments to be thrown away."

—Umberto Eco, *The Name of the Rose*

The genesis of creative endeavors and the cultural politics they unleash can be located in the anxieties, fears, and opportunities afforded by an intensely interdependent world. Globalization is nothing new; however, the depth of human interactions continues to increase, especially in the ways that people experience or voice their cultural identities. Such interactions might produce cultural events of global interest. On the other hand, such interactions might lead to protests and the burning of effigies. Both are examples of cultural politics. At the level of cultural identity, the affinity for a griot singer at Carnegie Hall in New York may stand for the emotive and hybrid ways in which our identities relate to artistic expressions from another part of the world. Alternatively, a song may prove controversial because it tears at the fabric of some shared sense of identity. Examples include the Dixie Chicks' opposition to President George W. Bush's Iraq war or Joan Baez's opposition to the war in Vietnam.

This book has traced the relations between creative forces and cultural politics at micro- and global levels. In doing so, it distinguishes the creative voice from cultural politics and policies. Not everything creative is cultural even if it is understood and reassigned in this way. The cultural politics this book examines include global controversies and rule making, especially in international organizations and forums where states tend to dominate deliberations. However, state and international policies encouraging creative products may be different from those encouraging particular types of cultural politics, especially those connected to national identity. A cultural identity arises from ideas of "groupness" that may be marginal to an artist's calculations. In conclusion I seek to further distinguish between creative and cultural voices and policies. I argue for innovative policies that encourage creativity through deliberative cultural politics that are inclusive and emancipatory.

The Creative Voice

Emancipation and voice are linked. George Eliot asks in *Middlemarch*, "Is there any yoked creature without its private opinions?" The opinions of great works of art are usually public. They voice a historical condition. They are reflections upon humanity. A similar sentiment is expressed in notions of cultural voice, when a group of people understands and represents its condition. While creative and cultural voices are not synonymous, they are often confused in speaking of cultural industries and policies. The presumption is that most creative expressions become cultural expressions when infused with commercial processes. Cultural industries then supposedly muffle cultural voices because the expressions they produce are too commercial, homogenized, and commodified. This is a fallacy and must be corrected.

The fusion of creative and cultural voices can be seen in Paulo Freire's *Pedagogy of the Oppressed*.[1] This seminal and revolutionary work is infused with the spirit of a critical consciousness, rooted in ideas of creative and imaginative representations. Such representations, which hold a mirror to the oppressed person's reality, arise from problem posing and dialogues that allow the meek to grasp the dimensions of their oppression. Critical pedagogies inspired by Freire's oeuvre often turn to aesthetic representations as a means of posing the problem of the world to the oppressed. Everything from graffiti on ghetto walls to the use of Internet by homeless populations can express or provide a counterpoint to conditions of oppression. In doing so, "people develop their power to perceive critically the way they exist in the world with which and in which they find themselves; they come to see the world not as static reality, but as a reality in process, in transformation" (Freire 1970/2000, 83).

Central to dialogic communication is the ability of the oppressed to name their world. This capability results from critical thinking following a series of codings and decodings that allow the oppressed to understand their limited situations and to try to transform them. The postcolonial imaginary, to which Freire is readily linked, grew out of precisely this need to understand and represent oppressive situations—and to represent them through media as varied as literature, pamphlets, posters, music, theater, radio, cassette tapes, loud speakers, telephones, television, and film. These media have been used to explore the possibility of a narrative or a discourse, however hybrid and syncretic, arising from within, rather than being imposed from the outside. They also offer an amazing ability to creators to be critical of the media used and to remain sensitive to local traditions of storytelling. The Kenyan-born Ngũgĩ wa Thiong'o switched to Gikuyu from English in many of his stories. Musicians all over the developing worlds have articulated through song and dance their everyday oppression. Cassette tapes with low production costs have been hugely important in conveying these new narratives. Freedom music in South Africa was the sine qua non of the struggle against Apartheid and the formation of a black consciousness. "What is Black consciousness?" asks Steve Biko. In a passage that harkens to Paulo Freire and Frantz Fanon, Biko declares: "At the heart of this kind of thinking is the realisation by blacks that the most potent weapon at the hands of the oppressor is the mind of the oppressed" (Biko 1973).

To deny that a cultural voice is necessary to overcome the conditions of oppression would be callous and, in fact, cruel . The belief, too, that all creativity is cultural is fraught with problems. Creativity may beget cultural politics but, equally, it may also make us question them. Tosca's Rome as depicted by Puccini upholds the musical expressions of its times but also questions the purposes of the state. Nicassio (1999, 5) notes that most Romans actually liked the republic of 1800 depicted in Tosca. However, Puccini used musical language a century later to question papal and state authority. Political authority will always find a compelling case for marshalling art for a variety of purposes but art, in return, will not always comply. Some art stirs discontent—it makes its witnesses unfit to play their roles and do the work the state wants done. Other artworks implant and support habits and attitudes the state finds congenial or thinks necessary for its own goals (Becker 1986/2000, 166). The relationship between art and patronage, public or private, is similarly complex and full of intended and unintended causes and effects.

Creative practices and cultural politics are connected, but in complex and multifaceted ways. For example, identities other than national cultural identities are also questioned in art. Tolstoy's *Anna Karenina* and Pushkin's Tatiana question gender roles, aristocratic cultures, and the divide between rural and urban. Premchand's *Nirmala* and Ba's *So Long a Letter* question colonialism, class, and gender. Art can question cultural identities, or it can simply reinforce them. To specify only a commercial reason for the stifling of cultural voices seems narrow, if not irresponsible. For every artwork that reinforces an identity, there is another that questions it. Postmodern artistic practices even unravel the idea of a coherent subject or identity even when confined to an individual, let alone an entire group. Instead, we are left with notions of decentered or fragmented subjects. Early examples of an impending postmodernity include the atonal scale, a Rauschenberg collage, or a nonlinear literary narrative. It is this postmodernity that Umberto Eco explores in his language of fragmented signs.

Sociologists often delink the practical and everyday from the languages and causes that named it so.[2] What now seems self-apparent was at one time constructed as anything *but* self-apparent. Thus, what we call a porcelain toilet is different from a marble water fountain. Or is it? This is precisely Marcel Duchamp's idea in elevating the urinal to a work of art and making us question the arbitrary and constructed languages we use to call something art. The Dadaist movement, with which Duchamp is associated, was explicitly anticulturalist in its deconstructions. Duchamp unravels the power of art institutions and institutionalized taste, themselves important to various conceptions of cultural identity.

The analysis above is a critique of neither the creative nor the cultural; it is merely a cautionary tale about keeping the two separate. Without art we would not topple dictatorships; at the same time, these regimes have employed great artists to reify their own dictatorial designs. Leni Riefenstahl's images glorifying Hitler are as etched on the historical consciousness as is Alexander Solzhenitsyn's *Gulag Archipelago* or George Orwell's *1984*.

Anglo-Saxon politics are often credited with keeping the creative and the cultural distinct. The Arts Council of the United Kingdom and the National Endowment for the Arts in the United States are independent arts-funding agencies designed to keep political interference at a minimum. But, as chapters 2 and 4 show, bureaucrats face heavy incentives to comply with the state that employs them or to employ experts in order to elevate institutionalized patterns of artistry and taste. Arts funding, therefore, is often critiqued for supporting high arts such as the symphony or the opera rather than street art and popular culture, although all may be important for creative expression.

Countries favoring creative-industry policies take caution in general in distinguishing creative industries from cultural policies. Often, this is carried out in the name of the economic importance of the arts. Tony Blair, former prime minister of the United Kingdom, supported a program for a "Creative Britain" or "Creative London" at the turn of the century, emphasizing the economic potential of creative industries in the United Kingdom. Arts lobbying groups in the United States similarly point to the arts as a legitimate and important economic activity in their petitioning for state funding. Thus, the $50 million in funding that arts groups received from the Obama administration legitimized artists "as part of the American workforce" in the words of the new NEA chairman, Patrice Walker Powell (Chang 2009). Worldwide, the copyright industry program at the World Intellectual Property Organization or the United Nations Conference on Trade and Development also speaks to the economic importance of creative industries (WIPO 2006; UNCTAD 2008). At a conceptual level, Florida (2002) and Currid (2007) underscore similar ideas. Both speak to the conditions of freedom, talent, and imagination that inform the creative classes and the environments that encourage them.

The distinctions that keep the creative and the cultural separate are not without their critics. Three critiques are often advanced with a view toward shaping cultural policies: that the arts are more than an economic activity; that the creative industry is broader in scope than cultural representations; and that the creative industry is too commercialized and its internal logic drives it toward economies of scale in domination and production and, therefore, homogenization and commodification rather than diversity. I take up each in turn.

First, as noted in chapter 2, art embodies various types of value, from the purely symbolic to the highly economic. Johannisson (2010) notes that the market-oriented economic discourses in policy must be balanced against the more humanistic and sociological discourses that preserve aesthetic values and broaden participation in the arts. Johannisson also acknowledges that these three types of discourse often coexist within various policy streams, although one might dominate the others. From this perspective, Florida's definition of the creative class—which grows through technology, talent, and tolerance—goes far beyond the economic design to which it is often relegated. Florida, in fact, ends by asking the following questions: "What do we *really* want? What kind of life—and what kind of society—do we want to bequeath to coming generations?" (2002, 325). Similarly, Currid's thesis about the creative "Warhol economy" in New York City is ultimately about defining the contours of individual and group identities through aesthetics and design rather than through finance and Wall Street. Thus, the case for thinking of arts as more than just an economic activity is made from both ends of the ideological spectrum, although one end always thinks the other is complicit in not going far enough.

The second critique aims at keeping creative industries distinct from cultural industries by showing that the output of cultural activities is primarily aesthetic even if provided through commercial means (for example, Broadway theater). This view asserts that creative industries tend to move toward design elements that include aesthetic considerations but are primarily geared toward other utilitarian functions, such as tourism, textile design or fashion, toys and games, and architecture. However, as noted in the introduction and chapter 1, the use of the terms "creative" versus "cultural" in this book is altogether different. "Creative" here stands for *aesthetic* activities assigned a particular intellectual property at both individual and group levels, even when the aesthetic is anti-art, as in the Dadaist movement. Meanwhile, the "cultural" is the group *identity* around these creative endeavors. As shown in the previous chapters, the move from the creative to the cultural entails deliberative politics. While I do not intend to provide any kind of a final word on the old distinction between creative and the cultural as design versus aesthetics, it seems to me that the distinctions are arbitrary, especially in digital environments and as more and activities take on commercial aspects. Drucker (2005, 247) notes, for example, that even the most progressive and radical fine arts now employ the same production techniques and institutions that conservative and market-oriented artists do: "Fine arts, artists, and critics exist in a condition of complicity with the institutions and values of contemporary culture."

The third critique regarding the economies of scale in production and domination is hard to dispute, especially in the face of overwhelming evidence of the domination of Hollywood's and the music industry's major companies—Sony, EMI, Universal, and Warner—which are organized globally. The extrapolation of such economies of scale is that transnational firms can destroy local creative expressions and can also lead to the commodification of every type of cultural activity. The latter, it seems to me, is an ideological position. The trope of commodification is often employed, as it has been since Adorno and Horkheimer's thesis, to show that commodification is a capitalist ideology, making the creative increasingly more commercial and divesting it of its imaginative and aesthetic aspects. However, the claim can hardly be dismissed as ideology alone. Liberal commentators such as Bill Ivey (2008), the former head of the National Endowment for the Arts, point out that copyright, the lack of public policy in the arts, and the increasing domination of entertainment industries are destroying the cultural life of the United States. Even libertarians such as Tyler Cowen worry that the long-run cost curves of broadcasting industries entail that they can dump relatively cheap programs on global and national markets. It is precisely maneuvers such as these that led to the audio-visual impasse at the WTO in 1993 and the framing of the UNESCO Convention on the Protection and Promotion of the Diversity of Cultural Expressions in 2005.

These three critiques have led globally to impassioned cultural debates as the ranks of cultural ministries and creative industries continue to grow. While we would have cause to worry about the decreasing diversity and increasing commodification of creative products, there is also enough empirical evidence presented here to caution us on two things. First, cultural politics are vulnerable to the influence of dominant cultural or creative groups, which may or may not lead to diversity or the lack of commodification. Therefore, one must examine cultural politics for the kinds of deliberations that they offer. Second, a blanket cultural policy that bans commodification or homogenization is impossible, if not laughable. We need policies that carefully encourage local production and distribution as well as participation in creative and aesthetic activities. The next section, therefore, attends to deliberative cultural politics and resultant cultural policies.

Toward Deliberative Cultural Politics and Policies

Creative products and expressions are different from cultural products. A sense of group identity is bestowed upon a cultural product, and it is tacitly or explicitly accepted as such by group members. Cultural politics refer to the deliberative processes through which questions of identity surrounding creative expressions are settled. Cultural policies are the result and can be understood as policies encouraging particular types of identity or specific measures that seek to encourage them.

There are two important considerations for cultural politics and policies: Who decides, and what is decided? While each question is answered separately here, a common normative thread links them: cultural politics and policies are ideally located in trust, transparency, and inclusion among the stakeholders and participants. As chapter 1 notes, the presence of these three elements in any kind of politics ensures that the resulting policies reflect problem posing and due consideration to multiple perspectives. The conceptual framework supporting such deliberations was detailed in the introductory chapters. The rest of this conclusion attends to the cultural policy outcomes posed in the four empirical chapters of this volume.

Table 7.1 summarizes the qualitative deliberative elements from the previous chapters. States seem to dominate cultural politics in most countries, with varying degrees of input from industry groups. Civil-society groups and individuals are mostly marginalized unless states invite them to participate. This holds true regardless of whether, from an international perspective, the policies are protectionist or trade-oriented. Thus commercialization, something that creative industries tend to favor, can happen regardless of whether the industry groups are protectionist or internationalist. The only difference is whether this commercialization favors domestic groups or international networks. This macrolevel snapshot does not capture all the nuances and complexities of international cultural politics discussed earlier, but it does allow two conclusions: cultural politics are largely exclusionary in most places, and the resulting cultural policies may or may not address the underlying problems that creative industries face. At a broad level, if creative diversity is desired, it is unclear how blanket protectionism or, in a few cases, trade policies will help diversity. They could even choke the process of diversification if production capacities are lacking in a particular context. On the other hand, if the aim is to distribute one's own products, it might be necessary to forge links or incentives to join global networks. Scott (2008, 319) notes that French-language films are stymied less in their production capacities than by the "competitive deficiencies of French film and marketing systems outside of France." Scott advocates that the French state ought to subsidize film distribution rather than production.

Creative-industry scholars and practitioners now accept that creative and cultural products are linked, but they are careful in advocating umbrella

TABLE 7.1

Cultural Politics and Policies

	CULTURAL POLITICS			CULTURAL POLICIES
	DEGREE OF TRUST	DEGREE OF TRANSPARENCY	DEGREE OF INCLUSIVITY	
Chapters 3–4: UNESCO-WTO debates	Fraught with us versus-them posturing: United States versus France-Canada	Deliberations fairly well publicized and known to stakeholders	Dominated by member states; perspectives from industry groups and academic experts	WTO: liberalization UNESCO: protectionism
Chapter 4: Developing-country perspectives	Ranging from mistrust of state to entrusting it with encouraging creative industries	Limited information made available	States decide; in some cases, limited input from industries; civil society groups ignored or uninvolved	Prioritization of creative/cultural policies; capacity building; access to global networks
Chapter 5: Cultural tourism	Debates worldwide on causes and consequences of cultural tourism	Biggest industry in the world, yet deliberations on tourism policies seldom publicized	Heterogeneity of cultural-tourism operations and preponderance of states ward against effective inclusion	Liberal and open policies welcoming tourists

policies in the name of the cultural. Tania Voon's recent volume on controversies surrounding international flows of cultural products accepts that
creative products are important for cultural identity and other social values
then turns to international measures that have been enacted to protect
these values (Voon 2007). She finds the existing set of measures address-
ing trade and cultural values to be insufficient or ambiguous not only at the
WTO or its predecessor, GATT, but also at the UNESCO. Her broad policy
prescription emerging from a survey of these measures is quite intuitive:
protect creative industries for the sake of producing unique cultural content or for the sake of diversity, but be careful of taking measures that only
make economic sense in terms of protecting cultural industries for their
own sake or to restrict trade. In other words, economic and cultural values
in creative products are compatible and Janus-faced rather than fighting
and incompatible twins.

Voon (2007, 50) notes that "justifications for government intervention
based on the special nature of cultural products *per se* are more likely to
endure than decrying the dominance of US cultural industries." She concludes by noting that the "the new scale of international trade has made
cultural homogenization a significant concern about globalization" (248).
The idea that the case for intervention *should* be made on the special nature
of creative products is apt: preserve and boost your own industries rather
than decrying those of others; enact measures that help with these goals
rather than merely restricting trade. A similarly compelling case can be
made for protecting and promoting social and cultural values through the
products that embody them.

Nevertheless, we also know that "protecting" diversity may be unnecessary; after all, cultural products are naturally hybrid and are thus, in some
sense, oblivious or immune to protection (Cowen 2002; García Canclini
1995). Tsutsumibayashi (2005, 110) goes further: efforts to protect cultural diversity could misfire and stymie the emergence of a global ethos
that facilitates intercultural dialogues and understandings. "Although it
is important to respect cultural diversity, since the alternative is cultural
hegemony or uniformity, too much emphasis on cultural diversity not
only could hinder the creation of a shared ethos but could, ironically, also
undermine cultural diversity itself by imposing uniformity within a so-
called cultural unit."

It is also empirically questionable whether a case for bridging the trade
and culture divide *can* be made solely on the basis of the "special nature"

of these products and not on "decrying the dominance of US cultural industries." The case for restricting trade in creative products has been made and will continue to be made directly and indirectly with reference to U.S. dominance. Hollywood is the dernier cri of critics—not just of creative industry trade but also of trade as a whole. It offers a framing device for the politics of collective action that underlie trade policy measures. When Jack Lang, the former culture minister of France, warned of a wall-to-wall *Dallas* during the Uruguay Round of trade talks (1986–94), he made his case by invoking Hollywood.

The emerging trend in thinking about cultural-policy instruments may be understood, at least at the microlevel, to favor policies designed to generate specific outcomes. Too often cultural politics focus on creative products and their effects, as they should, but in banning particular types of products, they commit a logical fallacy: banning products does not necessarily encourage creative production at "home." More appropriately, creative products follow a specific value chain, emerging from the creative imagination and moving through production, distribution, consumption, and finally into archiving and preservation (see figure 5.1). A few policies that might speak to specific aspects of the value chain are described in table 7.2. The table also lists representative works that speak to these policies along with a few measures that have been enacted to implement them. A preliminary list matching instruments and objectives must be illustrative rather than exhaustive, but it underscores the point that creative expressions and diversity are spurred by tailored cultural instruments rather than by umbrella cultural policies.

At the macrolevel, we will continue to witness dramatic articulations of threats to cultural identity and accusations regarding cultural domination and imperialism. This is understandable in an age driven by cultural anxieties and perceived losses to local or national identity. However, a robust response to these anxieties must involve—rigorously and effectively—the voices of the various communities that perceive threats to their ways of life. State policies designed to isolate communities from global flows and the resulting cultural hybridities will be unsuccessful and short-lived.[3] States have an incentive to delineate the borders of their national cultural identities. A first step toward divorcing such crude political objectives from creative-expression policies moves arts funding and instruments away from direct and continual legislative influences, toward independent creative-arts agencies and institutions. The ideal type in this volume

TABLE 7.2

Cultural Policy Targets and Instruments: A Value-Chain Perspective

CREATIVE VALUE CHAIN AND TARGET	POLICY OBJECTIVES AND INSTRUMENTS	EXAMPLES AND EXEMPLARS
Creative imagination	1. Tolerance and freedom 2. Creative flows and hybridity 3. Preserving arts in conflict 4. Security of life for artists	1. Creative cities (Florida 2002) 2. Openness to commerce (Cowen 1998) 3. Open cities during World War II; artist communes 4. Laws governing freedom of expression; grants and institutions encouraging creative expressions
Production	1. Existence of creative industry infrastructures and talent 2. Security of property rights governing creative production 3. Subsidies to cover revenue deficits and increasing costs of arts (Baumol's cost disease) 4. Creation of production capacities and institutions, esp. in developing worlds	1. Creative Britain (DCMS 2001) 2. Laws protecting options and incentives contracts (Caves 2002, Vogel 2007) 3. Numerous arts-agency policies from local to international levels (Cummings and Katz 1987); tax incentives for philanthropy and charitable donations (O'Hare, Feld, and Shuster 1983) 4. Emphasis in most national creative industry plans (UNCTAD 2008)
Distribution	1. Encouraging arts festivals 2. Access to distribution networks through institutional support 3. Subsidies or grants for creating or accessing distribution networks	1. Rationalizing demand and supply (Frey 2003); inclusion and expressions (Snowball and Webb, 2008) 2. Creating arts/creative-product distribution agencies such as South Africa's National Film and Video Foundation
Exhibition	1. State and market incentives for creating exhibition spaces 2. Cultural-tourism policies for exhibiting heritage	1. State led cultural policies 2. Tourism campaigns world wide (OECD 2008)
Archiving and preservation	1. Copyrights laws 2. Creative Commons 3. Creation of physical and digital archives	1. TRIPS and national copyright legislations (Watal 2001) 2. Creativecommons.org 3. National museums (Garcia Canclini 1995)

Note: The distinctions among constituent elements of the value chain can be arbitrary. The rationale for intellectual property, for example, is often located in rewarding imagination rather than in archiving and preserving it. UNESCO (2009) writes of a value circle rather than a chain connecting various elements to one another.

favors communities finding their cultural voices through reasoned delib-erations and building confident community identities.[4] However, the gap between community representations and elite deliberations is still quite wide in cultural policies across the world.

Our global anxieties can only be resolved through some delineation of multiculturalism in our daily lives: at a minimum the multicultural person spans and transcends several cultural boundaries while forming a sense of individual or social worth (Adler 1998). A multicultural person or commu-nity is networked with others but maintains distinct and flexible identities. Thus, in choosing among various types of patronage or market networks for creative expressions, the notion of networks must be maintained. If cultural policies specify arbitrary boundaries around culture, they will in-crease global anxieties in the long run. Fortunately, for every artifice that elevates one isolated identity, there's another that contests it. A wall or a fence confronts a bridge or a tunnel. Such is art!

Notes

Introduction: The Creative Voice and Cultural Identity

1. The cultural critic Lee E. Heller (1992, 340), writes that the gothic novel, in general, or Frankenstein in particular "reflects different cultural anxieties, focused around the kinds of disorder to which the community felt vulnerable."

2. See also Thussu (2008).

3. Huntington (1993), Barber (1995), Jameson and Miyoshi (2004).

4. This definition closely tracks that of Throsby (2001, 112–14), but I depart from his understanding by not necessarily equating the creative with the cultural and by including cultural tourism as an affiliated rather than an ancillary activity.

5. See, for example, Hesmondhalgh (2007) for cultural industries and DCMS (2001) for use of the term "creative industries" in similar terms as this book

6. On the positive correlation between markets and diversity of creative expressions, see Cowen 1998, 2000, 2006. For its pathology, see Miller and Yúdice 2000. Most critical understanding of cultural industries can be traced to Horkheimer and Adorno (1947/2002) who deployed this term to showcase the hidden exploitative nature of capitalism through the propagation of a mass consumer culture.

7. In detailing cultural politics, this book is indebted to political scientists such as Mulcahy and Wyszomirski (1995), Bradford, Gary, and Wallach (2000), Goff (2007), and Cherbo, Stewart, and Wyszomirski (2008), who have examined either the politics or the institutions involved in cultural policymaking. Broadly, it also leans upon

sociologists and communication scholars who speak to globalization and identity, such as Hannerz (1996), García Canclini (2001), Kraidy (2005), and political theorists concerned with the politics of cultural identity in general (Benhabib 2002).

1. Cultural Politics and Global Anxieties

1. The idea of a nonoppressed cultural voice comes from Freire. Its use in a market-driven context is informed by my own work on Freire's ideas (Singh 2008a).

2. The European Union came into being in 1992. Between 1985 and 1992, it was the European Community, and before that the European Economic Community. When referring to a particular period, I use the relevant appellation; in general, the term European Union is used here.

3. Arguably, Beethoven and Pink Floyd are both important in questioning authority but, curiously, the cultural elite often only emphasize the Beethoven concert.

4. Ruggie (1993) and Spruyt (1996) show that the nation-state was among the many solutions available for organizing and representing territoriality. As with creative expressions and identity, the final solution depended on imagination and politics.

5. For analysis of differences in negotiated outcomes resulting from diffused versus concentrated power and of the various types of power discussed in this section, see Singh 2008b. Stokes (1998) calls attention to the "pathologies of deliberations" resulting from those with materials resources. For further explanation on the role of metapower in cultural representations, see Singh (2010a).

6. This notion parallel notions of democracy described in termed of deliberations (Elster 1998) and discursive pluralism (Dryzek and Niemeyer 2008).

7. Power understood in the instrumental sense is control of resources to effect particular outcomes. Its obverse, structural power, constrains particular outcomes.

8. See Freire (1970/2000), and Habermas (1985, 1976).

9. Benhabib (1996, 68) holds "democratic legitimacy" and "unconstrained public deliberation of all about maters of common concern" to be almost coterminous.

10. Obama's comment was made on April 6, 2008, at a fundraiser in San Francisco as he sought to explain his difficulty in winning working-class and rural votes in Pennsylvania and the Midwest among people who are anxious about their economic conditions and job losses. He said: "And it's not surprising then that they get bitter, they cling to guns or religion or antipathy to people who aren't like them or anti-immigrant sentiment or anti-trade sentiment as a way to explain their frustrations." The comments were first reported in *The Huffington Post*, where the full text of the Obama speech can be found: http://www.huffingtonpost .com/mayhill-fowler/obama-no-surprise-that-ha_b_96188.html.

11. Of course, even where it does not lead to anger, the interlocutors might still feel a lack of authenticity or loss of innocence. "I think of the postmodern attitude as that of a man who loves a very cultivated woman and cannot say to her, 'I love you madly,' because he knows that she knows (and that she knows he knows) that these words have already been written by Barbara Cartland. Still, there is a solution. He can say, 'as Barbara Cartland would put it, I love you madly.' At this point, having avoided false innocence, having said clearly that it is no longer possible to speak innocently, he will nevertheless have said what he wanted to say to the woman: that the loves her, but he loves her in an age of lost innocence" (Eco 1995, 32).

12. If is often argued that performing and fine arts need public support much more than entertainment industries such as cinema and television that have commercial viability.

13. In an extreme version, identity is totally defined through acts of commercial consumption. Walker (2008, 8) asserts that people buy brand-name products to assuage their helplessness and isolation. "A potent brand becomes a form of identity in shorthand."

14. At a more general level, Price (2008) notes that morality in world politics must be adjudged according to some sense of empirical and deliberative progress rather than a moral absolute. He notes that critical theory, often informed by radical analyses, often clings to such absolutes.

15. In formal terms, the dependent variable in this book is cultural policies regarding identity, which varies from being singularly defined to being hybrid. When singular, patronage systems are usually the dominant form of cultural policies; hybridity reveals the intersection of state patronage and market incentives in cultural policies.

16. Wendt (1992) noted that anarchy in itself cannot help us predict the way nations would interact. The way nations constitute particular practices within anarchy is, therefore, important.

17. See Glazer 1997; Said 1978. Interesting debates also took place *within* particular ideologies. See Ahmad (1987) and Jameson (1986) on the left and Bloom (1988).

18. A few representative works may be listed: Birnbaum 2001; Khilnani 2001; Shumway 2001. Most accounts pay homage in to the historian Benedict Anderson, who examined the epistemic process of national-identity formation in the wake of print capitalism in local markets (1983).

19. Worldpublicopinion.org, "World Public Favors Globalization and Trade but Wants to Protect Environment and Jobs," April 25, 2007, http://www.worldpublicopinion.org/pipa/articles/btglobalizationtradera/349.php?lb=btgl&pnt=349&nid =&id=. Accessed January 9, 2009.

20. Worldpublicopinion.org, "Africans and Asians Tend to View Globalization Favorably; Europeans and Americans are More Skeptical," November 7, 2006,

http://www.worldpublicopinion.org/pipa/articles/btglobalizationtradera/273.php?l
b=btgl&pnt=273&nid=&id=. Accessed January 9, 2009.

21. See www.pollingreport.com/trade. Recent surveys also find a slight drop in support for the free market system, especially as the global slowdown began in 2007. See, for example, Worldpublicopnion.org, "Erosion of Support for Free Market System: global Poll." April 15, 2008, http://www.worldpublicopinion.org/pipa/articles/btglobalizationtradera/471.php?lb=btgl&pnt=471&nid=&id=. Accessed January 9, 2009.

22. Worldpublicopinion.org, "Muslims Positive About Globalization, Trade," August 27, 2008, http://www.worldpublicopinion.org/pipa/articles/btglobalizationtradera/528.php?lb=btgl&pnt=528&nid=&id=. Accessed January 9, 2009. The six countries where the sample noted that the effects of globalization are considered "mostly good" were Egypt (79 percent), Nigeria (78 percent), Azerbaijan (63 percent), Indonesia (61 percent), Iran (61 percent), and the Palestinian territories (58 percent). The exception was Turkey, with only 39 percent support.

23. "Europeans Want Tests for Immigrants," *FT*, December 14, 2007.

24. Scholars in the English school of international relations have long debated whether an international society made up of national identities is giving way to a world society with cosmopolitan populations (Linklater and Suganami 2006; Buzan 2004). Hannerz (1992) settles for a version of complex cosmopolitanism while others note that global humanity is an elite notion with which an isolated farmer in the developing world cannot empathize (Mazlish 2008).

2. Value, Markets, Patronage

1. Whether this music was secularized or Sanskritized is contested. The latter notion speaks to creation of a vocabulary of national heritage that goes back through history and asserts particular arts forms to be "pure" representations of this heritage (Gaston 1996).

2. Similar sentiments about art can be found throughout the history of economic thought. See Goodwin (2006).

3. For the former position, see Cowen (1998, 2002, 2006).

4. For these and other concepts of value, also see Hutter and Throsby (2008).

5. See Miller and Yúdice (2002, 7–12), for summary of literature on taste.

6. See Plattner (2003) for overview.

7. In the same vein, Polanyi (1944) wrote forcefully that even laissez-faire was invented and collectively understood by its practitioners.

8. See also Ekelund and Tollison (1997, chapter 4) for ideas regarding venal society.

9. Also see Andrault and Dressayre (1987), in the same volume.

10. Nevertheless, the Medici were as adept at controlling painters and sculptors to glorify the family's power, as the ancient *nobiles* in Rome used poets to mobilize voters in their favor. See Kent (2000) for Medici accounts and Williams (1982).

11. While Granovetter writes that sociological analysis differs substantially from neoclassical analysis, this may not be the case, as new institutional economics and its emphasis on cultural practices shows. Granovetter's mentor Harrison White has also shown (2008) that social forms and culture are themselves responses to uncertainty and the vicissitudes of life. Neither White nor Douglass North can be accused of functionalism as neither indicates that efficient social structures or economic institutions will always emerge, as in arguments based on the survival of the fittest. Cultural-path dependency can sustain inefficient processes for a long period of time.

12. The historical Hollywood studio system and current Hollywood films are often accused by their critics of using formulas. Hollywood's aesthetic style—long shots for context, close shots for story development—are also seen as formulaic.

13. Auber's *La Muette de Portici* from 1828 is widely accepted to be the first great enunciation of the grand opera style.

14. In this sense, according to Adorno, opera performed the functions that would be taken over by cinema in the twentieth century; cited in Gerhard (1998, 22).

15. See also Barbier (1995) and the Charlton (2003) for the social and political contexts in which grand opera grew.

16. See Kent (2000) for an account of Cosimo de Medici's patronage.

17. As noted in the last chapter, while there is a positive correlation between the market and diversity, my intent in this book is to highlight the politics underlying cultural policies rather than measuring their effects in terms of diversity.

18. Recent accounts of Florentine growth are not as praiseworthy. Emigh (2008) shows that urban growth in Florence impoverished rural Tuscan areas.

19. Balfe (1993) reaches similar conclusions.

20. See detailed explanations in Caves (2000) across various creative industries. As an aside, even these complex contractual forms are embedded in cultural understandings. Fine arts and design schools now regularly teach students how to survive in these complex environments. The enforceability of these contracts is often dependent on a reputation system rather than police power, although glamorous disputes concerning royalty payments and the like are often the subject of media attention.

21. Costs were as high as $200,000 per MIPS (millions of instructions per second) on a mainframe when introduced; they were less than $100 per MIPS on a PC by 1995 and were expected to decline to a few dollars per MIPS by 2010.

22. An early version of the globalization of copyright issues can be found in Putnam (1896).

23. For links between artists' property rights and copyright, see Rushton (2003, 2001).

24. My thanks to Arjun S. Ravi for introducing me to the independent music industry and bands and their relation to the music majors.

25. http://en.wikipedia.org/wiki/Colbie_Cailat, accessed May 2, 2009.

26. See, for example: http://blog.cleveland.com/metro/2009/04/seventyfive _people_rally_to_cr.html, accessed May 2, 2009. The original music video can be found at: http://www.youtube.com/watch?v=C5r4Oz4Nt20.

27. "Glocalism" originated in business practices in the mid-1990s to connote transnational and local community practices. Rosenau (1997) coins the term "fragmegration."

28. See Kim and Hart (2002) for an overview.

29. For an economic perspective on the formation of taste, see Throsby (2001, 114–16). For a progressive account of the construction of taste in producing docile subjects, see Yúdice and Miller (2002, 7–12).

3. Culture Wars

1. However, UNESCO's estimates are conservative, gathered from custom receipts that, for example, count the original value of a film as it crosses customs but not the balance of payments that accrue from licenses and royalties, which in turn produce major receipts for the motion picture or the television industry worldwide. One estimate calculated the value derived from intellectual property (including patents, copyrights, trademarks, and industrial designs) at $2.24 trillion in 1999 of which the U.S. share was 40 percent. MPAA (2006) estimates that total worldwide box-office receipts were $23.24 billion in 2005, up from $17 billion in 2001. Because Hollywood dominates worldwide exports, a large chunk of this $23 billion accrued to the United States and does not show up in the audio-visual figures provided by the UNESCO. Scott (2008) notes that Hollywood earned almost $9 billion from exports of film and tape rentals in 2000.

2. For an excellent history of Hollywood's export drive from 1920 to 1950, see Jarvie (1992). See De Grazia (2005) for the way the United States has used its cultural products in general to become an "irresistible empire." However, the United States is not alone in this. Katzenstein (2005, chapter 5) discusses the role of cultural products in the diplomacy between Germany and Japan. Nye (2004), concerning soft power, has ignited those who believe cultural diplomacy is important in resolving conflicts.

3. This paragraph builds on Jeancolas (1998).

4. See Van Grasstek (2006); Voon (2007); Singh (2010b).

5. See Feld (2001) for an understanding of intellectual property issues underlying world music, wherein Western artists repackaged and sold folksongs in the developing world. Outside of cultural products, two well-known cases are Texmati

Rice, which made a minor modification on basmati rice seed found in the Himalayas, and the neem tree, which has several medicinal qualities. Courts sided with Texmati in United States but not in Europe. Neem tree patents were denied in the United States as well.

6. See Rushton (2003) for overview of these issues.

7. As earnings from creative products come from intangibles such as license fees and royalties, they are considered services rather than goods in world trade definitions.

8. The MFN clause in international trade means that no nation is to be discriminated in application of trade measures. An MFN exemption thus allows Europeans to discriminate against any nation, in this case the United States.

9. This chapter does not assume that surpluses in trade will help to protect cultural diversity. Subsequent sections will show that many developing countries continue to produce culturally hybrid products that take advantage of globalization processes.

10. Philippines has long served as a source for architectural drafting. India and Taiwan are emerging as animation powerhouses. Video games are a big export from countries such as Korea and China.

11. Statistics cited from http://www.mpaa.org/researchStatistics.asp. Accessed March 4, 2009.

12. For the former position, see Goff (2007). For the latter, see Cowen (2002) and Kraidy (2005). For cultural studies perspectives on both issues, see King (1997), Jameson and Miyoshi (2004), and Yúdice (2004).

13. Based on interviews. Interestingly, the agreement was enforced by Centre national du cinéma et de l'image animée. CNC is responsible for the state aid given to film industry by a tax on box-office receipts and, from 1984 onward, a tax on TV network profits. These taxes on receipts and profits would become an issue during the Uruguay Round.

14. Of course, the idea of a European cultural identity was itself a framing device to help constitute this sense of identity. See Berezin and Schain (1999) for interesting context on this issue.

15. Robert (2000, 88), notes that Prime Minister Wilson similarly played a Canadian "unity card" in the midst of a constitutional crisis at home.

16. Interviews, June 2001–2007.

17. Only three developed countries are included: the United States, Japan, and New Zealand.

18. See Ross (1995) for the way Delors centralized the EC and exercised influence over its matters. The Delors presidency was thus quite different from that of Jacques Santer, who did not enforce such centralization.

19. The EC usually reflects member-state competencies, and the unanimity rule binds them to do so. In the past, the EC has usually played an entrepreneurial role in those areas where the member states lack competencies. This was the case with

intellectual property (TRIPS) and Internet domain name negotiations. The role of the Directorate General on Culture in playing an entrepreneurial role is unusual and has to do with the alliance of interests within its staff with the French position and, during the Uruguay Round, the Delors presidency.

20. *Washington Times*, November 24, 1994.

21. Interviews, 2001–2005.

22. Mickey Kantor was the U.S. trade representative during the audio-visual negotiation. The European Union representatives were Leon Brittan, EU commissioner for external relations, and Jonathan Scheele, the EU official responsible for negotiating services

23. *Washington Times*, November 24, 1993. Upon his death on April 26, 2007, several newspapers quoted Valenti's colorful language and noted the effect he had on Hollywood's global affairs. *The Guardian*, for example, noted: "During frequent trips to Europe, Valenti would stay at the embassies of US ambassadors while pursuing Hollywood's own foreign policy 'with the authority to negotiate on its own terms with governments' as he grandly defined it. His vociferous insistence on Tinseltown's rights to unimpeded free trade nearly wrecked world trade talks (GATT) in Geneva in 1993. Accusations of American cultural imperialism merely inspired Valenti to deliver lectures on the priority of freedom of expression" (April 30, 2007).

24. Writings on Paris as the locus of European identity go back to Victor Hugo.

25. Interview, Paris, June 2001.

26. Interviews, July–August 2001.

27. Interview, July 2001.

28. Lax and Sebenius (1986, 69, 231–32), suggests avoiding fundamental clashes in interest by focusing on issues instead.

29. Interview, October 2003.

30. Interview, November 2003.

31. Based on interviews.

32. A trade-off may have come into play in the endgame. In exchange for U.S. acquiescence on the cultural MFN exemption, the EU agreed to support Washington's demand for an eighteen-month exemption from the Uruguay Round obligation to open its markets to Asian financial services. (Washington was feeling pressure from banks and insurance firms on allowing foreign competition into the U.S. markets when they were not allowed to enter the foreign markets.) The Europeans also withdrew pressure for concessions on the protected maritime market in the United States.

4. UNESCO and the Europeans

1. Based on interviews, July 2005

2. In actuality, the push for antipiracy measures has also been divisive. The MPAA was squarely behind these moves in late 2009, but the RIAA was already beginning to back off.

3. World Trade Organization, "Proposals for the New Negotiations," http://www.wto.org/english/tratop_e/serv_e/s_propnewnegs_e.htm, accessed October 8, 2003.

4. Kantor (2004) cites a study estimating a $5.4 billion loss to film industry via piracy, calling it "a practice that is on the verge of exploding."

5. This paragraph based on interviews with various officials in Paris and Brussels, 2004–7.

6. Directive 89/552/EEC, adopted in October 1989 and amended June 1997 by directive 97/36/EC.

7. UNESCO, "Creative Industries," http://ortalo.unesco.org/culture/admin/ev.php?URL_ID=2461&URL_DO=DO_TOPIC&URL_SECTION=-512. Accessed May 1, 2007.

8. The MAI would have had a weak legal basis, and so U.S. and industry support for it became lukewarm. See Graham (2000).

9. Excerpt attributed to France and cited in Neil (1997).

10. Based on an interview with former OECD official, May 2007.

11. Based on an interview with former OECD official, May 2007, and Neil (1997).

12. See Sauvé and Stern (2000) for overview.

13. See www.incp-ripc.org and www.unesco.org/culture/pluralism/diversity.

14. Other declarations regularly cited by INCP include the Communiqué of the Summit of the G-8 in Okinawa, Japan, July 2000; the Declaration of the Summit of the Americas at Québec City, April 2001; the Declaration and Plan of Action of Cartegna de Indias adopted by Organization of American States, July 2002; and the Dakar Declaration on the Promotion of African Caribbean Pacific Cultures and Cultural Industries, June 2003. See INCP (2003).

15. France's support for cinema in Francophone countries via CNC is already well known. Recently, CNC is moving toward supporting cinema in non-Francophone countries and in languages other than French.

16. http://portal.unesco.org/culture/en/ev.php-URL_ID=33232&URL_DO=DO_TOPIC&URL_SECTION=201.html#III, accessed March 10, 2009.

17. See http://portal.unesco.org/culture/en/ev.php-URL_ID=35405&URL_DO=DO_TOPIC&URL_SECTION=201.html, accessed November 15, 2009.

18. Based on interviews in Paris and Brussels at French government agencies, the EU, and UNESCO, July 2005. Several groups within the INCD now view the draft convention to be too weak to be either meaningful or enforceable. One UNESCO official summed up many provisions of the convention as being symbolically rather than substantively important.

19. Philosophically, the French state's legitimacy in arguing for cultural diversity can be questioned. Historically, the state has a dismal record in accepting or promoting multiculturalism and remains uneasy about being seen as a multicultural society itself (Birnbaum 2001). French officials (based on interviews, 2001–2006) dismiss the notion that just because France has domestic problems does not mean that it cannot speak to cultural diversity issues at the international level. There is also a consensus in French intellectual and political circles that the idea of being French is consistent with the idea of being European, and now international and cosmopolitan. R. Frank (2002) contends that the idea of Europe has always been a tug of war between the French and German notions.

20. Cloonan (2007, 1) provides a review of the creative-industry policies of Blair's New Labor and begins his book by speaking of the politics linking creativity with culture: "This books is about power and powerlessness, politics and politicians, problems and policies." Blair himself declared in 2007 that he had fostered a "golden age" for the arts in Britain, increasing funding for the arts from 186 million pounds in 1997 to 412 million pounds in 2007 (http://www.thisislondon.co.uk/arts/article-23387800-details/Blair:+I+have+fostered+a+golden+age+for+arts/article.do; accessed March 10, 2009).

21. Interview, November 19, 2002.

22. Based on interviews.

23. See Singh (2007) for the position of developing countries in the GATS and UNESCO frameworks.

24. See Deibert (1997) for a reiteration of this story primarily through communication media.

25. Pan-European social movements, diasporic groups, and businesses all feature networked practices.

26. See essays in Berezin and Schain (2003); Wintel (1996).

27. Anthony Smith is often taken to be an exemplar of the primordial approach to local identity, though his analysis is based on emotive affinities rather than primordial stubbornness.

28. The principle of "subsidiarity" in EU cultural policy can be seen as the umbrella concept that deposes higher authorities, as in this case EU, to consult with lower authorities in making decisions (see Gordon 2007, 15, 27–28).

29. Statistics cited in Barrowclough and Kozul-Wright (2008, 7); Gordon (2009, 16).

5. Cultural Patrons in the Developing World

1. For the success of states as an organizational form in Europe, see Spruyt (1996).

2. The term "postcolonial" implies that this literature continues to be shaped by colonial history. However valid that claim may be it ignores many other influences, especially in the current period. I use the terms "postcolonial literature" and "developing-world literature" interchangeably.

3. While these narratives reveal enormous complexity, they are often misunderstood in the West as "national desire" as Frederic Jameson (1986) categorizes the Third World novel. A lively debate ensued as a result of Jameson's intervention. Aijaz Ahmad (1987) shares Jameson's progressive ideals but accuses him of missing the complexity of these narratives, in effect creating an Orientalizing stereotype that accuses the Third World narrative of doing something the Europeans purportedly did in the nineteenth century. In other words, the Third World novelist is here accused of being backward.

4. Not only is the issue of cultural voice brought up in these narratives, but the very medium of the written word is questioned when people like Dungarembga write screenplays and the Senegalese writer Ousmane Sembene moves to film. "Personally, I prefer to read because I learned from reading. But I think that cinema is culturally much more important, and for us in Africa it is an absolute necessity. There is one thing you can't take away from the African masses and that is having seen something" (Ousmane, in Perry et al. 1973, 37)

5. This underscores autonomous evolution from below as opposed to regulated interactions from above. For example, commercial exchanges between postcolonial and developed countries until recent times were heavily governed by the rules made by the latter. Only in recent time has the developing world begun to make these rules in its favor (Singh 2000).

6. Elsewhere (Singh 2002), I conceptualize as metapower the ability of networks to reconfigure, constitute, or reconstitute identities, interests, and institutions.

7. Again, postcolonial literature supports this claim. Chinua Achebe' *Things Fall Apart* and Jorge Amado's *Gabriela, Clove, and Cinnamon* are examples.

8. The idea of development as modernization is now heavily critiqued as the imposition of Eurocentric experiences upon a developing world, a practice in which countless elite scholars and development policymakers and organizations participated. Escobar (1995) calls it "a monologue from the heights of power."

9. For an excellent introduction to development communication, see Mody (2003).

10. A different position was taken by the négritude movement in Africa, which celebrated the continent's blackness in opposition to racism. However, négritude is now critiqued as not distinctively African but a binary response to the racism felt by Africa's elite, such as Léopold Senghor, when they studied in places like Paris. Galvan (2004) writes that in Senegal, négritude was understood in and confined to Dakar.

11. For NWICO debates, see Singh (2010b).

12. Interview May 15, 2006.

13. Soft power is the power to attract or to persuade others with the use of a country's political values and cultural exports. Joseph Nye, who coined the term, wrote an article in the weekly newsmagazine *India Today* arguing that India has an advantage in such soft power processes over China because of India's relatively open society. Nye (2006) concludes: "Despite its problems, it is a safe bet that India's hard and soft powers are likely to rise in the coming times. If India can combine the two successfully, it will be a 'smart power.'"

14. Copied by author, May 12, 2006.

15. Nevertheless, this does not mean that GATS instruments do not need to be amended to account for regulatory and market-based incentives, where necessary to boost creative industries. See Voon (2007) and Goff (2007) for comprehensive context and support for these notions.

16. This may be beginning to change. A recent UNESCO document (2009) acknowledges the role of both design industries and cultural tourism in fostering cultural diversity.

17. For an extension of Freire's ideas to a market-driven context, see Singh (2008b).

18. I am well aware of Freire's misgivings against capitalism, but I assert that there's no a priori epistemological reason that a cultural voice cannot be developed through commercial exchanges. See Singh (2008b).

19. For cultural complexity and transnational linkages, see Hannerz (1992, 1996).

20. Keynote speech given at "Culture and Development: Advancing Equality and Racial Inclusion," Inter-American Development Bank, December 10, 2008.

21. This paragraph also borrows its findings from Bouzas and Soltz (2005).

22. That networks are key to promoting tourism is borne out in a recent *Economist* article (2008), which notes that gay tourism now accounts for 25 percent of Argentinean tourism and is mostly supported through gay tourism networks.

23. Based on author's interviews in Geneva

24. This paragraph and the next one on Costa Rica rely on Singh (2005) including the interviews carried out with trade and tourism officials and executives during August 2004.

25. Based on interviews, May 2006.

26. Initially the Indian ambassador to UNESCO was lukewarm to the convention. By the time the convention was signed in 2005, she had become a major supporter. A European cultural-policy official interviewed in June 2005 specifically cited her as someone who needed persuasion. This may reflect the stance India took: signing the convention but also continuing to be supportive of the GATS framework. Similarly, South Korea's support of the UNESCO convention, while

signatory to the audio-visual framework, may also have been attributable to the vigorous diplomacy practiced by the French in courting them. However, in Korea there was also support from a coalition of defensive film interests, which had grown strong in the Korean market in the 1990s with revenues generated from taxes on Hollywood films.

27. According to UNESCO figures, India, with $284 million in exports, does not rank much higher than Malaysia. Both cases can then be seen as responding to either creative-industry pressures or thinking strategically about future sources of competitive advantage.

28. Several small developing countries, such as Bahamas, have high degrees of specialization in travel and tourism services. But, even strife-torn areas such as Sierra Leone and Haiti had high specialization ratios in 1997 (Gallagher et al. 2005, 44).

29. Among trade advocates, this is taken to be a weakness of the GATS framework because it allows countries to be protectionist.

30. At a recent trip to Dakar in December 2006, I had conversation with a griot singer at a local restaurant, who offered to make a CD of his singing for twenty-four dollars. He explained that the recording would be made at a local studio.

31. However, Cunningham et al. (2008) also bemoans that Latin American music is effectively "poached" by the international music majors: Sony, EMI, Universal, and Warner.

32. Based on interviews and field research in Dakar and Johannesburg, November–December 2006.

33. Mbye Cham's paper "Historical Challenges of African Cinema," summarized in Department of Arts and Culture and NFVF (2007, 8).

34. Interviews in Dakar, Senegal, and Johannesburg, South Africa, December 2006.

35. Interviews in Montevideo, August 2007. Also see Singh (2008c).

36. See Caves 2000 for an explanation of these contractual arrangements and their historical evolution.

37. Interview at Metropolis Films, 4 September 2007.

38. The information in this paragraph comes mostly from Hoefert de Turégano (2008).

39. This argument finds its support in the new philosophies of aesthetics that move beyond the binary posed by the traditional view of art as beauty and the progressive view of art as being nothing but a political artifact. Drucker (2005, 14) notes in the context of fine art that "artists work with the awareness of the critical ambiguities of their situation." She notes: "Slickly produced works with high production values and prepackaged imagery recycled from the realms of cultural industry, made up of material objects bought in malls and outlet stores or put

on display using modes copied from the highest end showroom environments all show up as regularly as do the 'unconstructed' works that flaunt their disregard for conventional art-making techniques" (13). Her word for such collaborations between fine arts and the cultural industry is "complicity."

40. Cowen (1998, 2000) reaches a similar conclusion from an economic point of view.

41. This argument can be traced back to Rosa Luxemburg (1951/2003), who located the sources of imperialism in underconsumption in imperial countries and the search for markets for products abroad. She was soundly critiqued by Marxists for ignoring the mode of production.

42. Quoted in Department of Arts and Culture and NFVF (2007, 18).

6. Culture by Any Other Name

1. Statistics cited from http://www.wto.org/english/tratop_e/serv_e/serv_e.htm, accessed November 10, 2009.

2. This number reflects customs receipts. If royalties were included, the number would be higher but still much lower than tourism dollars.

3. Consistent with standard usage, this chapter speaks of cultural heritage and cultural tourism. However, the argument in this book is that tourism and heritage are creative industries and become cultural only when imbued with some notion of a cultural identity. A recent OECD (2009) report employs the term "creative tourism" to include industries that privilege both a region's history and its future.

4. Van Grasstek (2006) makes the distinction between the software or the goods and services that comprise cultural products versus hardware or the equipment and ancillary activities necessary for producing the software.

5. If international sex trade were to be added, the tourism numbers would go up further and economies such as Thailand and the Dominican Republic would show up as top earners.

6. Statistics cited in Bonet (2003, 188). This author also notes: "If the term 'culture' is considered in a wider sense (as interests in the objects and lifestyles of other peoples), then the vast majority of tourists consume cultural products and services at one time or another (whether relatively authentic or largely commercialized in the style of theme parks)."

7. The connection of Disneyland to American cultural identity came through in the Chinese government's opposition to a park in Shanghai and to Disneyland's plans to broadcast the Disney Channel in China to introduce its characters to the Chinese population (Crothers 2007, 134). See, also Baudrillard (1995) for a critique of Disneyland.

8. McDowell, Steinberg, and Tomasello (2008 chap. 4), is an otherwise brilliant analysis of tourism, within the context of the liberalization of the global services economy, but it misses this important distinction. Countries have sought to protect flows of cultural products but not tourism.

9. This is not an argument for privileging particular aesthetics, especially if these arise out of deliberative processes that are inclusive and transparent, but only to call attention to fake claims of authenticity and heritage and to show how both are constructed.

10. Starbucks ignited controversy in 2007 and was closed. The McDonald's, despite controversies, stays open.

11. I have met several opera aficionados who prefer listening to opera CDs or watching the opera on DVD than going to the opera house itself. There are also the nostalgic purists who would argue to the superior authenticity of the vinyl recordings. Further twists come from the new-fangled machines that allow us to digitize vinyl recordings and cassette tapes.

12. Edensor (1998, 58) describes tourism as a "rich sensual encounter of the Western tourist moving through heterogeneous tourist space."

13. See *GLQ* 2002 for several case studies dealing with the formation of sexual identity and tourism and for postcolonial domination. Puar (2002, 103), notes that white gay male sexuality in particular is intricately linked with the idea of being able to travel to "safe havens."

14. It now remains to be seen if one day a country will argue for sex services to be included as part of its exports. Certainly, GATS could accommodate sex work as part of professional or tourism services (see table 5.1).

15. This argument builds on an increasing body of scholarship that studies the links between tourism and sex work. See, for example Seabrook (2001) and Brennan (2004).

16. The importance of place and locality to sex trade is made by Brennan (2004).

17. Economists define industry as a related set of economic activities that are commercial in nature. Cultural-studies scholars view these industries from an ideological perspective in which culture is commodified and sold to sustain capitalism. See Miller and Yúdice (2002); the classic reference is Horkheimer and Adorno (1947/2002).

18. There is a plethora of literature on sex trafficking and violations of human rights. For an overview, see Kara (2008).

19. Cultural-policies literature generally places pure creativity at the core of cultural activities, with the outer circles occupied by activities that serve other purposes and include heightened degrees of commercialism. In that sense, a painting might be placed more toward the core than architectural services that include creativity, other forms of utility, and commercial aspects. (See UNESCO [2005] for definitions of cultural activities. However, this document omits tourism.)

20. Gaston (1996, chap. 1) traces the *devdasi* dance connection to the Vedic days of ancient India; thereafter it grew with royal and wealthy patronage through the ages.

21. A version of this subsection was co-authored with Shilpa Alimchandani in 2006 and published in Singh and Hart (2007).

22. The rise of sex industry and its connection with foreign military presence is now explored in several works. See Enloe (2001).

23. On a broader level, Ma (1996) explores the ways in which the "Oriental" women use their liaison with Western men to get themselves out of patriarchal societies. These intercultural relationships end in failure because of the difference in expectations between the Japanese (in Ma's book) and mostly American men.

24. Internet search conducted on November 19, 2005.

7. The Creative Voice and Cultural Policy

1. For more on my homage to Freire, including details on ideas discussed here, please see Singh 2008a.

2. See Berger and Luckamann (1966). The concepts of practical and discursive consciousness in Giddens (1984) are also important in this regard.

3. There is an important commonsense exception: state policies may be equally ineffective at orchestrating diversity. Nevertheless, there may be instances where carefully designed policy instruments may help a community preserve important creative expressions and heritage. Or, to borrow from abroad, Ataturk's adoption of a Latin-based script for the Turkish language in 1928 or the Meiji restoration in Japan in the latter half of the nineteenth century embodies the creation of national cultural identity through explicitly hybrid cultural policies.

4. As Mahatama Gandhi wrote, "I do not want my house to be walled in on all sides and my windows to be stuffed. I want the culture of all lands to be blown about my house as freely as possible. But I refuse to be blown off my feet by any."

Works Cited

Abbinnett, Ross. 2003. *Culture and Identity: Critical Theories.* London: Sage.

Acheson, Keith, and Christopher Maule. 2004. "Convention on Cultural Diversity." *Journal of Cultural Economics* 28:243–56.

Ackerman, Ruthie. 2009. "All the President's Art." Artinfo.com. 22 June. http://www.artinfo.com/news/story/31760/all-the-presidents-art/. Accessed November 2, 2009.

Adler, Peter S. 1998. "Beyond Cultrual Identity: Reflections on Cultural and Multicultural Man." In *Culture, Communication, and Conflict: Readings in Intercultural Relations,* ed. Gary S. Weaver, 250–65. Needham Heights, Mass.: Simon and Schuster.

Ahmad, Aijaz. 1987. "Jameson's Rhetoric of Otherness and the 'National Allegory.'" *Social Text* 17 (Fall): 3–25.

Americans for UNESCO. 2004. *Prospects and Retrospects* 1.1 (Spring–Summer).

Anderson, Benedict. 1983. *Imagined Communities.* London: Verso

Andrault, Marianne, and Philippe Dressayre. 1987. "Government and the Arts in France." In *The Patron State: Government and the Arts in Europe, North America, and Japan,* ed. Milton C. Cummings and Richard S. Katz, 17–44. New York: Oxford University Press.

Appadurai, Arjun. 2004. "The Capacity to Aspire: Culture and the Terms of Recognition." In *Culture and Public Action,* ed. Vijayendra Rao and Michael Walton, 59–84. Stanford, Calif.: Stanford University Press. 2004.

———, ed. 2000. *Globalization*. Durham, N.C.: Duke University Press.

———. 1996. *Modernity at Large: Cultural Dimensions of Globalization*. Minneapolis: University of Minnesota Press.

Appiah, K. Anthony. 1994. "Identity, Authenticity, Survival: Multicultural Societies and Social Reproduction." In *Multiculturalism: Examining the Politics of Recognition*, ed. Amy Gutman, 149–63. Princeton, N.J.: Princeton University Press.

Associated Press. 1993. "France Claims Trade Victory, but Hollywood Wins at Box Office." 14 December.

Ba, Mariama. 1980. *So Long A Letter*. Reading, Berkshire: Heinemann.

Balfe, Judith Huggins, ed. 1993. *Paying the Piper: Causes and Consequences of Art Patronage*. Urbana: University of Illinois Press.

Barber, Benjamin R. 1995. *Jihad vs. McWorld: How Globalism and Tribalism Are Shaping the World*. New York: Ballantine.

Barbier, Patrick. 1995. *Opera in Paris, 1800–1850: A Lively History*. Portland, Ore.: Amadeus Press.

Barrowclough, Diana, and Zeljka Kozul-Wright. 2008. *Creative Industries and Developing Countries: Voice, Choice, and Economic Growth*. London: Routledge.

Baudrillard, Jean. 1995. *Simulacra and Simulation*. Trans. Sheila Faria Glaser. Ann Arbor: University of Michigan Press.

Baumol, William J., and William G. Bowen. 1966. *Performing Arts: The Economic Dilemma*. New York: The Twentieth Century Fund.

Becker, Howard S. 1986/2000. *Art Worlds*. 25th anniv. ed. Berkeley: University of California Press.

Benhabib, Seyla. 2002. *The Claims of Culture: Equality and Diversity in the Global Era*. Princeton, N.J.: Princeton University Press.

———. 1996. "Toward a Deliberative Model of Democratic Legitimacy." In *Democracy and Difference: Contesting the Boundaries of the Political*, ed. Seyla Benhabib, 120–35. Princeton, N.J.: Princeton University Press.

Benhabib, Seyla, Ian Shapiro, Danilo Petranovic. 2007. *Identities, Affiliations, and Allegiances*. Cambridge: Cambridge University Press.

Benjamin, Walter. 1935/1969. "The Work of Art in the Age of Mechanical Reproduction." In *Illuminations*, ed. Hannah Arendt, trans. Harry Johns, 217–52. New York: Schocken Books.

Berezin, Mabel, and Martin Schain, eds. 2003. *Europe Without Borders: Remapping Territory, Citizenship, and Identity in a Transnational Age*. Baltimore, Md.: Johns Hopkins University Press.

Berger, Peter L., and Thomas Luckmann. 1966. *The Social Construction of Reality: A Treatise in the Sociology of Knowledge*. New York: Anchor Books.

Biko, Steven. 1973. "Black Consciousness and the Quest for a True Humanity." Paper delivered at the Black Theology Conference, Edendale, South Africa, 13–16 Feb-

ruary. Available from http://www.sahistory.org.za/pages/governence-projects/
black-consciousness/biko/writings-humanity.htm.

Birnbaum, Pierre. 2001. *The Idea of France.* Trans. M. B. DeBevoise. New York: Hill
and Wang.

Bishop, R., and L. S. Robinson. 1998. *Night Market: Sexual Cultures and the Thai
Economic Miracle.* New York: Routledge.

Bloom, Allan. 1988. *The Closing of the American Mind.* New York: Simon and
Schuster.

Bonet, Lluis. 2003. "Cultural Tourism." In *A Handbook of Cultural Economics,* ed.
Ruth Towse, 187–93. Cheltenham, U.K.: Edward Elgar.

Boonchalaski, W., and P. Guest. 1998. "Prostitution in Thailand." In *The Sex Sector: The Economic and Social Bases of Prostitution in Southeast Asia,* ed. L. L. Lim,
130–69. Geneva: International Labor Office, International Labor Organization.

Bourdieu, Pierre. 1993. *The Field of Cultural Production.* Ed. Randal Johnson. New
York: Columbia University Press.

Bouzas, Roberto, and Hernán Soltz. 2005. "Argentina and GATS: A Study on the
Domestic Determinants of GATS Commitments." In *Managing the Challenges
of WTO Participation: Forty-five Case Studies,* ed. Peter Gallagher et al., 38–52.
Cambridge: Cambridge University Press.

Bradford, Gigi, Michael Gary, and Glenn Wallach, eds. 2000. *The Politics of Culture:
Policy Perspectives for Individuals, Institutions, and Communities.* New York: The
New Press.

Braudel, Fernand. 1963/1993. *A History of Civilization.* Trans. Richard Mayne. New
York: Penguin.

Brennan, Denise. 2004. *What's Love Got to Do with It? Transnational Desires and Sex
Tourism in the Dominican Republic.* Durham, N.C.: Duke University Press.

Brown, Ian. 2009. "Can Creative Industries Survive Digital Onslaught?" *Financial
Times.* 3 November.

Browne, Sandra. 2008. "The Film Industry in Nigeria." In *The Cultural Economy,*
ed. Helmut Anheier and Yudhishter Raj Isar, 95–96. London: Sage.

Buzan, Barry. 2004. *From International to World Society? English School Theory and
the Structure of Globalization.* Cambridge: Cambridge University Press.

Carter, Tim. 1997. "Lorenzo Da Ponte." In *The New Grove Dictionary of the Opera,*
vol. 1, ed. Stanley Sadie, 1073–76 . London: Macmillan Reference.

Castells, Manuel. 1998. *The Information Age: Economy, Society and Culture.* Vol. 1:
End of Millenium. Oxford: Blackwell.

——. 1997. *The Information Age: Economy, Society, and Culture.* Vol. 2: *The Power of
Identity.* Oxford: Blackwell.

——. 1996. *The Information Age: Economy, Society, and Culture.* Vol. 3: *The Rise of
Networked Society.* Oxford: Blackwell.

Caves, Richard. 2000. *Creative Industries: Contracts Between Art and Commerce.* Cambridge, Mass.: Harvard University Press.

Chagy, Gideon. 1973. *The New Patrons of the Arts.* New York: Harry N. Abrams.

Chang, Jeff. 2009. "The Creativity Stimulus." *The Nation.* 15 April. Available at http://www.thenation.com/doc/20090504/chang/single. Accessed 24 April 2009.

Charlton, David, ed. 2003. *The Cambridge Companion to Grand Opera.* Cambridge: Cambridge University Press.

Cheen, Lim Chze. 2005. "Malaysia: Strategies for the Liberalization of the Services Sector." In *Managing the Challenges of WTO Participation: Forty-five Case Studies,* ed. Peter Gallagher et al., 349–61. Cambridge: Cambridge University Press.

Cherbo, Joni M., Ruth Ann Stewart, and Margaret Jane Wyszomirski, eds. 2008. *Understanding the Arts and the Creative Sector in the United States.* New Brunswick, N.J.: Rutgers University Press.

Cipolla, Carlo M. 1980. *Before the Industrial Revolution: European Society and Economy, 1000–1700.* 2nd ed. New York: Norton.

Cloonan, Martin. 2007. *Popular Music and the State in UK: Culture, Trade, or Industry?.* Farnham, U.K.: Ashgate.

CNN.com. 1999. "France to Defend Film Trade from Hollywood at WTO." 29 November.

Cocq, Emmanuel, and Patrick Messerlin. 2005. "French Audio-Visual Policy: Impact and Compatibility with Trade Negotiations." In *Cultural Diversity and International Economic Integration: The Global Governance of the Audio-Visual Sector,* ed. Paolo Guerrieri, P. Lelio Iapadre, and Georg Koopmann, 21–95. Cheltenham, U.K.: Edward Elgar.

Commission of the European Communities. 2002. *Fifth Communication from the Commission to the Council and the European Parliament. On the Application of Articles 4 and 5 of Directive 89/552/EEC "Television Without Frontiers," as amended by Directive 97/36/EC, for the period 1999–2000.* Brussels. 8 November.

Cowen, Tyler. 2006. *Good and Plenty: The Creative Successes of American Arts Funding.* Princeton, N.J.: Princeton University Press.

——. 2002. *Creative Destruction: How Globalization Is Changing the World's Cultures.* Princeton, N.J.: Princeton University Press.

——. 1998. *In Praise of Commercial Culture.* Cambridge, Mass.: Harvard University Press.

Crosten, William Loran. 1948. *French Grand Opera: An Art and a Business.* New York: King's Crown Press, Columbia University.

Crothers, Lane. 2007. *Globalization and American Popular Culture.* Lanham, Md.: Rowman and Littlefield.

Cummings, Milton C., and Richard S. Katz, eds. 1987. *The Patron State: Government and the Arts in Europe, North America, and Japan.* New York: Oxford University Press.

Cunningham, Stuart, et al. 2008. "Financing Creative Industries in Developing Countries." In *Creative Industries and Developing Countries: Voice, Choic,e and Economic Growth,* ed. Diana Barrowclough and Zeljka Kozul-Wright. 65–110. London: Routledge.

Currid, Elizabeth. 2007. *The Warhol Economy: How Fashion, Art, and Music Drive New York City.* Princeton, N.J.: Princeton University Press.

Davidson, J. O. 1998. *Prostitution, Power, and Freedom.* Ann Arbor: University of Michigan Press.

Davis, Shelton H. 2004. "The Mayan Movement and Culture in Guatemala." In *Culture and Public Action,* ed. Vijayendra Rao and Michael Walton, 328–58, Stanford, Calif.: Stanford University Press.

DCMS. 2001. *Creative Industries Mapping Document.* London: Department of Culture, Media, and Sport. Available at http://www.culture.gov.uk/reference _library/publications/4632.aspx. Accessed 22 March 2010.

De Botton, Alain. 2002. *The Art of Travel.* New York: Vintage.

De Grazia, Victoria. 2005. *Irresistible Empire: America's Advance Through Twentieth-Century Europe.* Cambridge, Mass.: Belknap Press of the Harvard University Press.

Deibert, Ronald. J. 1997. *Parchment, Printing, Hypermedia: Communication and World Order Transformation.* New York: Columbia University Press.

Délégation Permanente de la France aupres de l'Organisation Mondiale du Commerce. 2002. "France, EU, and Cultural Diversity." Document. Geneva. 16 October.

Department of Arts and Culture and National Film and Video Foundation. 2007. *Africa Film Summit 2006 Report.* Johannesburg, South Africa: Mayibuye iAfrika.

Department of Trade and Industry. 2002. *Liberalizing Trade in Services: A New Consultation on the World Trade Organization GATS Negotiations.* October. Available at http://www2.dti.gov.uk/ewt/service.htm. Accessed 10 October 2003.

Dewey, Patricia. 2007. "Introduction." *Journal of Arts Management, Law, and Society* 37 (1): 3–9.

DiMaggio, Paul. 2000. "Social Structure, Institutions, and Cultural Goods: The Case of the United States." In *The Politics of Culture: Policy Perspectives for Individuals, Institutions, and Communities,* ed. Gigi Bradford, Michael Gary, and Glenn Wallach, 38–62. New York: The New Press.

Dominguez, Virginia R. 2000. "Invoking Culture: The Messy Side of 'Cultural Politics.'" In *The Politics of Culture: Policy Perspectives for Individuals, Institutions, and Communities,* ed. Gigi Bradford, Michael Gary, and Glenn Wallach, 20–37. New York: The New Press.

Drucker, Johanna. 2005. *Sweet Dreams: Contemporary Art and Complicity.* Chicago: University of Chicago Press.

Dryzek, John S., and Simon Niemeyer. 2008. "Discursive Representation." *American Political Science Review* 102.4 (November): 481–93.

Duneier, Mitchell. 1992. *Slim's Table: Race, Respectability, Masculinity*. Chicago: University of Chicago Press.

Dungarembga, Tsitsi. 1988. *Nervous Conditions*. New York: Seal Press.

Eco, Umberto. 1995. "'I Love You Madly,' He Said Self-Consciously.'" In *The Truth About the Truth: De-confusing and Re-constructing the Postmodern World*, ed. Walter Truett-Anderson, 31–33. New York: Putnam.

Economist. 2008. "Going Pinker on the Plata: A New Destination for Gay Tourists." 4 December. http://www.economist.com/displayStory.cfm?story_id=12725407. Accessed 4 May 2009.

Edensor, Tim. 1998. *Tourists at the Taj*. London: Routledge.

Ekelund, Robert B., Jr., and Robert D. Tollison. 1997. *Politicized Economies: Monarchy, Monopoly, and Mercantilism*. College Station: Texas A&M University Press.

Elster, Jon, ed. 1998. *Deliberative Democracy*. Cambridge: Cambridge University Press.

Emigh, Rebecca Jean. 2008. *The Underdevelopment of Capitalism: Sectors and Markets in Fifteenth-Century Tuscany*. Philadelphia: Temple University Press.

Enloe, Cynthia. 2001. *Bananas, Beaches, and Bases: Making Feminist Sense of International Politics*. Berkeley: University of California Press.

Escobar, Arturo. 1995. *Encountering Development: The Making and Unmaking of the Third World*. Princeton, N.J.: Princeton University Press.

Feigenbaum, Harvey. 2010. "The Political Economy of Cultural Diversity in Film and Television." In *International Cultural Policies and Power*, ed. J. P. Singh, 77–83. Basingstoke: Palgrave/Macmillan.

——. 2004. "Is Technology the Enemy of Culture?" *International Journal of Cultural Policy* 10 (3): 251–63.

Feld, Steven. 20001. "A Sweet Lullaby for World Music." In *Globalization*, ed. Arjun Appadurai, 189–216. Durham, N.C.: Duke University Press.

Felski, Rita. 1995. *The Gender of Modernity*. Cambridge, Mass.: Harvard University Press.

Financial Times. 2009a. "China Appeals Over WTO Ruling on Restricted US Media Imports." 23 September.

——. 2009b. "Malaysia Sees Chance to Put Model That Puts Knowledge First." 12 March.

——. 2002. "Media: A Closer Watch on All Channels." 18 November.

Florida, Richard. 2002. *The Rise of the Creative Class*. New York: Basic Books.

Frank, Marc. 2005. "Restructuring of Sugar Cane Industry Leaves Void in Cuban Soul." *Financial Times*. 12 October.

Frank, Robert. 2002. "The Meaning of Europe in French National Discourse: A French Europe or a Europeanised France?" In *The Meaning of Europe: Variety and Contention Within and Among Nations*, ed. Mikael af Malmborg and Bo Strath, 311–26. Oxford: Berg.

Frank, Thomas. 2004. *What's the Matter with Kansas? How Conservatives Won the Heart of America.* New York: Metropolitan.

Freire, Paulo. 1970/2000. *Pedagogy of the Oppressed.* New York: Continuum.

Frey, Bruno S. 2003. "Festivals." In *A Handbook of Cultural Economics*, ed. Ruth Towse, 232–36. Cheltenham, U.K.: Edward Elgar.

———. 2000. *Arts and Economics: Analysis and Cultural Policy.* Berlin: Springer.

Fulcher, Jane. 1987. *The Nation's Image: French Grand Opera as Politics and Politicized Art.* Cambridge: Cambridge University Press.

Galvan, Dennis. 2004. *The State Must Be Our Master of Fire: How Peasants Craft Culturally Sustainable Development in Senegal.* Berkeley: University of California Press.

Gallagher, Peter, et al., eds. 2005. *Managing the Challenges of WTO Participation: Forty-five Case Studies.* Cambridge: Cambridge University Press.

García Canclini, Nestor. 2001. "From National Capital to Global Capital: Urban Change in Mexico City." In *Globalization*, ed. Arjun Appadurai, 253–59. Durham, N.C.: Duke University Press.

———. 2000. "Cultural Policy Options in the Context of Globalization." In *The Politics of Culture: Policy Perspectives for Individuals, Institutions, and Communities*, ed. Gigi Bradford, Michael Gary, and Glenn Wallach, 302–26. New York: New Press.

———. 1995. *Hybrid Cultures: Strategies for Entering and Leaving Modernity.* Minneapolis: University of Minnesota Press.

Gaston, Anne-Marie. 1996. *Bharagnatyam: From Temple to Theatre.* New Delhi: Manohar Publishers.

Geertz, Clifford. 1973. *The Interpretation of Cultures.* New York: Basic Books.

Gerhard, Anselm. 1998. *The Urbanization of Opera.* Chicago: University of Chicago Press.

Ghosh, L. 2002. *Prostitution in Thailand: Myth and Reality.* New Delhi: Munshiram Manoharlal.

Giddens, Anthony. 1984. *The Constitution of Society: Outline of the Theory of Structuration.* Berkeley: University of California Press.

Glassner, Barry. 1999. *The Culture of Fear: Why Americans Are Afraid of the Wrong Things.* New York: Basic Books.

Glazer, Nathan. 1997. *We Are All Multiculturalists Now.* Cambridge, Mass.: Harvard University Press.

GLQ: A Journal of Lesbian and Gay Studies. 2002. "Special Issue on Queer Tourism: Geographies of Globalization." *GLQ* 8 (1–2).

Gmelch, Sharon Bohn. 2004. *Tourists and Tourism: A Reader.* Long Grove, Ill.: Waveland Press.

Goff, Patricia M. 2007. *Limits to Liberalization: Local Culture in Global Marketplace.* Ithaca, N.Y.: Cornell University Press.

——. 2000. "Invisible Borders: Economic Liberalization and National Identity." *International Studies Quarterly* 44:533–62.

Goffman, Irving. 1959. *The Presentation of Self in Everyday Life.* New York: Anchor Books.

Goldsmith, Ben, and Tom O'Regan. 2005. *The Film Studio: Film Production in the Global Economy.* Lanham, Mass.: Rowman and Littlefield.

Goodwin, Craufurd. 2006. "Art and Culture in the History of Economic Thought." In *Handbook of the Economics of Art and Culture,* ed. Victor A. Ginsburgh and David Throsby, 25–68. Handbooks in Economics 25. Amsterdam: North-Holland.

Gopnik, Blake. 2009. "1600 Pen and Ink: Obamas' Choice of Works on Loan to White House." *Washington Post.* 7 October.

Gordon, C. 2007. "Culture and the European Union in a Global Context." *Journal of Arts Management, Law, and Society* 37 (1): 11–30

Graham, Edward M. 2000. *Fighting the Wrong Enemy: Anti-Global Activities and Multinational Enterprises.* Washington, D.C.: Institute for International Economics.

Granovetter, Mark. 1985. "Economic Action and Social Structure: The Problem of Embeddedness." *American Journal of Sociology* 91.3 (November): 481–510.

Grosso, Massimo Geloso, Molly Lesher, and Enrico Pinali. 2007. *Service Trade Liberalization and Tourism Development.* OECD Trade Policy Working Paper No. 57. November. TD/TC/WP (2006) 37 Final. Paris: OECD.

Guerrieri, Paolo, and P. Lelio Iapadre. 2005. Introduction to *Cultural Diversity and International Economic Integration: The Global Governance of the Audio-Visual Sector,* ed. Paolo Guerrieri, O. Lelio Iapadre, and Georg Koopmann, 1–17. Cheltenham, U.K.: Edward Elgar.

Guyer, Jane. 2004. *Marginal Gains: Monetary Transactions in Atlantic Africa.* Chicago: University of Chicago Press.

Habermas, Jürgen. 1985. *The Theory of Communicative Action.* Vol. 1: *Reason and the Rationalization of Society.* Boston: Beacon Press.

——. 1976. *Communication and the Evolution of Society.* Boston: Beacon Press.

Halbwachs, Maurice. 1941/1992. *On Collective Memory.* Chicago: University of Illinois Press.

Halle, David. 1993. *Inside Culture: Art and Class in the American Home.* Chicago: University of Chicago Press.

Hamilton, A. 1997. "Primal Dream: Masculinism, Sin, and Salvation in Thailand's Sex Trade." In *Sites of Desire, Economies of Pleasure: Sexualities in Asia and the Pacific,* ed. L. Manderson and M. Jolly, 145–65. Chicago: University of Chicago Press.

Hannerz, Ulf. 1996. *Transnational Connections.* London: Rutledge.

———. 1992. *Cultural Complexity*. New York: Columbia University Press.

Hart, Jeffrey J. 2010. "Toward a Political Economy of Digital Culture: From Organized Mass Consumption to Attention Rivalry." In *International Cultural Policies and Power*, ed. J. P. Singh, 56–62. Basingstoke: Palgrave/Macmillan.

Heller, Lee E. 1992. "*Frankenstein* and the Cultural Uses of the Gothic." In *Frankenstein: Mary Shelley*, ed. Johanna M. Smith, 325–41. Boston: Bedford Books.

Hermann, Richard K., Philip E. Tetlock, and Matthew N. Diascro. 2001. "How Americans Think About Trade: Reconciling Conflicts Among Money, Power, and Principles." *International Studies Quarterly* 45:191–218.

Hesmondhalgh, David. 2007. *The Cultural Industries*. 2nd ed. London: Sage.

Hoefert de Turégano, Theresa. 2008. "Film Culture and Industry in Burkina Faso." In *Creative Industries and Developing Countries: Voice, Choice, and Economic Growth*, ed. Diana Barrowclough and Zeljka Kozul-Wright, 111–29. London: Routledge

Hope, Kerin, and George Parker. 2006. "Oldest Profession Helps Boost Greek National Output by 25%." *Financial Times*. 29 September.

Horkheimer, Max, and Theodor W. Adorno. 1947/2002. *Dialectic of Enlightenment*. Stanford, Calif.: Stanford: Stanford University Press

Houellebecq, Michel. 2004. *Platform*. Trans. Frank Wynne. New York: Vintage International.

Huntington, Samuel P. 1993. "The Clash of Civilizations?" *Foreign Affairs* 72.3 (Summer): 22–49.

Hurd, Ian. 1999. "Legitimacy and Authority in International Politics." *International Organization*. 53 (3): 379–408.

Hutter, Michael, and David Throsby, eds. 2008. *Beyond Price: Value in Culture, Economics, and the Arts*. Cambridge: Cambridge University Press.

INCP. 2003. *Draft International Convention on Cultural Diversity by the Working Group on Cultural Diversity and Globalization*. To be presented to Ministers at the 6th annual Ministerial Meeting of the International Network on Cultural Policy, Opatije, Croatoa, 16–18 October 2003. http://206.191.7.19/iicd/list_e.shtml. July 29. Accessed 10 October 2003.

Ivey, Bill. 2008. *Arts Inc.: How Greed and Neglect Have Destroyed Our Cultural Rights*. Berkeley: University of California Press.

Iyer, Pico. 2005. "One Night in Bangkok." *Financial Times*. 25 November.

Jameson, Frederic. 1986. "Third World Literature in the Era of Multinational Corporations." *Social Text* 15 (Fall): 65–88.

Jameson, Frederic, and Masao Miyoshi, eds. 2004. *The Cultures of Globalization*. Durham, N.C.: Duke University Press.

Jarvie, Ian. 1992. *Hollywood's Overseas Campaign: The North Atlantic Movie Trade, 1920–1950*. Cambridge: Cambridge University Press.

Jeancolas, Jean-Pierre. 1998. "From the Blum-Byrnes Agreement to the GATT Affair." In *Hollywood and Europe: Economics, Culture, and National Identity: 1945–95*, ed. Geoffrey Nowell-Smith and Steven Ricci, 47–61. London: British Film Institute

Johannisson, Jenny. 2010. "Making Geography Matter in Cultural Policy Research: The Case of Regional Cultural Policy in Sweden." In *International Cultural Policies and Power*, ed. J. P. Singh, 127–39. Basingstoke: Palgrave/Macmillan.

Johnson, J. 2006. "India's Resurrection of its Cultural Identity Reveals Ambition for 'Soft Power.' " *Financial Times*. 1 October.

Kammen, Michael. 2006. *Visual Shock: A History of Art Controversies in American Culture*. New York: Vintage Books.

Kantor, Mickey. 2004. "Film Pirates Are Robbing Us All." *Financial Times*. 19 November.

Kara, Siddharth. 2008. *Sex Trafficking: Inside the Business of Modern Slavery*. New York: Columbia University Press.

Katzenstein, Peter J. 2005. *A World of Regions: Asia and Europe in the American Imperium*. Ithaca, N.Y.: Cornell University Press.

Keck, Margaret E., and Kathryn Sikkink. 1998. *Activists Beyond Borders: Advocacy Networks in International Politics*. Ithaca, N.Y.: Cornell University Press.

Kelsey, Jane. 2007. "Globalization of Cultural Policymaking and the Hazards of Legal Seduction." In *Media in the Age of Marketization*, ed. G. Murdoch and J. Wasko. Cresskill, N.J.: Hampton Press.

Kent, Dale. 2000. *Cosimo De'Medici and the Florentine Renaissance: The Patron's Oeuvre*. New Haven, Conn.: Yale University Press.

Khilnani, Sunil. 2001. *The Idea of India*. New York: Farrar, Straus and Giroux.

Kim, Sangbae, and Jeffrey A. Hart. 2002. "The Global Political Economy of Wintelism: A New Mode of Power and Governance in the Global Computer Industry." In *Information Technologies and Global Politics: The Changing Scope of Power and Governance*, ed. James N. Rosenau and J. P. Singh, 143–68. Albany: State University of New York Press.

King, Anthony D. 1997. *Culture, Globalization, and the World System: Contemporary Conditions for the Representation of Identity*. Minneapolis: University of Minnesota Press.

Kleyemeyer, Charles David. 1994. *Cultural Expression and Grassroots Development: Cases from Latin America and the Caribbean*. Boulder, Colo.: Lynne Reiner.

Kraidy, Marwan M. 2005. *Hybridity, or the Cultural Logic of Globalization*. Philadelphia: Temple University Press.

Kurlantzick, Joshua. 2007. *Charm Offensive: How China's Soft Power Is Transforming the World*. New Haven, Conn.: Yale University Press.

Lamy, Pascal. 2002. *L'Europe en premiere ligne*. Paris: Editions Du Seuil.

Lang, Jack. 1998. "L'A.M.I., c'est l'ennemi." *Le Monde*. 10 February.

Lange, Andre. 1998. *Trends in World Audiovisual Market*. Strasbourg: European Audiovisual Market.

Lapid, Yosef, and Frederick Kratochwil, eds. 1996. *The Return of Culture and Identity in IR Theory*. Boulder, Colo.: Lynne Reinner.

Lax, David A., and James K. Sebenius. 1986. *The Manager as Negotiator: Bargaining for Cooperation and Competitive Gain*. New York: The Free Press.

Leahy, Joe. 2009. "Warner Brothers Tips Its Hat to Bollywood." *Financial Times*. 17 January.

L'Ecuyer, P., and Ken Rogerson. 2000. "Broadcast Policies of the European Union: Constraints on Globalization?" Paper presented at the International Studies Association, Los Angeles. March.

Lerner, David. 1958. *The Passing of Traditional Society: Modernizing the Middle East*. New York: Free Press.

Levy, David A. 1999. *Europe's Digital Revolution: Broadcasting Regulation, the EU, and the Nation-State*. London: Routledge.

Lim, L. L., ed. 1998. *The Sex Sector: The Economic and Social Bases of Prostitution in Southeast Asia*. Geneva: International Labor Office, International Labor Organization.

Linklater, Andrew, and Hidemi Suganami. 2006. *The English School of International Relations: A Contemporary Assessment*. Cambridge: Cambridge University Press.

Luxemburg, Rosa. 1951/2003. *Accumulation of Capital*. London: Routledge.

Ma, Karen. 1996. *The Modern Madame Butterfly: Fantasies and Reality in Japanese Cross-Cultural Relationships*. Tokyo: Charles E. Tuttle.

Martinez, Ibsen. 2005. "Romancing the Globe." *Foreign Policy* 151 (November/December): 48–56.

Mazlish, Bruce. 2008. *The Idea of Humanity in the Global Era*. Basingstoke: Palgrave.

McDowell, Stephen D., Philip E. Steinberg, and Tami K. Tomasello. 2008. *Managing the Infosphere: Governance, Technology, and Cultural Practice in Motion*. Philadelphia: Temple University Press.

McNamara, Kathleen. 2010. "Constructing Authority in the European Union." In *Who Governs the Globe*, ed. Deborah D. Avant, Martha Finnemore, and Susan K. Sell, 153–79. Cambridge: Cambridge University Press.

Mellor, N. 2005. "Girl Power." *Financial Times*. 11 November.

Miller, Toby, and George Yúdice. 2002. *Cultural Policy*. London: Sage.

Mody, Bella, ed. 2003. *International and Development Communication: A Twenty-first-Century Perspective*. Thousand Oaks, Calif.: Sage.

Mukherjee, Arpita. 2005. "Audio-Visual Policies and International Trade: The Case of India." In *Cultural Diversity and International Economic Integration: The Global Governance of the Audio-Visual Sector*, ed. Paolo Guerrieri, O. Lelio Iapadre, and Georg Koopmann, 218–58. Cheltenham, U.K.: Edward Elgar.

Mulcahy, Kevin, and Margaret Wyzsomirski. 1995. *America's Commitment to Culture: Government and the Arts*. Boulder, Colo.: Westview.

Neil, Gary T. 1997. "MAI and Canada's Cultural Sector." http://www.ccarts.ca/en/advocacy/publications/policy/mai.htm. October. Accessed 1 May 2007.

Newman, Barnett. 1947. "The First Man Was an Artist." *The Tiger's Eye*. October. Also available at: http://venetianred.net/2008/10/10/barnett-newman%E2%80%94the-first-man-was-an-artist/. Accessed 1 May 2009.

Nicassio, Susan Vandiver. 1999. *Tosca's Rome: The Play and the Opera in Historical Perspective*. Chicago: University of Chicago Press.

Niezen, Ronald. 2004. *A World Beyond Difference: Cultural Identity in the Age of Globalization*. Malden, Mass.: Blackwell.

Noam, Eli. 1991. *Television in Europe*. New York: Oxford University Press.

North, Douglass C. 1994. "Economic Performance Through Time." *American Economic Review* 84 (3): 359–68.

——. 1990. *Institutions, Institutional Change, and Economic Performance*. Cambridge: Cambridge University Press.

——. 1981. *Structure and Change in Economic History*. New York: Norton.

North Douglass C., and Robert T. Thomas. 1973. *The Rise of the Western World: A New Economic History*. Cambridge: Cambridge University Press.

Nuttail, Sarah, and Cheryl Ann Michael, eds. 2001. *Senses of Culture: South African Culture Studies*. New York: Oxford University Press.

Nye, Joseph S., Jr. 2006. "Springing Tiger." *India Today*. 25 September.

——. 2004. *Soft Power: The Means to Success in World Politics*. New York: Public Affairs.

Obuljen, Nina. 2005. *Why We Need European Cultural Policies: The Impact of EU Enlargement on Cultural Policies in Transition Countries*. Amsterdam: European Cultural Foundation.

OECD. 2009. *The Impact of Culture on Tourism*. Paris: Organization of Economic Cooperation and Development.

——. 2008. *Opening Up Trade in Services: Key for Tourism Growth*. February. Paris: OECD Policy Brief.

O'Hare, Michael, Alan L. Feld, and J. Mark Shuster. 1983. *Patrons Despite Themselves: Taxpayers and Arts Policy*. New York: New York University Press.

Olson, Mancur. 1982. *The Rise and Decline of Nations: Economic Growth, Stagflation, and Social Rigidities*. New Haven, Conn.: Yale University Press.

Ortiz Mena, Antonio. 2006. "Getting to 'No': Defending Against Demands in NAFTA Energy Negotiations." In *Negotiating Trade: Developing Countries in the WTO and NAFTA*, ed. John Odell, 177–216. Cambridge: Cambridge University Press.

Paillard, J. 2006. Talk given at the fourteenth International Conference on Cultural Economics. Vienna, Austria. 7 July.

Perry, G. M., et al. 1973. "Ousmane Sembène: An Interview." *Film Quarterly* 26.3 (Spring): 36–42.

Pitt, Charles. 1997. "India." In *The New Grove Dictionary of the Opera*, vol. 2, ed. Stanley Sadie, 796–97. London: MacMillan.

Plattner, Stuart. 2003. "Anthropology of Art." In *A Handbook of Cultural Economics*, ed. Ruth Towse, 15–19. Cheltenham, U.K.: Edward Elgar.

Pogrebin, Robin. 2009. "Arts Leaders Urge Role for Culture in Economic Recovery." *New York Times*. January 26.

Polanyi, Karl. 1944. *The Great Transformation*. New York: Rinehart.

Postman, Neil. 1985. *Amusing Ourselves to Death: Public Discourse in the Age of Show Business*. New York: Penguin.

Preeg, Ernest H. 1995. *Traders in a Brave New World: The Uruguay Round and the Future of the International System*. Chicago: University of Chicago Press.

Price, Richard. 2008. "Moral Limit and Possibility in World Politics." *International Organization* 62 (2): 191–220.

Puar, Jasbir. 2002. "Circuits of Queer Mobility: Tourism, Travel, and Globalization." *GLQ* 8 (1–2): 101–37.

Putnam, Geo. Haven. 1896. *The Question of Copyright*. New York: The Knickerbocker Press.

Raunig, Gerald. 2005. "2015." In *European Cultural Policies, 2015: A Report with Scenarios on the Future of Public Funding for Contemporary Art in Europe*, ed. Maria Lind and Raimund Minichbauer, 14–20. Vienna: European Institute for Progressive Cultural Policies.

Richardson, J. 1999. "Introduction by the Series Editor." In *Europe's Digital Revolution: Broadcasting Regulation, the EU, and the Nation-State*, by David A. Levy, xi–xiii. London: Routledge.

Rizzo, Ilde. 2006. "Cultural Heritage: Economic Analysis and Public Policy." In *Handbook of the Economics of Art and Culture*, ed. Victor A. Ginsburgh and David Throsby, 983–1016. Amsterdam: North Holland.

Robert, Maryse. 2000. *Negotiating NAFTA: Explaining the Outcome in Culture, Textile, Autos, and Pharmaceuticals*. Toronto: University of Toronto Press.

Rosenau, James N. 1997. *Along the Domestic-Foreign Frontier: Exploring Governance in a Turbulent World*. Cambridge: Cambridge University Press.

Ross, G. 1995. *Jacques Delors and European Integration*. Oxford: Polity Press.

Rosselli, John. 1984. *The Opera Industry in Italy from Cimarosa to Verdi: The Role of the Impresario*. Cambridge: Cambridge University Press.

Roy, Martin. 2008. "Beyond the Main Screen: Audiovisual Services in PTAs." In *Liberalizing Trade in Services: Bilateral, Regional, and Multilateral Perspectives in the Twenty-first Century*, ed. Juan A. Marchetti and Martin Roy, 340–77. Cambridge: Cambridge University Press.

Rudolph, Lloyd I. 1983. "Establishing a Niche for Cultural Policy: An Introduction." *Pacific Affairs* 56.1 (Spring): 5–14.

Ruggie, John Gerard. 1993. "Territoriality and Beyond: Problematizing Modernity in International Relations." *International Organization* 47.1 (Winter): 139–74.

Rushton, Michael, 2003. "Artists' Rights." In *A Handbook of Cultural Economics*, ed. Ruth Towse, 76–80. Cheltenham, U.K.: Edward Elgar.

Rushton, Michael. 2001. "The Law and Economics of Artists' Inalienable Rights." *Journal of Cultural Economics* 25 (4): 243–57

Saatchi, Maurice. 2008. "Freud's Law and the Angry English." *Financial Times*. 6 February.

Said, Edward. 1978. *Orientalism*. New York: Vintage Books.

Sandholtz. Wayne. 1992. *High-Tech Europe: The Politics of International Cooperation*. Berkeley: University of California Press.

Sauvé, Pierre, 2006. Introduction to *Trends in Audiovisual Market: Regional Perspectives from the South*, United Nations Educational, Scientific and Cultural Organization, 7–20. Paris: UNESCO.

Sauvé, Pierre, and Robert M. Stern, eds. *The GATS 2000: New Directions in Services Trade Liberalization*. Washington, D.C.: Brookings.

Scott, Alan J. 2008. "Cultural Economy: Retrospect and Prospect." In *The Cultural Economy*, ed. Helmut Anheier and Yudhishter Raj Isar, 307–23. The Cultures and Globalization Series 2. Los Angeles: Sage.

Seabrook, J. 2001. *Travels in the Skin Trade: Tourism and the Sex Industry*. 2nd ed. London: Pluto Press.

Sheth, Jagdish, and J. P. Singh. 1994. "The Future of Telecommunications Services at the Local Level." In *Telecommunications Policy in Georgia*, ed. Georgia Institute of Technology. Atlanta: Georgia Institute of Technology.

Shumway, Nicholas. 2001. *The Invention of Argentina*. Berkeley, Calif.: University of California Press.

Singh, J. P., ed. 2010a. *International Cultural Policies and Power*. Basingstoke: Palgrave/Macmillan.

——. 2010b. *United Nations Educational, Scientific, and Cultural Organization: Creating Norms in a Complex World*. London: Routledge.

——. 2008a. "Paulo Freire: Possibilities for Dialogic Communication in a Market-Driven Information Age." Key Thinkers in the Information Age Series. *Information, Communication, and Society* 11 (5): 699–726.

——. 2008b. *Negotiation and the Global Information Economy*. Cambridge: Cambridge University Press.

——. 2008c. "GATS Plus or Minus? Services Commitments in Comparative Contexts for Colombia and Uruguay." In *Opening Markets for Trade in Services: Coun-*

tries and Sectors in Bilateral and WTO Negotiations, ed. Juan A. Marchetti and Martin Roy, 505–36. Cambridge: Cambridge University Press.

——. 2005. "Services Commitments: Case Studies from Belize and Costa Rica." In *Managing the Challenges of WTO Participation: Forty-five Case Studies,* ed. P. Gallagher, P. Low, and A. L. Stoler, 78–94. Cambridge: Cambridge University Press.

——. 2007. "Culture or Commerce? A Comparative Assessment of International Interactions and Developing Countries at UNESCO, WTO, and Beyond." *International Studies Perspectives* 8:36–53.

——. 2002. "Introduction: Information Technologies and the Changing Scope of Power and Governance." In *Information Technologies and Global Politics: The Changing Scope of Power and Governance,* ed. James N. Rosenau and J. P. Singh, 1–38. Albany: State University of New York Press.

——. 2000. "Weak Powers and Globalism: The Impact of Plurality on Weak-Strong Negotiations in the International Economy." *International Negotiation* 5:449–84.

Singh, J. P., and Shilpa A. Hart. "Sex Workers and Cultural Policy: Mapping the Issues and Actors in Thailand." *Review of Policy Research* 24.2 (2007): 155–73.

Skrobanek, Siriporn. 2003. "Human Trafficking: From Vertical to Horizontal Journey." *Voices of Thai Women* 20 (May): 2–5.

Smith, Adam. 1776/2003. *The Wealth of Nations.* New York: Bantam Classics.

Snowball, J. D. and A. C. M. Webb. 2008. "Breaking into the Conversation: Cultural Value and the Role of the South African National Arts Festival from Apartheid to Democracy." *International Journal of Cultural Policy* 14.2 (May): 149–64.

Spruyt, Hendrik. 1996. *The Sovereign State and Its Competitors.* Princeton, N.J.: Princeton University Press.

Steinfatt, T. M. 2002. *Working at the Bar: Sex Work and Health Communication in Thailand.* Westport, Conn.: Ablex Publishing.

Stokes, Susan. 1998. "Pathologies of Deliberation." In *Deliberative Democracy,* ed. Jon Elster, 123–39. Cambridge: Cambridge University Press.

Taylor, Charles. 1994. "The Politics of Recognition." In *Multiculturalism: Examining the Politics of Recognition,* ed. Amy Gutman, 25–73. Princeton, N.J.: Princeton University Press.

Throsby, David. 2001. *Culture and Economics.* Cambridge: Cambridge University Press.

Thussu, Daya Kishan. 2008. *News as Entertainment: The Rise of Infotainment.* London: Sage.

Towse, Ruth. 2008. "Why Has Cultural Economics Ignored Copyright?" *Journal of Cultural Economics* 32 (4): 243–59.

Trofimov, Y. 2006. "White-Skinned Black African Singer Uses His Fame to Help Fellow Albinos." *The Wall Street Journal.* 6–8 January.

Tsutsumibayashi, Ken. 2005. "Fusion of Horizons or Confusion of Horizons? Intercultural Dialogue and Its Risks." *Global Governance* 11.1 (January–March): 103–14.

UNCTAD. 2008. *The Creative Economy Report 2008: The Challenge of Assessing the Creative Economy.* United Nations. UNCTAD/DITC/2008/2.

———. 2002. *Report of the Expert Meeting on Audiovisual Services: Improving Participation of Developing Countries.* United Nations. TD/B/COM.1/56. 4 December.

———. 1999. *Lessons from the MAI.* UNCTAD Series on Issues in International Investment Agreement. United Nations Conference on Trade and Development. New York: United Nations.

UNESCO. 2009a. *UNESCO World Report: Investing in Cultural Diversity and Intercultural Dialogue.* October. Available at http://portal.unesco.org/en/ev.php-URL_ID=46731&URL_DO=DO_TOPIC&URL_SECTION=201.html. Accessed November 10, 2009.

———. 2009b. *The 2009 UNESCO Framework for Cultural Statistics.* Available at http://uis.unesco.org/template/pdf/cscl/framework/FCS_2009_EN.pdf.

———. 2005a. *International Flows of Selected Cultural Goods and Services, 1994–2003.* Institute for Statistics. Montreal: UNESCO Institute for Statistics. Available at www.uis.unesco.org/ev_en.php?ID=6372_201&ID2=DO_TOPIC. Accessed 15 November 2009.

———. 2005b. *Convention on the Protection and Promotion of the Diversity of Cultural Expressions.* http://portal.unesco.org/en/ev.php-URL_ID=31038&URL_DO=DO_TOPIC&URL_SECTION=201.html. Accessed 15 November 2009.

———. 2001. *UNESCO Declaration on Cultural Diversity.* Adopted at the 31st session of the UNESCO General Conference. Available at: http://www.unesco.org/culture/pluralism/diversity. 2 November.

UNESCO Institute for Statistics. 2007. *The 2009 UNESCO Framework for Cultural Statistics: Draft.* December.

United Nations Conference on Trade and Development. 2002. *Audiovisual Services: Improving Participation of Developing Countries.* Trade and Development Board: Commission on Trade in Goods and Services, and Commodities. TD/B/COM.1/EM.20/2. 27 September.

UNWTO. 2009. *Tourism Highlights 2009 Edition.* Madrid: WTO. Accessed from www.world-tourism.org.

———. 2006. *Tourism Highlights 2006 Edition.* Madrid: WTO. Accessed from www.world-tourism.org.

Urry, John. 2002. *The Tourist Gaze.* London: Sage.

USTR. 2007. "WTO Dispute Settlement Regarding China—Measures Affecting Trading Rights and Distribution Services for Certain Publications and Audiovisual Entertainment Products." Docket No. WTO/DS-363. *Federal Register* 72 (71): 20143–20144. 23 April. Available at http://wais.access.gpo.gov.

Vanaspong, C. 2002. "A Portrait of the Lady: The Portrayal of Thailand and Its Prostitutes in the International Media." In *Transnational Prostitution: Changing Patterns in a Global Context*, ed. S. Thorbek and B. Pattanaik, 139–55. London: Zed Books.

Van Grasstek, Craig. 2006. "Treatment of Cultural Goods and Services in International Trade Agreements." In UNESCO, *Trends in Audiovisual Markets: Regional Perspectives from the South*, 89–153. Paris: UNESCO.

Vatsayan, K. M. 1972. *Some Aspects of Cultural Policies in India*. Paris: UNESCO Press.

Vogel, Harold L. 2007. *Entertainment Industry Economics: A Guide for Financial Analysis*. 7th ed. Cambridge: Cambridge University Press.

Voon, Tania. 2007. *Cultural Products and the World Trade Organization*. Cambridge: Cambridge University Press.

Walker, Rob. 2008. *Buying In: The Secret Dialogue Between What We Buy and Who We Are*. New York: Random House.

Watal, Jayashree. 2001. *Intellectual Property Rights in the WTO and Developing World*. The Hague: Kluwer Law International.

Wendt, Alexander. 1992. "Anarchy Is What States Make of It: The Social Construction of Power Politics." *International Organization* 46:384–96.

White, Harrison C. 2008. *Identity and Control: How Social Transformations Emerge*. 2nd ed. Princeton, N.J.: Princeton University Press.

Willemen, P. 1992. "The Making of African Cinema." *Transition* 58:138–50.

Williams, Gordon. 1982. "Phases in Political Patronage of Literature in Rome." In *Literary and Artistic Patronage in Ancient Rome*, ed. Barbara K. Gold, 3–27. Austin: University of Texas Press.

Wintel, Michael, ed. 1996. *Culture and Identity in Europe*. Aldershot: Avebury.

World Intellectual Property Organization. 2006. *National Studies on Assessing the Economic Contribution of the Copyright-Based Industries*. Creative Industries Series No. 1. Geneva. May.

WTO. 2005a. Communication from Hong Kong, China, Japan, Mexico, The Separate Customs Territory of Taiwan, Penghu, Kinmen and Matsu; and United States. Joint Statement on the Negotiation of Audiovisual Services. TNS/S/W/49. 30 June.

——. 2005b. *International Trade Statistics, 2004*. Geneva: World Trade Organization.

——. 2002. Trade in Services. The People's Republic of China: Schedule of Specific Commitments. GATS/SC/135. 14 February.

——. 2001a. Declaration on the TRIPS Agreement and Public Health. Ministerial Conference, Doha, WT/MIN(01)/DEC/W2. 14 November.

———. 2001b. Communication from Brazil: Audiovisual Services. Council for Trade in Services. Special Session. s/css/W/99, 9 July.

———. 2001c. Communication from Switzerland: GATS 2000: Audio-visual Services. Council for Trade in Services Special Session. S/CSS/W/74. 4 May.

———. 1998a. Audiovisual Services: Background Note by Secretariat. Council for Trade in Services. S/C/W/40. 15 June.

———. 1998b. Electronic Commerce and the Role of the WTO. Geneva: World Trade Organization.

———. 1997a. *Canada—Certain Measures Regarding Periodicals.* Report of the Appellate Body. WT/DS31/AB/R. 30 June

———. 1997b. *Canada—Certain Measures Regarding Periodicals.* Report of the Appellate Body. WT/DS31/R. 14 March.

———. 1996a. Press Brief: Basic Telecoms. 8 December.

———. 1996b. Report of the Group on Basic Telecommunications. 30 April.

———. 1996c. Minutes of the Meeting. Dispute Settlement Body. 19 June. WT/DSB/M/19. 10 July.

———. 1994a. General Agreement on Trade in Services. Argentina: Schedule of Specific Commitments. GATS/SC/4. 15 April.

———. 1994b. General Agreement on Trade in Services. Belize: Schedule of Specific Commitments. GATS/SC/10. 15 April.

———. 1994c. Trade in Services. Costa Rica: Schedule of Specific Commitments. GATS/SC/22. 15 April.

———. 1994d. General Agreement on Trade in Services. India: Schedule of Specific Commitments. GATS/SC/42. 15 April.

Wyszomirski, Margaret Jane. 2008. "The Local Creative Economy in the United States." In *The Cultural Economy,* ed. Helmut Anheier and Yudhishter Raj Isar, 199–212. Los Angeles: Sage.

Young, Iris Marion. 1996. "Communication and the Other: Beyond Deliberative Democracy." In *Democracy and Difference: Contesting the Boundaries of the Political,* ed. Seyla Benhabib, 120–35. Princeton, N.J.: Princeton University Press.

Yúdice, George. 2004. *The Expediency of Culture: Uses of Culture in the Global Era.* Durham, N.C.: Duke University Press.

Yuk, P. K. 2006. "Bollywood: A Broader Audience for Song and Dance." *Financial Times.* 28 June.

Zachary, G. Pascals. 2000. *The Global Me: New Cosmopolitans and the Global Edge—Picking Globalism's Winners and Losers.* New York: PublicAffairs.

Index